CHICAGO PUBLIC LIBRARY

R01011 10689

DISCARD

D1361129

MADE IN ILLINOIS

A STORY OF ILLINOIS MANUFACTURING

BY ROLF ACHILLES

Published in honor
of the
Illinois Manufacturers' Association
Centennial

Copyright 1993, Illinois Manufacturers' Association

All rights reserved.

Edited by Patricia John

Book design by Dianne Burgis, Burgis Risinger Design Corporation

All names of corporations and products
indicated in the text are the copyright and trademark of the companies.

First Edition, October 1993

Library of Congress Care Number #93-61095

Illinois Manufacturers' Association

209 West Jackson Boulevard, Suite 700

Chicago, Illinois 60606-0998

220 East Adams Street

Springfield, Illinois 62701-1123

R01011 10689

TABLE OF CONTENTS

FORWARD

Made in Illinois: A Story of Illinois Manufacturing depicts something more than the history of Illinois-made products. It also is a story about revolutionizing and capitalizing on the growth, ideas and dreams of American workers and leaders.

Former Illinois Gov. James R. Thompson often extolled the virtues of the Land of Lincoln in his rhetoric. He would describe Illinois as the quintessential state of all the United States — the large megalopolis of the Chicago region in the northeast, the Mississippi bluffs to the west, the central prairies, the coal mines of Little Egypt in southern Illinois. He is right. No other state in the union represents the pride and pulse of America than Illinois does. That is why, we at the IMA, thought it was so important to produce *Made in Illinois,* to try to recapture the excitement, vibrancy and ingenuity of the American spirit during the rise of manufacturing in Illinois.

Made in Illinois is the first attempt to chronicle a portion of one of the most important segments of our economy: Manufacturing. Centuries ago, people migrated to Illinois not only because of its natural resource abundance, but of the state's ability to transport products to any region of the world. Rich, central Illinois plains inspired farmers to look for ways to unlock the state's agricultural wonders. Once farmers truly discovered the value of Illinois land, they began processing livestock, which added value to grain. And soon, the rest of the world witnessed the dawn of Illinois' reputation as a transportation hub.

By transporting goods worldwide, Illinois flourished and became home for several businesses including those in the steel and meat packing industries. As immigrants arrived, the abundance of labor attracted new industries including mining in southern Illinois and other service-related industries. Whether it was the Civil War, the Industrial Revolution or advent of the assembly line, Illinois manufacturing has played a key role in most major historical events of our nation's history.

In 1893, during the height of the Industrial Revolution, a small, but ambitious group of Illinois manufacturers met in a dimly lit room in the Medinah Temple on Wells Street in Chicago. The group's purpose: What manufacturers could do to influence the various laws and regulations proposed and passed in the Illinois General Assembly. The manufacturers strongly believed in the need to organize and form one voice for manufacturing, and thus, the IMA was born. Today, as in 1893, private enterprise and manufacturing, in particular, are under constant scrutiny by lawmakers. From its birth to the present, the mission of the IMA has been to educate the public and elected officials on the challenges of producing a quality product at a competitive price. The IMA believes that if Illinois citizens, including the state's children, understand the past, they may better understand the future and what could happen if the Illinois manufacturing base is not nurtured.

The IMA provides information about the ever-changing regulatory arena and offers employee training to member companies so they may compete in the global economy. For the small manufacturer — under 100 employees and 70 percent of the membership — the IMA is just a telephone call away, ready to answer questions on almost any subject affecting the workplace. The IMA is the manufacturers' voice in the state Capitol and through its Manufacturers Political Action Committee, supports the business community's interests by electing pro-business officials.

It is the hope of the IMA Board of Directors that *Made in Illinois* is used as a blueprint for future state leaders to foster a friendlier climate in which Illinois manufacturers may flourish. Illinois must better educate its children. We also must provide a stable business climate in which to create jobs, employ our workforce and improve the quality of our environment in a balanced and sensible fashion. It is not an easy mission. But as you read the following pages, clearly our forefathers overcame great obstacles to tame and build a home called Illinois. Our challenge as citizens of this great state is to build on those successes and conquer the obstacles in our path as we enter the 21st century. Together, we can achieve.

Gregory W. Baise
President
Illinois Manufacturers' Association
November 1993

AUTHOR'S PREFACE

Though this publication carries the name of only one author, hundreds of people were involved in the development and production of this book. Without the assistance of many voices, known only over the telephone and mostly anonymous, agreeing to send information, look up some fact or statistic, or send photographs, the one author could not have completed this task.

Given the nature of this publication and the time constraints of a centennial, the help manufacturers provided was absolutely essential. From promptly answering the initial questionnaire sent out by the IMA, to returning telephone calls, providing documentation or archival photographs, the women and men who make up the manufacturers in Illinois have all been very helpful. Many went out of their way to assist this project. To all, I would here like to say thank you for your help.

Writing history is usually done in libraries and archives, rarely at the source of events. For this book, some statistics and early historical information came through traditional means, while the histories that some corporations have commissioned of themselves, the brochures they have prepared, the archives they have maintained and the memories of individuals stand at the very core of this book. Interestingly enough, very few of the corporate publications are to be found in public libraries, university libraries or have made it into the public sector in general. The stories of the products and the people that invented them are the very fiber of our lives; yet it can be safely said, without fear of serious contradiction, that manufacturing is the unknown cornerstone of America, which has held the rest of the world in awe for more than a century.

A special thank you to Barry MacLean, president of MacLean-Fogg, who set the book in motion, and to Gregory Baise, president of the Association, for following through on the ideas and suggestions and for his trust. Jane Carpenter, vice president of public affairs, Karen Klemens, director of communications and Karen Rigg, executive secretary have been especially helpful, and between them provided me with many suggestions and contacts to scores of companies.

Outside the IMA, a very special thank you to Sally Forthe, Steve Bigolin and the many archivists, librarians and historians who have been very helpful. Of special note are those in the State Library and State Archives in Springfield, the Chicago Historical Society, the Newberry Library, the Rockford, Peoria, Decatur and Chicago Public Libraries have been most helpful in making this publication possible. After all is said and done, it is of course understood that all mistakes and inaccuracies are solely those of the author.

A very special thank you to Patricia John, for her editing and reading of the text, and to Dianne Burgis, for making the manuscript into a book.

The section on Caterpillar is based in part on *The Caterpillar Story*, published in 1984 by Caterpillar Inc.

The McCormick Reaper Factory on the north branch of the Chicago River, 1847

RIVERS, ROADS AND TRADE BRING IN THE SETTLERS

Viewed from the East, Illinois was the middle of the country, the gateway to the west, a cornucopia of natural and man made resources, and the Mississippi its most important road. For many, the idea of manufacturing in Illinois was a natural one, favored by God.

Until the 1840s Illinois' importance lay in its southern towns: Kaskaskia, Cairo, Cahokia, Vandalia and Shawneetown. Vandalia was for 20 years (1819-1839) the political and social capital of Illinois. All these towns were the centers of commerce, manufacturing and culture in their areas. Their settlers were predominantly Southerners. One such Southerner was Edward Coles, second governor of Illinois (1822-26), who also served as secretary to President Madison and was the son of a wealthy Virginia planter. When Coles arrived in the Edwardsville area in 1819, he immediately freed his slaves and gave each 160 acres of land. Though the population increased and the towns prospered, it was the opening of the Erie Canal and the transfer of the state capital to Springfield, in 1837, that ultimately caused the tide of commerce and politics to sweep northward until, as shown by the 1930 census, 80 percent of the population was massed in the northern half of the state.

The first American community of the old Northwest, as the Illinois Territory was known prior to the Louisiana Purchase by the United States in 1803, was the tiny settlement of Bellefontaine, now called Waterloo, but this is not the oldest town in Illinois. That honor belongs to Cahokia, founded in May of 1699 by Father Jean Francois Buisson de St. Cosme, a member of the Seminar of Foreign Missions, who had completed a house and a chapel at Cahokia, to the great distress of the Jesuits, who had thought they had a claim on the whole of the Mississippi valley. For the next century Cahokia prospered with trade to and from New Orleans in flour, lumber, pork, lead and pelts.

Trade brought with it manufacturers, and possibly the earliest documented manufacturer in Illinois was a tannery established for buffalo skins by the Frenchman Charles Juchereau de St. Denys, Lieutenant General of the jurisdiction of Montreal, in 1702 at Va Bache. The following summer an epidemic ripped through the Illinois area. Many died, including half the inhabitants of Va Bache, among them Juchereau. The tannery was abandoned the following year.

Another important French settlement was the village of Renault, named for Phillipe Francois Renault, director-general of mining operations for **John Law's Western Company**. Law had formulated a plan for the colonization and commercial exploitation of the Mississippi valley for the French, but overspeculation and haste brought its collapse. The scheme is known to history as the "Mississippi Bubble." Renault left France in 1719 with

The earliest documented manufacturer in Illinois was a tannery established for buffalo skins in 1702.

200 miners to search for precious stones and metals in the Louisiana Territory. En route, he stopped at Santo Domingo (now Haiti) and bought 500 slaves, some of which he brought to Illinois. After an unsuccessful treasure hunt, Renault sold his slaves to French colonists in Illinois and returned to France in 1742. Until early in the present century there were blacks living in the vicinity of Renault and Prairie du Rocher who clung to French customs and spoke a mixture of French and English.

On the other side of Illinois, in the Wabash River basin, the French, too, were the first Europeans to settle. A few of them entered Illinois from Vincennes, an old French settlement and the capital of the Indiana Territory. But it was the Ohio River, to the south, that provided the earliest avenue of entry for larger numbers of Europeans and Americans into southern Illinois. These settlers were much more homogeneous, clannish and aware of their historical background than those that would follow later in the north.

The first towns in Illinois were small, and manufacturing depended on converting local natural resources into trade goods. Water powered saw mills converted trees to rough planks, grist mills turned grain into flour and butchers turned pigs into pickled pork. When local needs were satisfied, trade followed. Towns of importance, such as Palestine, had 30 families, five stores, two taverns, a steam saw and grist mill.

Along the Mississippi a site such as Andalusia, the place were Clark's Ferry crossed the river to Buffalo, Iowa, the most important crossing above St. Louis in the 1830s, quickly drew land speculators whose elaborate plans showing a thriving town with many lots were sold to the unsuspecting in the East. Before the scheme collapsed, the "metropolis of the Middle West" had found many investors and even a few settlers. Other schemes followed, most of them legitimate.

Among the most common points of origin for the early American settlers in Illinois was New England. These settlers brought their own traditions with them. Pierce Downer was from Rutland, Vermont, and in 1832 lived in what was to become Downers Grove, incorporated in 1870. Carpentersville was settled in 1834 by Angelo Carpenter of Uxbridge, Massachusetts. The Ottawa area, the junction of the Fox River with the Illinois River, was settled after the Black Hawk War (1832) by New Englanders who brought with them their political, educational and religious beliefs. Kewanee's older section was long known as Wethersfield, which in 1836 was an enterprise born of the Connecticut Association, which deemed it its duty to foster Protestantism in the rapidly growing state and to counter already thriving Roman Catholic communities. Wethersfield was named after a community in Connecticut. Shares were sold at $250 each for title to 160 acres of prairie, 20 of woodland and a town lot. Galesburg was conceived as a city in 1835, by George Washington Gale in Oneida, New York. The site was chosen after a careful examination of land in Indiana and Illinois, and its plan was laid out before its proprietors-settlers came west. 50 families contributed $20,000, bought 20 square miles at $1.25 per acre, and in 1836-37 moved to the area. An early settler was Jonathan Blanchard, a New Englander and early President of Knox College. Jacksonville was first settled by Southerners, but by the late

Manufacturing depended on converting local natural resources into trade goods.

1830s so many New Englanders lived there that its character was more New England than that of any other community in Illinois. Byron, named for the English poet, was founded in 1835 by New Englanders and mostly settled by them. And in 1835 Major Leonard Andrus of Vermont settled Grand Detour. He built a dam for water power, erected a saw mill and a flour mill. John Deere, too, soon arrived from Vermont.

John Deere compound in Grand Detour in 1875

Settlements
that prospered
usually
had some
manufacturing
as their
central enterprise
and mainstay.

Before the railroads brought floods of people, goods and commerce to the state, rough roads, originating elsewhere and usually following ancient trails, crossed the region and were a main source of communication. Travel was slow but constant, with eastern migration into Illinois being uninterrupted until the great depression of 1837 slowed its pace, slightly, for a year.

Along these roads settlements developed, most of which did not survive the fast cultural changes that marked the first few decades of Illinois' nineteenth century. But those that prospered and became towns usually had some manufacturing as their central enterprise and mainstay.

Among the important early roads was the Trace Road — today United States 50 — which connected Bear Grass (now Louisville, Kentucky) with Cahokia on the Mississippi, a few miles below East St. Louis. For two decades, from 1805-1825, post riders on horseback carried mail over the road. In 1824 a four horse stage and mail route was established.

Illinois was promoted to statehood in 1818. The following year at the first assembly, meeting in the original capital, the village of Kaskaskia at the mouth of the river of that name, the legislature voted to move. It was decided to move to a new town where sales of real estate from a federal land grant might benefit the infant state's treasury. Thus the archives were hauled by wagon in 1820 to Vandalia, more than 111 miles on the primitive Vincennes Trace. This new capital was in the heart of the then populous area of the state. As the population of the state shifted northward after the Black Hawk war into the recently acquired Indian lands, the legislature voted, in 1837, to move a second time, to Springfield, near the center of the state. The assembly met for the first time there on December 9, 1839.

In 1837 under an ambitious State improvement program, the Trace Road was graded. Bridges and culverts were hewn from white oak felled along the road. Between Vincennes, Indiana and Lawrenceville miles of trestlework were constructed. But the many expensive improvement schemes, and the Panic of 1837, plunged the young state into near bankruptcy, and the Trace Road was turned over to a private company, which completed the work and planked the treacherous swamp section.

The planking of roads was a Canadian development that reached Illinois in the late 1840s. To pay for the planks, toll gates were set up and all travelers had to pay tribute to the owners. These were Illinois' first tollways. For less than a decade these tollways, built of three-inch planks laid on stringers in the mud, eight feet wide and with frequent gravel turnouts, were the recognized way to easy travel and easy money up and down the state. One of the longest plank tollways was from Graceland in Lakeview (now part of Chicago) to Geneva, by way of Elgin.

Another road, and a much more famous one, was the National or Cumberland Road, a major transcontinental highway begun in the East in 1811 and completed in Vandalia by 1839. Today the National Road is a railroad route, United States 40 and I-70, and for most of the nineteenth century the Cumberland Road was the most traveled road in the United States, if for no other reason than that it was America's east - west mail route. In 1839, it took about 94 hours to travel from Washington, D.C. to St. Louis, Missouri. Many of the stagecoach stops along the way blossomed into villages. Then with the railroad these villages either died or grew into towns and cities. In Vandalia a Madonna of the Trail monument, 18 feet high, was erected by the Daughters of the American Revolution in 1928 to mark the western end of the Cumberland Road.

The stagecoach was, for a time, a reliable means of communication and transportation (if not a comfortable one) and from it, too, settlements began. Warren developed at the junction of the Chicago-Galena Stagecoach Road and the Old Sucker Trail, which ran from St. Louis to Wiota, Wisconsin. Belvidere was a significant stop on the Chicago-Galena route. Astoria was once a station on the four horse stagecoach line between Peoria and Quincy. And early communication between Chicago and River Forest was made possible through **Frink & Walker**, whose stagecoach drawn by four horses carried 10 passengers and charged 50 cents for adults, 25 cents for children.

In the northern part of the state, the ancient path between what would become Chicago and Janesville, Wisconsin became a principal road to the northwest in 1845, and was

To pay for the planking of roads, toll gates were set up and all travelers had to pay tribute to the owners.

known as the United States Mail Route, while the Hubbard Trail which led from Vincennes to Fort Dearborn was the main early route to Chicago from the southeast. Momence, platted in 1844, was an important stop on the Hubbard Trail. As many as 200 wagons and pack trains sometimes camped here overnight.

The Sauk Trail, for centuries the route to Detroit, became the westward artery for trappers, soldiers, settlers and the mail. Covered wagons traversed it to lands beyond the Mississippi, the 49ers followed it to California, New Englanders struggled over it, abolitionists followed it, and slaves used it to escape from Missouri to Indiana. Where the Sauk Trail crossed the Hubbard Trail became known as Thorn Grove in the 1830s. German settlers renamed it Bloom in 1849, honoring Robert Bluehm, a German patriot executed for democratic thoughts in Vienna in 1848. Its current name, Chicago Heights, dates from 1890 when the Chicago Heights Land Association induced manufacturers to establish plants there.

Grist and flour mills were usually powered by water.

While the roads brought people to Illinois, it is water power that was a principal factor in attracting settlers to northern Illinois. Among the earliest descriptions of Illinois is one of a river. In 1673, the famous French explorer Louis Jolliet described the Illinois River valley as "most beautiful and most easy to be settled. This river is wide and deep... it is stocked with brills and sturgeons. Game is in abundance. There are prairies three, six, ten, and twenty leagues in length and three in width... A settler would not be required to spend 10 years cutting down and burning timber." Although the Illinois River valley was not settled as a French colony, it was an early avenue of exploration and then commerce, and when it was settled by Europeans they did it for just the reasons Jolliet gave.

WATER POWER

The rivers moved goods, but also provided power to manufacturers in towns along them. Many towns can lay claim to a waterwheel powered grist or flour mill as their first industry, which then attracted other industry until the place became a manufacturing center. Along the Rock River there were mills in Rockford and Dixon, and a few places in between. Along the Fox River, Batavia began its industrial life in 1837 with a flour mill. Although Decatur was first settled by Europeans around 1820, it was not until 1832 that the first dam and saw mill were built by David D. Allen, above a ford in the Sangamon River. Soon other manufacturers followed. Marseilles was an industrial community that used Illinois River waterpower to turn waterwheels that powered machines almost exclusively for most of the nineteenth century.

The first settler in DuPage County was Bailey Hobson, who staked a claim in 1830; returning the following year, he established a grist mill. In 1832 Joseph Naper arrived and built the first saw mill and platted the town site, now called Naperville, along the Des Plaines River. Warrenville, now a part of Naperville, was a crossroads hamlet with a tannery and grist mill that drew trade from as far away as Galena in the 1840s.

Carpentersville, on the Des Plaines River, had a sawmill, grist mill, woolen mill and grocery store when it was platted in 1851. A sawmill and grist mill was built on the east side of the river, north of what is now Lake Street, in River Forest. The mill finished much of the lumber that went into the building of early Chicago. Just east of Oquawka, in Henderson County, on the Mississippi at Henderson Creek, stood the Radmacher Mill, built in the 1830s. Operated by water power from Henderson Creek, the mill ground feed, flour, corn meal and buckwheat. Its California redwood woodwork was admired well into the twentieth century.

As settlements developed along the roads and rivers, each had a family of local importance, a clutch of houses, a store or two, and each settlement thought of itself as an important site with a glorious future. The differentiation, the survival or death of a community, eventually depended on events outside the control of the community, and usually had to do with commerce and manufacturing.

Two cities, for example, that saw themselves as important, and they were for a time, were Havana and Naples. By 1836 some 35 steamboats were operating on the Illinois River at Havana, though there were no regular Mississippi-type boat manufacturers on the river. Naples was the one place on the Illinois River where a steamboat was built. She was the *Olitippa*, and ran long before there was any regular steamboat service on the river. By the end of the century both cities had settled into a comfortable small town status, with some regional importance.

Much of the industrial development of Illinois occurred outside of Chicago. Carpentersville is a good example. The city was founded as Carpenter's Grove on the east bank of the Fox River in 1837 by Charles and Daniel Carpenter. Angelo, Charles' son, had industrial ideas. He built a sawmill (the first industry) and a dam. Surrounding timberland provided black walnut trees that were cut into lumber at the mill and then shipped to Chicago by ox teams. With the dam he controlled the area's water power. Angelo also bought a wool mill in what was then Dundee and moved it to Carpentersville. He turned the mill into a factory for spinning and dying yarn, flannel and cashmere. The mill remained in business until the 1880s, when it burned down. He owned the **Atlantic Flour Mills**, which were built in Carpenter's Grove in 1845.

Later, in partnership with his father-in-law, Alfred Edwards of Dundee, Carpenter bought out a small reaper manufacturer. That company he made into the **Illinois Iron & Bolt Co.**, which became a major industry in the village for years, and an IMA member from 1899 on. In 1851 Carpenter built a bridge across the Fox River, at a $10,000 cost to himself. Carpenter died in 1880 a wealthy man. His widow later married George P. Lord, who headed the **Elgin National Watch Company**. She died in 1905.

By 1900 Carpentersville had a population of about 1,000, and three large industries: **Illinois Condensing Co.**, **Star Manufacturing Co.** and Illinois Iron & Bolt Co. — the largest of the three. The bolt company originally made iron parts designed to reduce wear on wagon wheel axles. Carpenter and Edwards took controlling interest of it in 1868 and

Much of the
industrial
development
of Illinois
occurred outside
of Chicago.

expanded its production to a variety of iron implements with a national market. In 1873, he and others organized Star Manufacturing Co., built of yellow "Dundee bricks," to manufacture plowshares, cultivator shovels, mold boards, discs and a general line of soil tilling replacement parts. Star and Illinois Iron & Bolt merged in 1912. The Star Manufacturing Co. complex was acquired by **Otto Engineering, Inc.** in 1977 and has since been

Moving the goods in Carpentersville

Water transportation was an irresistible lure to industry.

After this initial growth, Carpentersville remained fairly quiet until the mid-1950s, when Leonard W. Besinger's Meadowdale housing development gave Carpentersville affordable houses, attracting many War veterans eager to live and own a home outside the city of Chicago. Besinger also built one of the nation's first large shopping centers.

It should be kept in mind that water transportation was such an irresistible lure to industry in the early days that even when canal traffic declined most of the factories remained. Steamboats and railroads got underway in the state at almost the same time, around 1838, and for the next forty years the two systems developed side by side. It was not until in 1878, when receipts on the Illinois & Michigan Canal fell below operating costs, that locomotives for the first time seriously threatened the supremacy of the boat.

In 1827 plans for the Illinois & Michigan (I & M) Canal were set. The long awaited celebration of the opening of the I & M Canal occurred on April 16, 1848 when the *General Fry*, loaded with passengers, arrived in Chicago. The boat had been launched earlier at Lockport and it had made the twenty-nine mile voyage to Bridgeport at a speed of five miles an hour. The first boat to arrive from La Salle, the western terminus of the Canal, was the *General Thornton* (as with the *General Fry*, named for a canal commissioner), which came in on April 24th. It was loaded with produce from New Orleans.

The *General Thornton* was built and owned by Isaac Hardy, a contractor who built the first lock at Lockport and a brother-in-law of William Gooding, chief canal engineer. Hardy's ship made history doubly, for the produce it carried was reloaded onto a steamer bound for Buffalo, New York — where it arrived two weeks before the Erie Canal was opened to navigation. Knowing full well that construction of the Erie Canal had begun in 1817, almost twenty years before the construction of the their own Canal started, Illinoisans cheered the news, and a proud Abraham Lincoln brought it to the attention of the nation in a speech before the House of Representatives.

Most immigrants arrived in Illinois by boat.

CANALS LINK ILLINOIS TO THE WORLD

The opening of the I & M Canal was greeted with enthusiasm or apprehension by Midwestern cities, depending on their locations. The rich central prairies of Illinois now poured their crops into Chicago rather than St. Louis. Within four years, Chicago was receiving almost four times as much corn as the Mississippi port. Across Lake Michigan sawmills began to buzz in the wooded sections of Michigan, and lines of steamers puffed across the lake and into the canal with much needed lumber for the booming prairie towns.

From the opening of the La Grange lock on October 21, 1889 to the end of June 1896, the amount of business on the Illinois River was up 200 percent. During the year 1896, 504 steamboats and barges passed through the La Grange lock. For over four decades the canal pumped money and prosperity into north central Illinois. For the early economic development of Chicago, the I & M Canal proved crucial because it was from there, along the banks of the Chicago River, that the city's original industrial, warehousing and commercial sites were located.

Henry M. Flint, in his History of the Mississippi Valley, published in 1832, wrote: "On account of the universality and cheapness of steamboat and canal passage, more than half the whole number of immigrants now arrive in the West by water. This remark applies to nine-tenths of those that come from Europe and the Northern States. They thus escape much of the expense, slowness, inconvenience, and danger of the ancient, cumbrous, and tiresome journey in wagons. They no longer experience the former vexations of incessant altercations with landlords, mutual charges of dishonesty, discomforts from new modes of speech and reckoning money, from breaking down carriages and wearing out of horses. Immigrants from Virginia, Georgia and the two Carolinas still immigrate after the ancient fashion, in the Southern wagon. Perhaps more than half the Northern immigrants now arrive by way of the New York canal and Lake Erie."

The Erie Canal opened in 1826. It was an important factor in the Great Lakes development. In 1836 there were about 3,000 canal boats on the Erie Canal. That meant one per hour leaving Albany, New York.

In 1826 or 27 the first steamboat sailed on Lake Michigan. It was a pleasure boat out of Green Bay. In 1833 two steamboats landed in Chicago. The next year, the Detroit-Chicago run became very lucrative. In 1839 a regular line of eight boats was formed between Buffalo and Chicago. The trip took 16 days. The rate from Buffalo to Chicago in 1841 was $20 per passenger in a cabin, $10 in steerage. Horses were $15 each.

The first direct clearance from Lake Michigan to Europe was made in 1856. The consignor, C.J. Kershaw of Montreal, hoped to ship a full cargo of wheat from Chicago, but there he could obtain only 5,000 bushels and was forced to seek the balance of 9,320 bushels in Milwaukee. The steamer *Dean Richmond*, a new vessel, left Chicago about July 14th, had her full cargo on the 18th, and sailed for Europe on the 19th, arriving in Liverpool September 29th. Others soon followed. The owners of these earliest vessels were individuals or companies of large financial resources.

A River and Harbor Convention was held in Chicago on July 5, 1847 in reaction to President Polk's veto on August 3, 1846 of the River and Harbor Bill. Cities and towns with harbors along Lake Michigan and ports on Illinois' rivers had wanted federal subsidy to help keep them dredged. Reaction in the *St. Louis Republican* in early September, 1846 was that the men of the West urge the men in office of the moral force of the popular will "that this government was framed for the benefit of the people," — and suggested a convention be held at a central point. While there were insufficient votes to override the President's veto, it became clear that this was an issue which had widespread and substantial impact on many aspects of commerce and industry.

Horace Greeley, famed editor and founder of the *New York Tribune* (1841), reported that at the convention: "Chicago is the only harbor on that lake, the shores of which comprise a development of coast of about 900 miles. Milwaukee affords no shelter, ...the mouth of the Kalamazoo river is dangerous. ...Thus, from the time a vessel leaves Chicago, she has no place of shelter till she reaches the northern outlet of the lake at the straits of Mackinac." To ease the access of the Quad Cities with Chicago and the I & M Canal, an Illinois & Mississippi Canal was proposed in the late 1880s. After much discussion, in which all the local engineers were in opposition, the canal was completed in 1907 at a cost of $7 million. The object of the improvement was to furnish a navigable waterway from Lake Michigan to the Mississippi, at the mouth of the Rock River, in connection with the upper Illinois River. But the Rock Island Railroad followed the same path and did the job better. The canal was declared obsolete in 1951 and closed to traffic. It now offers fishing, boating and picnicking.

The Corps of Engineers report of 1898 told its readers that "The commerce of the river amounts to from 10,000,000 to 11,000,000 tons per annum. Of this probably 70 percent originates in the form of manufactured articles in Chicago, or lodges permanently within the city limits and is consumed by its population or put in other forms by manufacture. The remaining ⅓ or ¼ freight simply handled at Chicago or in transit at Chicago such as grain, salt, coal, lumber, especially grain and salt." In 1899, everyone knew "the Great Lakes are developing a manufacturing growth in America that is lifting the new continent to a commanding supremacy in the markets of the world." The Calumet/South Chicago

Horace Greeley wrote "...Chicago is the only harbor on that lake..."

Harbor was the finest on Lake Michigan in 1900. The Chicago Shipbuilding Co. was located on the Calumet River at South Chicago.

In 1897, the total shipment of grain by lake came to 168,131,000 bushels; receipts of lumber aggregated 906,241,000 feet; iron ore receipts were 1,800,000 tons. There were only two other ports in the world which outranked Chicago in the volume of tonnage handled in 1897 — London and New York. In 1897 New York handled 15,333,398; London, 14,433,580; Chicago, 12,965,832 tons of cargo.

The **Bessemer Steamship Co.** was organized in 1896 and was then the most powerful transportation company on the lakes. It was a John D. Rockefeller interest, and ran between Duluth and Chicago and Lake Erie ports. Its largest ship, the propeller *Samuel F.B. Morse*, was also the largest on the Great Lakes. It was 476 feet in length, had a 50 foot beam, was 30 feet deep, had quadruple engines, 3,000 h.p. and a capacity of 7,500 net tons on a mean draft of 17 feet 2 inches.

The lake carriers formally organized in 1895 as the Association of Lake Lines. The Lumber Carrier's Association was organized in Detroit in 1898 for the purpose of fixing minimum rates for carrying lumber. The iron companies of Lake Superior organized their own lake transport system and built their own vessels, while coal mines and grain companies never became vessel owners.

In the early 1870s the Calumet River (12 miles south of the mouth of the Chicago River) was improved to provide a harbor for industry. In 1880 the **North Chicago Rolling Mills**, better known as the south works of **US Steel Corp.**, were opened on the north bank of the mouth of the Calumet River. Housing construction in the area boomed, and the town of Hegewisch was founded in 1883. The Calumet area developed rapidly as a site for heavy industry and, by 1915, it was one of the most important centers for heavy industry in the world.

In 1900 the Chicago Sanitary and Ship Canal was opened. To date it is one of America's great engineering feats because of the difficulty of cutting it through rock. Its immediate effect was to reverse the flow of the Chicago River, from into the lake to out of the lake. The immediate reasons for the need to reverse the flow of the river were industry on the North Branch and the stock yards on the South Branch of the Chicago River. The Stock yards were primary polluters and even though the river was slow, many a dead bit of cow, steer, pig or horse found its way to the lake shore. Also, sanitation being what it was in the city, the river and lake were the easiest, most direct dumping sites. At the same time the lake was the source of most of the city's drinking water. After numerous epidemics and much searching for causes, some civic leaders came to the realization that the contents of the Chicago River just might be a factor in local health. They came to the conclusion that if the River were turned around, that is, flowed out of the lake, the sparsely populated down river country would benefit, especially if it were a canal. Construction began immediately on an improved canal linking the south branch of the

In 1897 only two cities in the world handled more tonnage than Chicago.

Chicago River with the Illinois River and that provided a water route to Joliet. The canal was opened in 1900 and has proven itself a major asset to Chicago and the cities along it. Another plan, to link the Calumet River with the Sanitary and Ship Canal, led to the cutting of the Calumet Sag Channel. It was completed in 1922 and has since carried treated domestic and industrial waste of the Calumet steel district towards the Mississippi. By 1969 the Calumet Sag Channel had been widened from 60 feet to 225 to accommodate shipping and the ever increasing waste from industry and newly expanding towns along it.

Another water route, known as the Gulf to Lakes Waterway, linked the Sanitary and Ship Canal with the Illinois River in 1934. The last major waterway development was the opening of the enlarged and deepened St. Lawrence Seaway in 1959.

Throughout the 1960s Chicago's harbors boomed. Navy Pier, which projects into the Lake near the mouth of the Chicago River, experienced a rebirth after lying dormant for decades after the advent of trucks, automobiles, and the Great Depression of the 1930s killed off the excursion trade and the "package freight" business.

The Sanitary and Ship Canal proved itself a major asset to all cities along its route.

Calumet Harbor in 1990

In the mid-1960s, between six and seven hundred ships arrived in downtown Chicago and Calumet Harbor each year. Changes in shipping methods and the continuing growth in the size of ocean ships reversed this trend. In 1975 there were fewer than three hundred arrivals. Ten years later it was down to a few dozen ships per year.

The three waterways, the Chicago Sanitary and Ship Canal, the Calumet River and Lake Calumet, and Indiana Harbor, became the location of five steel and iron production plants, three steel fabrication plants, five chemical production plants, one auto assembly plant, one cereal producer, eight grain elevators and terminal facilities, two cement shipping terminals, eleven general warehouses and a variety of small manufacturers and firms.

The first major occupant along the Chicago Sanitary and Ship Canal was **International Harvester Company** in 1902. Others soon followed. The waterway was ideal for moving bulky freight. Railroads and electrical utilities followed quickly.

During the 1890s Chicago was the lumber capital of the United States.

Since then, highly specialized loading and unloading equipment at the dockside kept pace with the improvements in ships. One ore-loading machine lifted railroad cars bodily, tilted them, and dumped their cargo into the mouths of chutes. In the 1950s cargo could be moved in and out of ships at the rate of 10,000 tons per hour. In less than a day, even the largest of the lake ships, 59,000 tons capacity could be filled or emptied.

By the middle of the nineteenth century rivers, roads and railways had begun to create a great wheel of manufacturing and commerce which would turn for more than another century around its hub, Chicago.

LUMBER IN CHICAGO

Chicago as a central trading post was recognized before 1700 by the French. In the treaty of Greenville, 1795, it was noted that a fort had stood at Chicago but that there was none presently. By 1803-04 the United States Government had built a fort. John Jacob Astor established a branch of the **American Fur Company** there in 1809. The massacre of 1812 scattered the few settlers for a time. In 1832 a post office was established, and though the population stood officially at 350, only 12 citizens voted upon the question of incorporating the town in 1833, while in 1834, in a second election for trustees, 111 votes were cast. The official census of 1837 reveals a population of 4,170.

In 1832 Ezra Adams, a soldier who was a carpenter by trade and who may have built the first frame house in the city, purchased a small raft of square timber of suitable building size, which had been hewn on the Calumet River and wrecked in the endeavor to tow it up the lake to the fort. Adams was more successful in bringing it into port, and this was the first manufactured lumber or timber for which records exist in Chicago.

From its start, Chicago was a lumber town. While the population of Chicago grew from 4,470 in 1840 to 1,698,575 in 1900, the total lumber receipts rose from 60,000,000 feet to 2,250,000,000 feet.

In 1833 all the lumber in Chicago was white wood brought from St. Joe River, Michigan. The following year a steam saw mill was erected along the North Branch near Clybourn Avenue, which was built by George E. Walker and George Hickling. Every able-bodied man in town was there. The mill was of the 'sash' or gate single (upright) saw type, and could probably cut 2,000 feet of board in 12 hours from cottonwood, oak and elm, which were indigenous. In 1832 or 1835 a Mr. Walker, of Walker's Grove, built a water saw mill on the DuPage River, 1 ½ miles from the present site of Plainfield. There he manufactured oak, walnut, hackberry, cottonwood and elm boards, which he teamed forty miles to Chicago. S. B. Cobb went to that mill in 1833 and got the lumber with which to build the first harness shop on the west side of the river. The mill operated until about 1842. In 1838 the sash and door factory of Francis McFall was established on Market Street in Chicago.

Frederick William Norwood introduced "yellow pine," a product of Southern forests, to Chicago. Shortly after the Civil War, he bought lumber in the South to be sold in the North. In 1884 Norwood was joined in business by Mr. Butterfield and, in 1886, purchased the **Boon & Sargent Mill**, with 3,000 acres of land in Brookshaven, Mississippi. This mill continued in operation until 1890, when the local trees were exhausted. **Norwood & Butterfield** then platted the town of Northfield, Mississippi, where they erected a double band mill, the first in the South, having capacity for manufacturing 100,000 feet per day, together with dry kilns of equal capacity. The lumber was used for flooring in Chicago.

During the 1890s there were a number of important lumber yards in Chicago. Among them were **John Spry Lumber Co.**; the **T. Wilce Co.**; **George Farnsworth**; **H. Witbeck Co.**, founded in 1868.; **Spalding Lumber Co.**; and **Francis Beidler**.

Probably the most successful of the Chicago lumber men was Edward Hines. Hines was born in Buffalo, New York, in 1863 of Irish parents, and came to Chicago in 1865. At 14, he became a "tally boy" for the lumber firm of **Fish & Brothers**. In 1884 the **S.K. Martin Lumber Co.** was formed and Martin made Hines a partner in that business, as secretary and treasurer. Hines retired April 15, 1892 and immediately organized his own business, **E. Hines Lumber Co.**, specializing in shingles, lath and pickets. In 1893 a year of great economic turmoil, the founding of the Illinois Manufacturers' Association and the World's Columbian Exposition, the company sold 102,525,625 feet of lumber, with a proportionate quantity of shingles and lath, the largest amount handled by any Chicago lumber house that year. Considering the business depression which prevailed during 1893, involving all classes of commercial industry, and the fact that it was only the firm's second year of existence, this was a very impressive showing.

Lumber was also important to other Illinois towns. Rockwood was a major center of the southern Illinois timber market on the Mississippi. The wood was used to fuel steamers. The town was also a flat bottomed boat manufacturing center. Karnak, in southern Illinois, was largely a company built logging and milling town.

While converting trees into planks was the dominant form of manufacturing during the 1830s, Illinois also saw the development of brick production and potteries. In Rushville, north of Beardstown, there were 18 potteries employing 200 workers during the three decades preceding the Civil War. Then the clay ran out. Today nothing of the kilns remains.

Southern "yellow pine" became Chicago's flooring.

For much of the nineteenth century Illinois was a major producer of pottery, supplying most of the needs of the trans-Mississippi trade. White Hall, founded in 1820, was the center of an important clay field that has been used since 1824, when William Heath began manufacturing redware there. One hundred years later, the pottery still made sewer pipes and drain tiles. In 1865 a large pottery works was established in Peoria. The town of Anna had a pottery manufacture in the 1880s that was very well known for the odd forms of its creations. Just as today, earthenware served many functions in the past. If it was used just for storage it did not have to be decorated much, but it did have to be functional and sturdy. This use of earthenware generally survived until replaced by a more efficient material, such as plastic, from the 1920s onward. Decorative earthenware was intended to be seen. It could also be functional, but its surface had to be decorated. The decoration required artisans with greater skill than just throwing a pot and applying a basic glaze. These manufacturers tended to be shorter lived because the demand for their products was mostly driven by fashion and taste set in a larger cultural context, outside the industry, and made known through magazines, newspapers and catalogues.

One pottery that made the transition all the way from bricks to art pottery was Haeger of Dundee, now known as **The Haeger Potteries Inc.** In 1871 and 1872 the bricks David H. Haeger manufactured in Dundee helped rebuild Chicago after the Great Fire. The Fox River's banks provided the clay for the bricks. From this start developed one of the great potteries of America. Haeger introduced its own distinctive form of art pottery in 1914. One of David's sons, Edmund H. Haeger, set up a complete working ceramic factory showing both ancient and contemporary modes of production at the Century of Progress Exposition, 1933-34. At their facility in Macomb, established in 1938, Haeger manufactured porcelain for a time, but more important, the plant still produces a complete line of pottery for florists.

Haeger of Dundee began as a brickmaker.

Haeger molders at work, 1993

In 1833 **Blodgett & Lampman** opened a brick yard in Chicago, along the north bank of the river between Clark and Dearborn, opposite the first brick house built in Chicago, also of that year. Belleville was also a major brick manufactory in the 1830s. In 1838 John Smith, his wife and eight children arrived in Savanna from Louisville, Kentucky, and he started a brick kiln. In 1853 George W. Penny came to see the red clay in what was to become Park Ridge, and he opened a brickyard. Penney alone produced over five million bricks annually and, with **Elston & Co.** and several smaller companies, the clay deposits yielded over 20 million bricks annually before they ran out at the end of the decade. In Penny's honor, the town became known as Bricktown. At the time, Chicago bricks sold for $6.00 to $6.50 per thousand, sharply underselling Philadelphia, then the leading brick manufacturing city.

By 1870, 20 Chicago brickyards employed 1,093 people, paid $256,055 in wages and $130,030 for materials on sales of $583,575. Most of the brick manufacturers producing in 1870 had been open for no more than three years. On October 1, 1871 there were an estimated 60,000 buildings in Chicago. Most of the materials used to build these structures were not manufactured in Illinois. The lumber was milled in Wisconsin and Michigan, the hardware and nails were imported from the East, and bricks were just coming into fashion. Then came the Great Chicago Fire, October 9 and 10, 1871, and much of Chicago north of Roosevelt Road and east of Halsted burned down. Where the city had to rebuild, brick was the material of choice. Up to this time, Philadelphia had been the center of United States brick production but, about the time of the Fire, Philadelphia's brick costs increased markedly at the same time that the railroads began to charge higher freight rates. Brick production immediately shifted to Chicago and as it rebuilt, Chicago became the pressed brick center of the United States.

At the same time Chicago also became the center of the nation's terra cotta production. The **Chicago Terra Cotta Company**, the first permanent terra cotta works in the United States, was established in Chicago in 1868, at Laflin and 15th Street, by two florists and seed dealers, Albert H. Hovey and J.F. Nichols, and manufactured horticultural urns, garden statuary and some architectural ornament.

Prior to the Great Fire stone, iron and brick were commonly believed to be fireproof building materials. Inspection of the ruins, however, showed broken bricks, crumbled granite walls and twisted iron columns which had melted and given way. From the disaster, architects learned the need to protect all cast iron structural work with a sheathing of fire clay, terra cotta or brick. The innovative use of terra cotta as a fireproof material has been attributed to three different men: George H. Johnson, John M. Van Osdel and Sanford E. Loring. The first, George H. Johnson, had immigrated in 1852 from England to New York City, where he became manager of the **Architectural Iron Works**. Eight years later Johnson moved to Chicago and, in partnership with architect John M. Van Osdel, built four cast iron front buildings on Lake Street. In 1870 Johnson obtained the first of four patents on fireproof hollow tiles.

> After 1871 Chicago became the pressed brick center of the United States.

When the Great Chicago Fire broke out, Johnson was in New York. He returned immediately to Chicago to survey the fire ruins on October 12th, and soon thereafter came up with the idea of using hollow, hard burned clay as a covering for cast iron columns and beams, as well as for creating a fireproof floor by putting terra cotta tiles between the beams. He also devised terra cotta tiles for partitions and for backing up exterior walls. A year later these ideas were incorporated by Van Osdel in the construction of the Kendal Building. On the interior, iron I-beams and vertical columns were encased in terra cotta tiles and elongated tiles were fitted together to form arched ceilings, partitions and floors, which inaugurated a system of fireproof construction that would become universal until the adoption of reinforced concrete around 1910. In 1886 the passage of a city ordinance requiring all buildings in Chicago over ninety feet high to be absolutely fireproof further stimulated the expansion of the terra cotta industry. The third inventor, Sanford E. Loring, was a partner in the architectural firm of **Loring & Jenny,** who assumed the position of Treasurer in the newly formed **Chicago Terra Cotta Company**. Loring gradually moved the production away from pots and urns and towards architectural elements.

In 1877 John R. True, John Brunkhorst, Gustav Hottinger and Henry Rohkam, all former employees of the Chicago Terra Cotta Company, founded the **Northwestern Terra Cotta Works** to produce architectural terra cotta and garden ornaments. The firm incorporated as the **Northwest Terra Cotta Company** in 1888 and by 1927 had become the largest terra cotta manufacturer in the United States with a main factory at 2525 North Clybourn and branch factories in Denver, St. Louis and Chicago Heights. Northwest furnished the terra cotta for many important Chicago buildings, including the Rookery, the Tacoma, the Railway Exchange Building, the Wrigley Building, the Blackstone Hotel, the Merchandise Mart and the Carbide & Carbon Building. The company survived until 1956.

Outside of Chicago the town of Crystal Lake has a small suburb known as Terra Cotta, named after its once chief manufacturer, the **Terra Cotta Tile Works**. Founded by William Day Gates in 1881, the company made sewer tiles and architectural terra cotta. Just before World War I its brand of ceramic, TECO ware, became very popular. During the Depression the firm was purchased by George A. Berry II, who began to use its kilns for the heat treating of steel. The last terra cotta and ceramic were produced in 1966.

When it wasn't animals, water in the form of rivers or steam powered most of the machinery built in nineteenth century America. But there were alternatives. Some of the northern Europeans who came to North America brought with them the technology of windmills and erected a good many in the East as early as the seventeenth century. Their use was localized and they never really offered a viable alternative to water power in the United States. Of the four windmills constructed in the middle of the nineteenth century in DuPage County, **Holsteins Mill** in Bloomingdale and the Heidemann in Addison are gone, but two have survived. **Fischer Mill**, built between 1847 and 1850 by Frederick Fischer, is on its original site by Grand Avenue, one mile east of York Road. In the 1920s it was still capable of producing about thirty barrels of flour a day. Today, it is a monument to its age.

TECO ware made Terra Cotta, Illinois famous.

The Old Holland Mill, built by Louis Backhaus in the 1850s, worked well on its site along York Road until it began falling apart. In disrepair in 1914, it came to the attention of "Colonel" George Fabyan, a wealthy businessman originally from Boston, who had an estate on the Fox River at St. Charles and was keen on consuming naturally milled flour. He bought the mill and had it transported to his estate, where it survives. In 1915 the mill was home to William Friedman, a student from Cornell University interested in genetics, who with his wife, Elizabeth Smith, worked for Fabyan on projects in cryptography to such effect that they became leading experts for the federal government during both world wars.

Wind was an alternative to water and animal power.

Near the end of the century, another kind of windmill was invented by LaVerne Noyes, born 1849. He was a farmer's son by birth, an inventor by nature and, fortunately, a good business man. When he was twenty five years old, in 1874, he established a business in improved haying tools at Batavia. Among the things he then invented, manufactured and sold were hay forks, hay stacking frames and carriers, and gate hangers. Along with his wife, Ida, Noyes was very interested in words and always kept the Webster's Unabridged Dictionary at hand. Ida Noyes found the dictionary very heavy and cumbersome. To make looking up words easier Noyes patented the wire dictionary holder and began to manufacture and offer it on the market. The demand was almost immediate and the wire dictionary holder sold so well that the Noyes' moved to Chicago and established a manufacturing facility for it there. Meanwhile he continued to work on new inventions and sell them to farm machinery manufacturers. Thus he met William Deering, founder of the company carrying his name, and a core firm in the creation of **International Harvester Company.**

Noyes' great invention improved on an old one — the windmill. His experiments and improvements transformed the passive windmill into an "air motor," a machine that could run on very light wind. His new firm was named the **Aermotor Company**, with manufacturing beginning in 1888 on West Monroe Street in Chicago. The business grew so fast that by 1890 new space was needed. The business expanded to include the making of the towers which supported the aermotor. These towers also functioned for carrying cables of electric transmissions lines from the hydro or steam generating plants, as radio station antennas and electric flood lights. Noyes also experimented with using the aermotor to transform wind into electricity, which could be stored in batteries that would in turn power electric motors to turn the aermotor when there was no wind. He died in 1919, before he could perfect this scheme.

Noyes was a president of the IMA from 1909-10. As a member of the IMA he visited the West and South. His close association with the University of Chicago is remembered in Ida Noyes Hall.

Whether it was the pistol to avenge one's honor, the Kentucky rifle for shooting squirrels and other things at long distances, or the hand gun to make your day, guns of all sorts have always been important to Americans. Much of America's west, starting from the

Atlantic coast, was "tamed" by guns and the bullets that made them effective were of lead. Throughout the nineteenth century lead was in great demand and any place that had it prospered. So it should not come as a surprise that mining, the first industry in Northwest Illinois, depended on lead. On a very small scale, and then only for use as ornament, Indians mined lead north and south of the mouth of the Wisconsin River from time immemorial, and the French, who used lead for shot, were active in this area from the 1690s on.

Galena's lead helped make guns important.

By 1810 lead was mined in a small way on the Fever River in Galena and shipped in flatboats down the Mississippi. But it was not until 1822, when the federal government leased a tract to Colonel James Johnson, who brought twenty miners and fifty slaves from Kentucky to work his claim, that mining really took off. The next year the *Virginia* became the first steamboat to reach "the point" on the upper Mississippi that would become Galena in 1826. Lead production increased markedly until 1845, when a record fifty-four million pounds of lead were shipped from Galena, which by that time had become one of the largest towns in Illinois and was the largest supplier of lead in the United States. As the lead production slowly declined and cheaper sources were found further west, the hills began to erode severely, silting up the river to such a degree that steamboats could not travel on it. Galena fell into a slumber that has preserved its historical past like no other city in Illinois.

GRAIN HELPED MAKE ILLINOIS GREAT

The greatest changes since ancient times in farming and grain harvesting in particular came about in the course of the nineteenth century when the manufacture of farm machinery came into its own in Illinois. It was here that the steel plow was perfected, that reapers were made, and that farmers brought their machine harvester grains to market.

Chicago was the first new city to grow to international prominence after the advent of the commercial age. Chicago grew because through it the world could be fed. Grain was Chicago's most dependable source of prosperity. Grain and lake boats made Chicago the hub of the nationwide railroad network. Grain served as collateral for commerce, and as commerce increased, so did the diversity of raw, semi-finished and finished materials moving through the Chicago River port.

While nature favored Chicago's location, man's industry was required to raise the city to unrivaled status among the world's entrepots. Over New Orleans, the first of its two competitors as "stacker of wheat," Chicago enjoyed a dual natural advantage. One was climate; the heat and humidity of the city on the Gulf often condemned grain in storage to rot or to be eaten by rodents. In Chicago, in contrast, grain put in storage during the fall and winter remained safely cool during the period when lake navigation was shut down for the winter. As late as 1880, 80 percent of the grain shipped through Chicago was stored before shipped.

Grain elevators along Calumet River in 1990

In 1838
78 bushels of
grain were shipped
from Chicago.

The second advantage was geography, which linked St. Louis to New Orleans by the Mississippi River, while leaving Chicago as an independent linchpin in a different geographical complex. To reach the rapidly growing cities on the East Coast and in northern Europe, the route from the grain producing prairie down the Mississippi River to St. Louis, through New Orleans, and around Florida was much longer than the route by rail or along the Illinois and Michigan Canal to Chicago. There it could then enter the Great Lakes system and reach New York via Buffalo and the Erie Canal or be shipped to Europe directly via the St. Lawrence River. Also, Chicagoans liked to boast that they could throw themselves into commerce unhindered by traditional ways of doing things, in contrast to St. Louis, where custom dictated that grain be handled in bags, each of which was graded, labeled and carried by hand.

The first consignment of grain from Chicago, 78 bushels shipped to Buffalo in 1838, was the last to be handled in this way in Chicago. The 3,768 bushels shipped the next year were elevated in buckets with ropes and pulleys to the second story of a frame riverside building for storage, then they were carried by way of bucket brigade to a chute which deposited the grain into four-bushel boxes on the deck of the vessel, which were then weighed and dumped straight into the ship's hold.

Over the next decade and a half, Chicagoans perfected this procedure into a system of which the elevator became the most essential and conspicuous physical embodiment.

In the traditional system it had been known which farmer grew the grain that was packed in any particular bag; in the new system developed in Chicago, the bagged grain was poured into bins to commingle with grains grown by many farmers. Central to this system was a nexus of trust among grain dealers and their clients, a trust that was policed and enforced by the **Chicago Board of Trade**, founded in 1848 and chartered in 1850, whose members had devised the system and subsequently controlled the grain it handled.

Chicago grain secured loans from the East that built railroads.

The storage capacity was essential to the system. While stored in Chicago, grain served as the basis for credit for both the businessmen and the farmers. In times of economic turmoil, when eastern paper lacked gold backing, Chicago paper was supported by grain. Chicago grain secured loans from the East that built railroads and the cities that sprang up along the railroad lines. While large, the elevators were otherwise unspectacular. They needed equipment to collect and elevate loose grain, bins to store it and chutes to deposit it into carriers. Irishmen wielding buckets did the first collecting and elevating, but after many of them moved on to dig the Illinois and Michigan Canal, horses and mules powering bucket chains took over.

The increase in railroad transportation brought the demand for more elevator storage. New technology such as the bucket conveyor at the **Bristol Elevator** was driven by a steam engine made at a Chicago iron foundry operated by Elihu Granger. The Bristol Elevator, constructed of brick, held a mere 80,000 bushels, only a small portion of the 2,160,000 bushels of wheat and 615,770 of corn and oats that moved through Chicago in 1848.

By 1854 when Chicago shipped thirteen million bushels, more than Odessa in the Ukraine, to become the world's greatest grain port, steam would drive a screw hoist and the city's two newest elevators would dwarf their predecessors. These two elevators, built on the basis of recent experience, would serve as models for the next half century. Standing on the north bank of the river opposite the commercial district, the **Armour, Dole and Co.** Elevator held 300,000 bushels, while the **Gibbs, Griffin and Co.** Elevator held 500,000 bushels.

A year later a larger elevator joined them across the river nearer the lake, the **Sturges, Buckingham and Co.** "A" Elevator holding 700,000 bushels brought by the Illinois Central Railroad. In a single day, the elevator's four great steam engines could unload 236 carloads of grain, measuring 80,000 to 90,000 bushels, while discharging even more in a day into lake steamers.

The Great Fire of 1871 consumed seven of the city's seventeen giant elevators, but replacements were quickly rebuilt on their old sites. Others soon joined the ranks; some of these were even larger than before, holding up to 2,000,000 bushels each.

In 1898 Chicago was equipped with twenty-two giant elevators with the combined capacity of thirty-two million bushels, but new shipment patterns were making Milwaukee and

Duluth more important grain ports than Chicago. In Chicago itself the task of moving and storing grain was shifting from the harbor to outlying railyards. New, fast, rail transportation obviated the need for storage and transshipment to lake boats. At the same time, new construction techniques using the stark, cylindrical, reinforced concrete bins were providing larger and more efficient structures. Gradually, the elevators disappeared from the central city.

In 1846 there were 177 manufacturing concerns in Chicago, employing in all 1,400 persons, about 10 percent of the total population; 250 persons were employed in packing houses; 71 in foundries; 50 in tanneries; 46 in cooperages; 61 in wagon shops; 190 in shoe shops; 59 in saddle and harness shops; 44 in cap and fur factories; 121 in tailor shops; 83 in cabinet and chair shops; 16 in soap, candle and oil factories.

Small shops became factories, expanding output and products. At Canton, William Parlin expanded the shop in which he turned out the first steel-bottomed plow that did away with the wooden moldboard. William Worth Burson invented a grain binder that featured machine-tied knots, but he had not yet perfected the automatic knitting machine that would make Rockford famous for its socks.

Edward Hegeler and Frederick W. Matthiessen, recent arrivals from Germany, decided that because of its coal supplies, water and proximity to Galena, La Salle County would be an ideal site for the nation's first zinc smelter. The zinc ore, shipped by the Illinois Central Railroad, was a by-product of the Galena lead mines. Established in 1858, the **Matthiessen and Hegeler Zinc Co.** of La Salle was the source of the principal revenue of the city after 1900. Early in the 19th century Stockton, by Rockford, was an important lead smelting town for the mines in JoDaviess County. Missouri zinc ore was smelted in Collinsville after the introduction of the railroad made possible the exploitation of local coal. Fairmont City, now in East St. Louis, was incorporated in 1914, when it became an important zinc smelting center. After a strike in 1918 it introduced Mexican workers, who by 1940 had become 25 percent of the population. Since the 1840s the manufacture of metals, mainly iron and steel has been very important to other Illinois cities such as La Salle, East St. Louis, Joliet and Chicago.

Until the invention of the reaper, advances in farming methods were so slow as to be almost imperceptible. In spite of its status as humanity's basic industry, agriculture failed to progress or even to undergo much study in ancient times. It was still a laborious, unrewarding pursuit in the 1830s — one offering little promise of leisure or security to anyone engaged in it. The farmer was completely at the mercy of the soil and the elements. If circumstances caused him to fail, he was confronted with the specter of famine. It was a world in which the overwhelming majority of the population toiled unceasingly to supply its mere physical needs.

Of all problems of the farmer, the harvesting of the grain was the most stubborn, having throughout history resisted every effort to apply any but human power to its solution.

Missouri zinc ore was smelted in Collinsville.

Horses and oxen had been used to pull plows, harrows and carts, but were of no avail at harvest time, when only countless hours of backbreaking toil could cut and bind the grain before it rotted on the ground.

Since the earliest recorded days of harvesting, the sickle had been the tool of choice. The scythe, practical only for cutting standing grain, was introduced sometime in antiquity and made it possible for a man to cut two acres a day. During the eighteenth century, the scythe was improved by the addition of wooden fingers. With this implement, called a cradle, grain could be cut and at the same time gathered and thrown into swaths, making it simpler for others following to bind it into sheaves.

The reaper revolutionized harvesting.

The greatest single boost to Illinois' farm implement use and production came with the McCormick reaper in 1847, when the company moved to Chicago. It immediately became the largest implement manufacturer in the city and state. Cyrus H. McCormick was born in 1809, in Rockbridge County, Virginia and died in May, 1884, in Chicago. He changed farming forever and played an important role in industrializing Chicago. McCormick didn't know there were forty-seven patents for reapers at the time he and Jo Anderson, a slave, built one in the smithy of his father's farm in 1831. Three years later he patented his design and by 1840, after many improvements and waging numerous battles over patent violations, began to manufacture and sell his reaper. McCormick claimed that his reaper could harvest as much as ten acres per day, eight more than with a scythe.

The first reaper of which there is a record was patented in England on July 4, 1799 by Joseph Boyee. Its immense weight and cumbersome proportions rendered it impractical and it was soon abandoned. Around the year 1826, Rev. Patrick Bell of Carmyville, Scotland, brought out a machine which was the first to use a vibrating cutter in place of a revolving circular plate. Up to this time the plate had done all the cutting. The vibrating cutter quickly proved to be the only efficient method for cutting grain or grass. One of these machines was brought to the United States and used.

An American named Hawkins was the first in this country to obtain a patent on a reaper. The year was 1810, and eastern farms were modest. The success of this machine was not proved; farmers preferred the scythe.

Over the next two decades many patents were granted to Americans, one of them to William Manning in 1831. He applied several new features to former machines, but did not find it practical to produce his experiments. Obed Hussey, in Cincinnati, Ohio, conceived the idea, in 1832, of a slotted guard for the knife or sickle to work in. This principle was adopted in all subsequent developments. Hussey produced the first practical reaper known. Following Hussey came McCormick who, in 1845 and after combining all the practical features developed so far, including Hussey's, introduced his own practical machine.

McCormick's reapers sold, but the Virginias were not the right base of operations. The demand for machinery was in the west and McCormick settled on Chicago as a suitable manufacturing site in 1847. Why he chose Chicago remains something of a mystery. Other western cities in Pennsylvania and Ohio had much better manufacturing facilities, but whether by luck or shrewd booster logic, his timing could not have been better. He formed a partnership with Charles M. Gray, bought land on the North Branch of the Chicago River, and built a factory there. His brother, along with Leander J. and William Sanderson, joined him. In the first year of production McCormick's factory produced 500 reapers. By 1871 production at the **McCormick Harvesting Machine Co.** stood at 10,000 units annually. By 1900 214,000 reapers were produced every year and the factory had moved to Blue Island and Western Avenues. Among his important innovations in marketing his product was the extension of liberal credit to the buyers. In 1859 McCormick started the *Chicago Times* newspaper, the leading antiwar paper in the North. Hailing from Virginia, McCormick had certain sympathies for the South, which he expressed in no uncertain terms. After his death in 1884, his wife, Nettie Fowler McCormick, took over the business, which merged with the **Deering Harvester Company**. to form the foundation of the **International Harvester Company** in 1902. The new company was big. Its plant in Canton alone manufactured more than 1,400 types of plows, harrows, discs and other agricultural implements.

In Rockford the **Talcott Emerson & Co.** built the Manny Reaper. Other farm machinery improvements followed, such as the self-rake, developed in principle by Dorsey and Young of Maryland. There was also the self-rake with two driving wheels and a hinged cutter bar. This was the invention of Augustus Adams and his partner, Mr. Silla, both of Sandwich.

Another important invention was the harvester. C.W. and W.W. Marsh, farmers living in Shabbona Grove, obtained a patent on August 17, 1858 for an entirely new method of harvesting by machine. The cut grain fell upon a revolving platform, was elevated up over

> In 1847 McCormick produced 500 reapers.

THE NEW MARSH HARVESTER AND TWINE BINDER.

the drive wheel and delivered upon the receiver, beside which two men stood and alternately bound the grain up. The automatic binder eventually replaced the two men.

The Marsh harvester established the most economical and rapid manner for gathering and binding grain known at the time. For the years 1858 through 1871 no other harvester was on the market. Built initially in a shop in Plano, the company opened extensive facilities in Sycamore in 1869. Their success was so strong that the old reaper manufacturers fell into line one by one and built harvesters, too.

Attention was also focused on automatic binding, but nothing much developed until in 1861 or 1862 when Mr. Burson of Rockford brought out a practical machine. Only a few machines were built, production being severely restricted by the Civil War. The same year a Mr. Sherwood, of Auburn, New York, demonstrated a wire binder which showed much promise, but it also became a casualty of the Civil War. The Marsh harvester filled the gap. Meanwhile the large manufacturers started producing harvesters under license from C.W. and W.W. Marsh, or without. Competition became fierce and by 1890 hand binding was virtually extinct.

In 1870 Charles Whitney and his brother, John II, built two original and complete machines for cutting and automatically binding grain with wire at the **Sycamore Marsh Harvester Company**. The machine worked well, but the sickness and death of John put a stop to developments. Eight years later Charles Whitney asked the Marsh Brothers to start up development again. The first machine was used that year, and though lacking great capacity it showed promise. In 1880, after some changes, 40 of them were put to the test in various harvests from Texas to Montana. They stood the test, but they were wire binders and other companies had shown twine to be faster, cheaper and a better material to work with, so twine binders were developed and introduced by Marsh in 1882. From the first acre of wheat cut in Texas to the last in Dakota, the Whitney designed and S.W. and W.W. Marsh manufactured binders proved such a success that a new firm was formed, the **Marsh Binder Manufacturing Company**. The new company bought the works of the Sycamore Marsh Harvester Manufacturing Co. and immediately went into production. The machine proved an immediate success.

In 1850 Illinois had 33 farm implement manufacturers; Pennsylvania had 337; New York, 306; Maine, 118; Ohio, 107; Massachusetts, 64; New Hampshire, 52; Maryland, 40; and Kentucky, 36. Ten years later there were four manufacturers in Chicago producing implements valued at $529,000 from raw materials valued at $118,100. The same year, New York City had one implement manufacturer producing $33,500 worth of machinery; Cincinnati had ten producing $221,700; Philadelphia had seven implement factories producing $103,850; and Detroit eight, with a total production of $35,268. Truly the production of farm machinery had moved to Illinois.

Much of the production was centered in Chicago. The Census of 1880 shows Chicago with three firms producing farm machinery worth $2,699,480. While the 910 implement factories in the United States and their 42,544 employees produced $81,271,651 worth of farm implements in the year ending June, 1890, Chicago's six produced about one-seventh of the total of the country. In the 1890s, Deering Harvester Works was the largest of its kind in the world.

Between 1870 and 1880 new implement manufacturers started up in Moline, Quincy and Rockford. By 1890 Quincy had five implement manufacturing companies and Channahon was an important farm equipment manufacturing center. Canton was a major center of farm implements and machinery development. Such machines as the corn stalk cutter, the disc harrow with concave discs and the lister were invented and developed there.

> Canton was a major farm implement center.

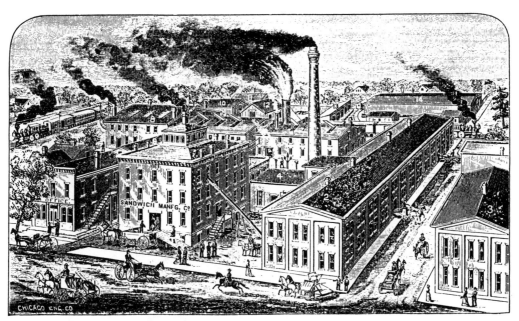

SHOPS AND OFFICE OF THE SANDWICH MANUFACTURING COMPANY.
SANDWICH, ILLINOIS.

Among the now forgotten important early farm implement manufacturers was the **Sandwich Manufacturing Co.** In 1840 or 1841 in the then small village of Elgin, the only iron foundry west of Lake Michigan was located. It was there that Augustus Adams and a Mr. Gifford opened business in a rode water-powered mill, melting iron one ladle at a time, and casting plow points and sled shoes for the new settlers. To melt more iron, a hotter fire was needed, and that meant harder coal. After much persuasion, **Norton & Co.,** of Chicago, was induced to import two hogsheads of hard coal from Pennsylvania for use in this shop. This coal may have been the first to ever have landed in Chicago.

In the 1840s wheat was grown in this area of Illinois and Augustus Adams was among the many inventors of reapers and other harvesting equipment. But when the wheat failed and corn became the staple farm product, corn shellers were needed. Small and inefficient hand shellers were being made in Elgin shops, but production could not keep pace with the ever increasing demand.

To manufacture his own shellers, Adams started a small shop in Sandwich on the Chicago, Burlington & Quincy railroad line. With a small steam engine introduced into Illinois agricultural manufacturing in 1489 to run the machinery, he developed his ideas for a practical portable Power Corn Sheller. He called it the "Veteran" and, by 1857, Adams had moved his family to Sandwich and was producing corn shellers as fast as his shop would permit.

The Sandwich Adams Corn Sheller was in great demand by 1861.

By 1861 the reputation of the Sandwich Adams Corn Sheller was so extensive that the firm employed about 100 people and became known as **A. Adams & Sons**. The company prospered and in 1867 was reorganized as the Sandwich Manufacturing Co. The company produced a line of shellers, the simplest being the "Veteran," a two hole, feed table sheller, with wire cob rake and fan. It easily adapted to light power and was much used in custom mills and small warehouses, where its capacity of 250 to 300 bushels of corn per day was adequate.

The Veteran Corn Sheller

Other hand shellers included the "Prince" and the "Comet." Larger shellers were run by the "Fast Motion One Horse Power, Reliance" which could also be used for feed grinders, root and straw cutters, and churns. For years the standard jobbing sheller was the four or six hole "Gear Mounted Sheller." The capacity of this machine was from 1,500 to 2,000 or 2,500 to 3,000 bushels respectively of shelled corn per day. These machines were in great demand for mills and warehouses where they were driven by belt from an engine or any other power source that is fitted onto a band wheel proportioned to the speed and size of the pulleys by which they are driven. There were also self feed and elevator models.

The 1890s saw the Sandwich Manufacturing Co. produce the "Appleby" binder which was placed on the Adams & French Harvester. This harvester differed from all others in moving the grain by using sets of vibrating rakes. Sandwich Manufacturing Co. also held the patent on and made the only hot-forged Machine Keys, which they supplied to manufacturers of implements, engines and heavy machinery from New England to Minnesota and far into the South.

The ability to mechanically harvest large fields of crops presupposed the ability to plant them. And before the harvester could be put to work, the plow had to prepare the soil. The first plows were made to order at the local blacksmith's forge. These proved inadequate, yet the time was fortunate because the prairies of Illinois were just being seduced and farmers demanded all the machinery they could get. With the new developments in production, output increased markedly and demand for farm machinery rose accordingly, which in turn increased farm productivity, and which in turn created greater markets for farm produced goods.

A number of Illinoisans claim to have produced the first steel plows. **Maple & Parlin**, a local enterprise in Canton, began the production of steel board plows in 1846. In 1852 William J. Orendorff supplanted Maple and the **P. & O. Plow Works** came into being. In 1919 P. & O. Plow Works became part of the International Harvester Company and by the 1930s was one of the largest manufacturers of plows in the world.

John Deere developed the world's first self-scouring steel plow.

"IF WE DON'T IMPROVE OUR PRODUCT, SOMEBODY ELSE WILL."

Though others may claim precedence, the accepted fact is that in 1837 an innovative young blacksmith named John Deere developed the world's first commercially successful, self-scouring steel plow. Today, John Deere's development is credited with opening the prairies to modern agriculture by enabling pioneer farmers to till the tough but rich Midwestern soil.

John Deere was born in Rutland, Vermont, in 1804. Later, moving to Middlebury, Vermont, he learned the blacksmith trade and served a four-year apprenticeship. In 1825 he began his career as a journeyman blacksmith and soon gained considerable fame for his careful workmanship and ingenuity. His highly polished hay forks and shovels were in great demand with farmers throughout western Vermont.

John Deere Low Down manure spreader in 1927

But as business conditions became depressed in Vermont in the mid-1830s, Deere's future looked bleak. At the same time, tales of golden opportunities in the "new west" began to circulate in the east. Several pioneers returned to Vermont from trips west hoping to persuade neighbors to relocate their business in Grand Detour, which had been settled by Leonard Andrus and others from Vermont. Grand Detour, so called by French voyageurs, lies in an oxbow bend in the Rock River Valley, a wide paradise teeming with game, fish, wild nuts, fruits, and home to Indians for many centuries who had grown corn, squash and other native crops.

John Deere was a blacksmith from Vermont.

With a small bundle of tools and very little money, Deere crossed the frontier to Grand Detour in 1836. The need for a blacksmith was so great that just two days after he arrived, Deere had built a forge and was in business serving the community with skillfully fashioned equipment and shoeing horses and oxen. From the farmers, Deere soon heard that the cast iron plows they had brought with them from the east were virtually useless in the rich, moist Midwestern soil. These plows were designed for the light, sandy New England soil. Every few steps, the farmers were forced to stop and scrape off the soil that clung to parts of the plow. As a result, cultivation was a slow and laborious task. Desperate, many farmers considered leaving the Midwest in search of soil conditions better suited to their equipment.

Deere was convinced that the sticky soil would fall, or scour, from a highly polished and properly shaped moldboard and share, allowing the plow to turn a clean furrow slice. Soon he had fashioned just such a plow from a broken saw blade of high quality English steel. Deere's "self-polishing" steel plow was successfully tested on the farm of Lewis Crandall near Grand Detour in 1837. It proved to be the solution needed for farming in what was then "the West."

Deere's contribution to the growth of American agriculture far exceeded just development of a successful steel plow. It was the practice of that day for blacksmiths to build tools for customers on order. But John Deere went into business manufacturing plows before he had orders for them. He would produce a supply of plows and then take them to the country to be sold — an entirely new approach to manufacturing and selling farm equipment.

This new sales approach and the need for a new plow spread the word quickly of the wondrous new invention. Farmers throughout the Midwest placed orders. Claiming they could hear the Deere plow sing as the share bit cleanly through the earth and soil fell from the moldboard, farmers dubbed it the "singing plow."

There were many problems involved in attempting to operate a manufacturing business on the frontier — few banks, poor transportation and a scarcity of steel. These firsts plows were built of whatever steel Deere could get. In 1843 he secured a shipment of special rolled steel from England. This steel had to be shipped across the Atlantic Ocean by steamship, up the Mississippi and Illinois Rivers by packet boat, and overland by wagon 40 miles to the little plow factory in Grand Detour. From this shipment Deere fashioned

Reliving the Deere experience

In 1846
the first slab
of cast plow steel
was rolled in the
United States
for John Deere.

400 plows. In 1846 the first slab of cast plow steel ever rolled in the United States was made for John Deere and shipped from Pittsburgh to Moline, where it was ready for use in the factory Deere opened there in 1847 to take advantage of the water power and transportation provided by the Mississippi River. A decade after the first plow was developed, John Deere was manufacturing 1,000 plows a year.

One of Deere's early partners chided him for constantly making changes in design. The fellow thought it was unnecessary because the farmers had to take whatever they produced. Deere replied: "No, they don't. If we don't improve our product, somebody else will." In 1868 Deere's business was incorporated under the name **Deere & Company**. By 1911 the company was making a wide range of steel plows, cultivators, corn and cotton planters, and other implements when six non-competing farm equipment companies were brought into the Deere organization, establishing the company as a full-line manufacturer of farm equipment. In 1918 the company purchased the Waterloo Gasoline Engine Company of Waterloo, Iowa, and tractors became an important part of the John Deere line.

Over the next decade modern farming would develop, and even during the depression Deere achieved record sales, breaking $100 million gross for the first time in 1937, the year of its centennial. By the mid-1950s Deere was firmly established as one of the nation's 100 largest manufacturing businesses. Over the next two decades, Deere would experience its greatest growth and establish manufacturing and marketing worldwide, becoming the world's largest manufacturer of farm equipment, and a leading supplier of construction equipment. Deere is also the North American market leader in forestry equipment, and lawn care and outdoor power products. The 1980s were a difficult time. The company restructured, and posted record sales and earning in the last three years of the decade. Today, John Deere is a multinational corporation doing business in more than 160 countries and employing 34,000 people worldwide.

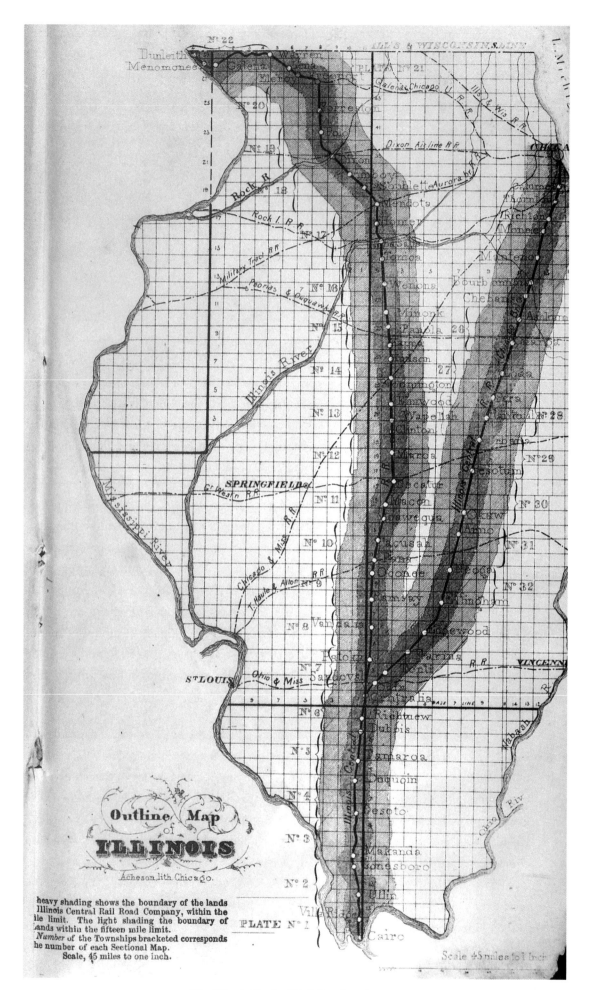

The Illinois Central Rail Road route

RAILROADS PUT MANUFACTURERS AND MARKETS ON A SCHEDULE

During the 1850s railroads brought about the distribution of manufactured products as it had never before been seen in Illinois or the nation. As rails rushed west from the East Coast the nation's population followed along them and towns easily popped up in places convenient to the trains' schedules. For the first time in human history, people could move faster than animals and carry more.

All along the railroutes change occurred. New lands became available through railroad right of ways. These lands, in turn, allowed rural populations to be closely bound to urban needs. With the development of farm machinery, farmers could now produce specifically for a market and not just for themselves and a few immediate neighbors. In turn, as ever more feed became available, hogs and cattle could be raised in quantities that surpassed all previous notions of meat production. To meet the food requirements of the rapidly increasing population, its production became industrialized.

Manufacturers, too, could realize their ideas and have access to markets via the rails. This allowed them to be located in small towns, some of which, in turn, became production centers of national importance. The traditional requirement of having natural resources immediately at hand before an industry could develop was no longer a rule. The railroads had changed that. From the 1850s on, Nature's abundance would come to man and be his servant. In Illinois the actualization of this dream came quickly and stayed for the next hundred years.

From the mid-1830s on, there were proposals to build railroads in many different parts of Illinois, but it was not until the late 1840s that intentions became deeds. The first successful railroad can be dated to 1836, when William B. Ogden, a Chicago based capitalist, acquired the dormant charter for a railline to the lead mines, the Galena and Chicago Union. The name of the line indicates the comparative importance of these two cities at the time.

Ogden's **Galena and Chicago Union Road** brought in the first locomotive, a used one called the *Pioneer*, on a sailing vessel from Buffalo, New York, in October, 1848. The next spring, the Pioneer made its run along the old stage route as far west as Elmhurst. The rails the Pioneer rode on were wooden riders sheathed in iron; the ties were small and widely spaced. They broke easily. The following year the track reached Elgin, then Garden Prairie, between Marengo and Belvidere. In 1852 tracks were laid in Belvidere and the next year in Freeport. There the Galena and Chicago Union stopped and connected with the Illinois Central Railroad, which already had reached Galena. Ogden's railroad returned big dividends, averaging 16 percent between 1850 and 1855. This return did not go unnoticed and soon eastern money was investing heavily in Illinois railroads.

The Pioneer was the first locomotive in Illinois.

Within a few years of the arrival of the first locomotive, the **Chicago Locomotive Co.** was organized and built the first locomotive in Chicago, the *Enterprise*. It was completed for the **Galena & Chicago Union Railroad Co.**

As the need for locomotives grew, the Galena & Chicago added its own locomotive building department. The **American Car Co.** opened its shops on the lake shore about three miles south of the Chicago River. This plant was followed by the Union Car Works of **A.B. Stone & Co.** These were built on the prairie to the west of the River. An iron bridge builder, **Stone & Boomer**, the builders of the Howe Patent Truss Bridge, erected their works nearby. By the mid-1850s Chicago was a major industrial center.

Railroads united Illinois markets to the East and Europe.

The arrival of the *Pioneer* in Chicago had set a precedent that would have a most profound impact on the city throughout its history. The concentration of railroad lines into Chicago was partly the result of intense political lobbying and partly the inevitable result of geography. Lines from the East had to pass the southern tip of Lake Michigan, from where Chicago had the only satisfactory port with transshipment possibilities. Lobbying helped establish lines that led west from Chicago. The city as a world transportation hub was being fixed. This development of railroad lines quickly led to the opening up of vast areas of agricultural land in Illinois and greatly increased economic activity in Chicago itself. It also had consequences on a national scale, for the fertile lands of the Midwest would no longer be tied in with the Mississippi Valley, as they had been with river and canal traffic. When the railroads reached the lake port they organized lake lines to cooperate in land-water transportation. Through the railroads, the great markets of the Plains and the East and Europe were united. Within one decade the eastwest axis had replaced the north-south one. The political and economic consequences would be profound.

When the Civil War came, in spite of the heavy mix of settlers from the South, Illinois followed its economic partners in the east. The north-south length of Illinois formed a sort of spearhead, penetrating Confederate territory. It should also be remembered that both Lincoln and Grant were from the state.

During the Civil War the southern terminal of the Illinois Central Railroad at Cairo became a huge advance base for the Union forces. Seemingly inexhaustible supplies were brought quickly by the railroads from the distant and well-protected north. Chicago became a great arsenal during the war, providing not only foodstuffs, but also enormous quantities of uniforms and equipment transportation, much of it locally or regionally produced or arriving through the port on Lake Michigan from points east.

Once the war was over, Chicago became the starting point for many a westward venture, with the result that many railroads merged in the vicinity of Chicago and made the city the head of an economic empire stretching as far as the Rocky Mountains and Los Angeles. As recently as 1965, 18 trunk lines provided freight services to all parts of the continental United States on 27 routes from Chicago.

The proliferation of railroads had an important impact on other Illinois towns, too. With the arrival of the railroad in Savanna in 1850, the town became a principle trading center for livestock and grain destined for the Chicago markets. In the 1930s Savanna was the third largest terminal of the Chicago, Milwaukee, St. Paul and Pacific line, with over 50 miles of track in the city. It was also the terminal point of three main line divisions of the Chicago, Burlington & Quincy.

The 1850s saw the chartering, construction and acquisitioning of many railroads in Illinois: the Wabash, which took over the ill-fated Springfield and Meredosia line; the Chicago and Northwestern; the Chicago and Alton; the Chicago, Burlington and Quincy, and the Chicago, Rock Island and Pacific. Interstate lines also came through Illinois: the Baltimore and Ohio; the Michigan Central; the Cleveland, Cincinnati, Chicago and St. Louis.

The first steel rails made in the United States were rolled in May, 1865 at the **Chicago Rolling Mills**. Half a decade later, in 1871, Illinois had 4,648 miles of steel track. And in 1874 alone 1,398 miles of steel track were laid. Thirty years later, in 1901, the state had 8,577 miles. By 1935 Illinois track mileage had swollen to 24,993 miles, the peak of track in Illinois. This rapid increase in mileage was a strong argument for commercial grain and livestock farming, for coal mining, for fuel, railroad car construction, steel mills, manufacturers of farm implements, restaurants, hotels and large wholesale trade in all manufactured goods.

Though the milling of grain had lost its importance in Chicago, the storage and shipping of grain, especially by railroad, soon made up for the difference. In 1832, 70 bushels of wheat were shipped from Chicago; eighteen years later it was two million and in 1870, 16 million. Places like Sheldon grew from a railroad switch established in 1860 by the Toledo, Peoria & Western Railroad to become an important shipping point for grain where eventually a 1,200,000 bushel terminal grain elevator was built.

While the railroads spiderwebbed across Illinois, the I & M Canal did not immediately loose importance. Channahon, founded in 1832, became an important I & M Canal town which in its heyday had six grain elevators within four miles of town. From there several steamboats carried corn to Chicago, but most of the freight was carried in canal boats drawn by mules from along the towpath.

The increase in railroad service brought with it new needs out of which industries developed. As railroads were used by more and more passengers, the need to validate tickets arose. A one-hole paper punch proved the ideal solution. The punch was born in 1878 to the **Chicago Ticket Punch Company**, today known as the **McGill Metal Products Company** of Marengo. McGill still manufactures this product, and is today the only manufacturer in the United States of a one-hole paper ticket punch. McGill is also the only company in the world making mechanical coin changers, the ones used by newspaper sellers and other vendors. And while they didn't invent the wood based mousetrap,

The ticket punch was born in 1878 to the Chicago Ticket Punch Co.

McGill was one of the world's largest manufacturers of them from the 1930s to the 1960s. In 1990 McGill sold the mousetrap division, though they remain closely associated with the product in the public's mind.

10,000 workers laid 705.5 miles of Illinois Central track.

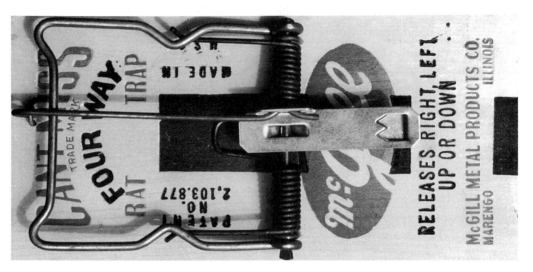

A McGill four way rat trap

A major construction project of the late 1860s was the Eads Bridge, named for its first builder, James B. Eads (1820-1887). The bridge spans the Mississippi between St. Louis and East St. Louis. Completed in 1874 after five years work, it marks the first use of steel in a truss-bridge and embodies the longest fixed end metal arch in the world. The central arch measures 520 feet long, the two other arches are 18 feet shorter. In building the piers on bedrock under the river, Eads was the first engineer in the United States to employ compressed-air caissons.

THE ILLINOIS CENTRAL R.R. OPENS THE MIDDLE OF ILLINOIS

In 1850 Congress granted Illinois 2,500,000 acres for the construction of a central railroad. Robert Rantoul of Massachusetts, with a group of Eastern capitalists, organized the **Illinois Central Rail Road Co. (IC)** and promised to give the state seven percent of the gross receipts from the main line and the branch, which was then a major source of state tax revenue. A Y-shaped system was planned, beginning in Cairo and branching at Centralia, with one line going up to Chicago and the other to Galena. Rails were brought from England through New Orleans, the Erie Canal and the Great Lakes. Quarries were opened along the way, and forests were cut in Michigan, Wisconsin and southern Illinois.

Just before the first massive wave of European immigrants who knew America to be paved with gold arrived, almost 10,000 laborers worked on the 705.5 mile railroad, which cost $25 million. The number of workers employed on this single project resulted in a noticeable shortage of labor in other sectors of manufacturing and helped draw the young and strong men away from the farm and into the wage-labor market. It also gave the impression to European travelers and writers that Illinois was the land of boundless energy. They described what they saw in terms that Voltaire and Rousseau would have recognized when they philosophized the Enlightenment into being. Those writing about Illinois began to know that it was blessed by God. When put into common language, these noble concepts drew countless Irish and Germans, then Italians, Russians and Poles to America. The various famines, economic swings and political repressions also helped these Europeans see America as a land where a man could express his opinions, own land and through work support his family. It was a land were women did not have to fear conscription for their sons or the Lord of the Land's designs upon her daughters.

At its completion, in 1856, the IC was the world's longest railroad. Its construction had been a bigger project than digging the Erie Canal. One benefit was that by cutting through the middle of the state, land previously almost inaccessible became available for cultivation. Beginning in 1855, before the completion of the track, the IC offered for sale 2,400,000 acres of "selected proven farm and woodlands in tracts of any size to suit the purchaser, on long credit at low rates of interest, situated on each side of the railroad, extending all the way from the extreme North to the South of the State of Illinois" (from an 1855 prospectus). By the next year, 1856, the ancient prairie lands and forests of Illinois were doomed. Eventually about thirty-five thousand different families bought land. Dozens of towns developed along the IC's right-of-way, many of them named for the superintendent or engineer responsible for the section. One of them, Odin, was known in the 1860s as the "hell-hole of the Illinois Central" because of a form of piracy practiced by some locals. Concealing themselves along the railroad embankment until the train stopped, they would scramble on board and scuttle off with the passengers' luggage.

Among the great boosters of the IC idea was Darius Holbrook, who had bought land in Cairo in 1835. He argued that by linking Galena with Cairo, Cairo would become a great metropolis. Its location, where the Ohio and Mississippi meet, held promise and in 1839 Holbrook succeeded in raising over one million dollars in London to meet his ends in building this fabled city. But not only do the two rivers meet at Cairo, they flood there. Within a season or two the investors lost almost everything. Among the investors in Cairo was the English novelist Charles Dickens, who visited the United States in 1842. He had written about Cairo as "a place without one single quality, in earth or air or water, to recommend it." This was after, of course, the floods. Eventually the railroad did come and for a few decades the IC made Cairo important. Holbrook was vindicated.

Some community leaders saw the railroads as just another fad. Often they realized their mistake too late. Most communities that were passed by the railroads had a choice: to move themselves, houses and all, to the line or to wither away. One that withered was Ewington, today only a historical marker and cemetery about two miles from the center of Effingham. Ewington's future seemed secure when it was chosen as the seat of Effingham County in the days when Vandalia was still the capital of Illinois. Its prosperity and importance hemorrhaged when, in 1852, the Illinois Central's tracks passed it by and continued into neighboring Effingham, then a brand new town. Seven years later Effingham plucked the county seat from under Ewington. The resulting change was so total that the old courthouse was transformed into the county poorhouse. In 1880 even that was aban-

In 1856, the Illinois Central was the world's longest railroad.

doned. A town that moved was Millville. When the **Frink & Walker** stage line through town was replaced by a railroad through nearby Warren in 1854, most of Millville's families moved to the now more prosperous Warren.

The IC, under the presidency of William H. Osborn, helped Illinois recover from the Civil War. The railroad took a loss at the start of the war by accepting corn at Chicago prices, minus transportation charges, so that farmers could meet payments on their land contracts. As a result, farmers easily unloaded the surplus from their abundant 1860 and 1861 crops. The corn went to Chicago and helped establish it as a grain center. The IC was also a pioneer in agricultural promotion when it turned to the new cause of crop diversification during the Civil War by urging farmers to plant cotton, sugar beets and flax. Crop diversification helped soften nature's impact on the farmer, who with the help of the new farm implements was better able to avoid the all or nothing aspects of traditional agriculture. Crop diversification also helped spread the idea that Illinois was the land in which anything could grow. For a while even tobacco became an industry when in 1858 **Michel's Tobacco Co.**, the first of its kind in Illinois, was founded in Decatur.

Another important development in agriculture was the state and local fair. The fair brought rural and town people and ideas together in one place. Right from its inception, the IC helped promote state fairs in Chicago in 1855 and in Centralia in 1858 with free transportation and special trains.

Trains ran strawberries express from Irvington to Chicago.

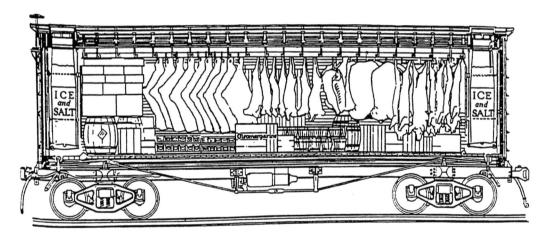

Early refrigerated railroad car

Centralia's location in the heart of the southern Illinois fruit belt resulted in early attempts to produce refrigerated cars and in 1867 the *Thunderbolt Express*, the first temperature controlled fruit train in America, began regular operation between Centralia and Chicago. In Cobden it is claimed that the refrigerator car was an outgrowth of a strawberry refrigerator box invented by Parker Earle. But it is also documented that in 1857 refrigerated railroad cars for hauling beef were being perfected in Chicago and that by 1866 fruits and vegetables were being shipped in refrigerated cars, too. In the 1890s, when Irvington was the strawberry capital of southern Illinois, the IC ran special non-stop trains to Chicago with the fruit during the season.

Many towns were born of the railroad or profited from the maintenance and manufacture of railroad parts. Clay City, a shipping and trading center, came into existence with the building of the Ohio & Mississippi Railroad. La Grange, incorporated in 1879, was the first suburb to be developed along the Chicago, Burlington & Quincy line; while Fairmont City, an industrial suburb of East St. Louis, began life in 1910 when a roundhouse of the Pennsylvania Railroad was built there. By the 1930s the Alton Railroad Shops were the largest industrial establishment in Bloomington, covering some 124 acres and employing about 1,500 people. There the entire process of rehabilitating railroad stock was done. In the 1930s Beardstown was an important railhead of the B & O and was the point where the Burlington crossed the Illinois River.

The Proviso Yards, near Melrose Park, of the Chicago & Northwestern were, in 1939, three miles long and half a mile wide, covering 960 acres. The yard had 59 tracks, each with a capacity of 70 cars — 4,000 daily. Lights allowed night operations. At the time they were said to be the largest railroad yards in the world.

By 1900 innovative technology made possible by electricity began to effect the railroads as much as it did other industries. Electric powered railroads were introduced into Illinois for passenger service between rural communities and larger urban centers. By 1927 there were 47 companies competing on 2,000 miles of electrified track. This good idea could not compete with a better one, the automobile, and by 1937 there were only six companies left with 536 miles of track.

Another innovation came in 1935 when streamlined diesel powered passenger trains were introduced into Illinois. Capable of speeds up to 120 mph, the streamlined diesel made America the world leader in railroad technology for a while. These design marvels never really caught on and were always only a visible minority among railroad machinery. Each of the major roads had one or more of the fast trains. Each had a dramatic name such as Burlington's all silver *Zephyr*; Rock Island's *Rocket*; Alton's *Abraham Lincoln*; Illinois Central's *Green Diamond*; Northwestern's *400*; Chicago, Milwaukee and St. Paul's red and yellow *Hiawatha*; and Atchison, Topeka and Santa Fe's *Superchief*.

In 1940 the IC had 1,406 steam engines and only 33 diesel units. *The City of New Orleans* was put into service in early 1947. This streamlined all-coach diesel powered train made possible a record schedule of less than 16 hours between Chicago and New Orleans. Its image of speed was important and quickly became the stuff of folk lore and song. For better visibility, it ran only during daylight hours. In the same year, 1947, the IC hauled 52,250 cars of bananas from New Orleans, an all-time record for such traffic. By the 1960s agricultural products, especially grain, made up one-sixth of all IC freight.

Much of the new freight equipment of the 1950s and 1960s was constructed at the IC's yards in Centralia. Along with the ever increasing freight traffic came new tracks. By 1970 more than 1,200 of the over 10,000 miles of IC track in Illinois were of continuous-welded rail. Two years later Illinois Central became the Illinois, Central Gulf and extended

Streamlined
diesel trains
could go
120 mph
in 1935.

westward across Iowa to Sioux City and southwards to New Orleans, but the core of the activity remained focused on the Y-shaped Illinois portion created in the 1850s.

One of the great Illinois railroads, the Atchison, Topeka & Santa Fe, was built in the 1880s. As a latecomer it fathered many legends, developed the system of railway sponsored eating places and inns along its route and set up an out-of-work miner, called Death Valley Scotty, to help obtain railway mail contracts by dramatizing the first run ever made from Los Angeles to Chicago in less than 40 hours. Scotty — whose only mine was an almost worthless hole called the *Golden Ophir*, in what is now Joshua Tree National Monument in California's desert — was established as the owner of a fabulously wealthy mine in Death Valley more than 150 miles away. The publicity resulting from this spectacular dash as the sole passenger from Los Angeles to Chicago gave the Santa Fe a lever for mail contracts that could not be disregarded and, from 1906 until mid-October 1967, Santa Fe mail trains made daily Chicago to Los Angeles runs in just over 39 hours.

Railroads were not the only important industry in Illinois during the 1850s and 1860s, just the most visible one. It was in the 1860s that Peoria came of age with not one, but seven distilleries. When the first seven New England farmers arrived in Peoria in 1819, French fur traders had already lived there for more than 100 years. In 1825 Peoria County was created and the community of Fort Clark was renamed in French-Indian, Peoria. For the next six years the county had jurisdiction over about one fourth of Illinois, including the small village of Chicago. Within the decade Peoria had a population of over 500 and was incorporated as a town. Ten years later its 2,000 inhabitants had adopted a city charter. Peoria was also an important regional center of pork packing and its factories produced plows, threshing machines and fanning mills.

BEER WAS FOR IMMIGRANTS, WHISKEY FOR "AMERICANS"

In 1850 there were 176 distilleries in Illinois, while Ohio was the leading producer in the West with an estimated 867. That decade saw the introduction of distillation of liquors to Chicago when **D. Ballantyne**'s and **A. Crosby**'s distilleries became local producers. In 1858 their production amounted to $3,600,000. In 1870 Chicago had eight distilleries, producing whiskey valued at $2,751,221, while its great competitor, Cincinnati, had 10 that produced $2,714,114 worth of whiskey. Ten years later, in 1880, Chicago had seven distilleries producing $4,387,545 worth of whisky, while Cincinnati had 10 distilleries producing $3,143,500. The nation's whiskey production shifted to Illinois in the 1880s.

In 1860 Peoria had seven highly competitive distilleries, which twenty years later were organized by Joseph Greenhut into the Cattle Feeders' and Distillers' Trust, also known as the "Whiskey Trust." The trust was so effective that by 1890 the number of distillers in Illinois had declined from 45 to seven, six of these being in Peoria. That year Peoria led the nation in whisky production with 10,778,000 gallons distilled. Nationwide there were 12 members of the Trust that survived until the Trust busting years of World War I.

The "Whiskey Trust" helped make Peoria famous.

GOTTFRIED ✦ BREWING ✦ COMPANY

THE LARGEST BREWERY IN ILLINOIS NOT CONNECTED WITH SYNDICATES.

JOHN H. WEISS, President.

C. M. GOTTFRIED, Secretary.   **F. GUNDRUM**, Vice-President.

Brewers and Bottlers of the celebrated "GOLDEN DROP" Beer, which is the ideal beverage of all those enjoying a pure, healthy and nourishing drink.

OFFICE AND BREWERY

CORNER ARCHER AND STEWART AVENUES,

CHICAGO.

Almost from its beginning, Chicago was a major beer town, too. The city's first brewery was established in 1838 at the corner of Pine and Chicago by William Lill and William Haas, with capital provided by William B. Ogden. Nine barrels of brew a week were produced. By 1880 Chicago had nineteen breweries which provided work for over 1,000 employees who produced 450,000 barrels of beer that year.

In 1855 Chicago had 675 "liquor establishments."

In 1855, according to the *Literary Budget*, Chicago had 675 "liquor establishments." Of these, 625 were owned by Germans and Irish, leaving 50 for "native Americans," read: white men born in the United States. This caused a problem which became known as the "Beer Riot." In March of 1855 the former physician Levi Boone, a colorful distant relative of Daniel Boone, rode into the mayor's office on the anti-foreign Know-Nothing party ticket. He immediately enforced the party's motto "America for Americans" by issuing a proclamation on March 17, 1855 by which he notified tavern keepers that the Sunday closing law would be strictly enforced by the police which, incidentally, were almost exclusively "Americans". The next day, March 18, was a Sunday. The police arrested many German innkeepers, who sold primarily beer, for violating the order while they did not bother to arrest respectable "American" barkeepers in such places as the "Young America" which sold whiskey. Beer, of course, was seen as the new immigrants' drink and was therefore not American, while whiskey, preferred by English speakers even if they were fresh out of Ireland, was perceived of as an American tradition.

In addition to this, on March 27, the liquor licenses for tavern owners were raised from fifty to 300 dollars and they were to be in effect only until July 1, three months. Very few German innkeepers, who catered primarily to workers, were able to pay the fee and many were forced to give up their businesses. Others defied the order and sold beer without having the new license. Over 200 transgressors were arrested. Trials were set for April 21. On that day a large number of Germans armed themselves with every conceivable weapon and massed before the courthouse. They wanted to show that they would not yield to the threat on their rights as provided by the constitution. Some fifty special police agents tried to disperse them with clubs. Chaos followed. A number of Germans were killed and many arrested before the mob dispersed. Soon the remainder and others gathered again on the North Side of the River, while militia General R.K. Swift made battle plans by alerting some 200 deputies and by placing two cannons at the corners of La Salle and Washington Streets and on Randolph and Clark Streets. However, it was the Irishman who was in charge of the Clark Street Bridge who thwarted the Teutons by swinging open the bridge when they approached. After much shouting and many threats, the Germans retreated to their favorite inns to wash down the day's memories with their favorite beer. Conflicts between Germans and Americans or foreign groups continued to flare up sporadically for many decades to follow.

By 1890 all but two of Chicago's leading breweries were German. Some of the more prominent ones were those of Michael Brand, Valentine Busch, **Gottfried Brewing Company**, Paul Pohl, William Ruehl, Peter Schoenhofen, Conrad Seipp and Frederick Wacker.

In many towns across the state breweries flourished, especially where there were significant German, Bohemian or Czech populations. For example, the **Star Union Brewery** in Peru was founded in 1845 and was well known until the 1960s for its brands Star Union and Sepp'l Brau.

Amboy was another town with potential. It was home to a small-town grocery store out of which developed **Carson Pirie Scott & Co.** The Amboy store was opened in 1854 by Samuel Carson and John T. Pirie, Scotch-Irish immigrants. Four years later their fellow countryman J.E. Scott joined them in Amboy and the firm was established. By 1865 they had a branch store in Mendota and Polo with headquarters in Chicago. By the late 1890s Carson Pirie Scott & Co. was one of the leading department stores in Chicago and with that a leader in the nation, rivaled only by **Marshall Field and Company**.

Until the 1850s industrial manufacturing was in its infancy in all parts of the United States and had not extended much beyond the East Coast. For instance, metal pipe fittings were not even made in the United States until 1845, and then only in a few small foundries in New York, Philadelphia and Boston. But once industrial manufacturing got underway, Illinois was the natural place for it.

> Since the 1850s the Kewanee Boiler Co. has been in business.

HEAVY INDUSTRY SETTLES IN ILLINOIS

For all of the nineteenth century steam was the byword for power and heating. By mid-century, steam was common, but ways to control it often proved elusive. Many ideas were tested and developed, only a few eventually proved practical.

In 1858 Richard Teller Crane got the contract for "steam warming" the new Cook County Court House in Chicago. Almost overnight he and his brother developed, designed and manufactured their first globe and check valve. They successfully completed the project and were paid their $6,000 contract, the largest of its kind paid out up to that time in Chicago. Crane, born in Paterson, New Jersey, in 1832, began a brass foundry in a corner of his uncle's lumberyard in Chicago in 1855. The following year he bought a 20 x 40 lot at 102 W. Lake St. By the next spring the company got involved with steam, selling steam heating, iron pipes and fittings. **R.T. Crane Brass & Bell Foundry** quickly became a major manufacturer. In 1858 Crane won the contract for the Cook County Court House and six years later, in 1864, he built a pipe mill — the first west of Pittsburgh. The Crane brothers incorporated in 1865 and renamed themselves **Northwest Manufacturing Co.** and continued making valves well into the next century.

In Kewanee the **Kewanee Boiler Co.** began manufacturing steam and hot water equipment in the 1850s. The company is still in business manufacturing heating and process steam boilers, burners and other boiling room equipment.

During the 1850s Chicago was growing very fast and manufacturing of all types of products boomed. **H. Whitbeck** manufactured buggies, wagons and plows, producing over 1,000 plows and 589 vehicles in 1852 alone. C. Morgan had a five story furniture manufactory building on Lake Street. **Scammon & Haven** established the **Chicago Oil Mill** in 1852 and produced 40,000 gallons of oil from flax seed supplied by the farmers of the immediate territory. Over 3,000 barrels of oil cake and 200,000 pounds of putty were also produced annually. The same year, 1852, the Clearville soap and candle factory produced one million pounds of soap and candles, 43,500 gallons of lard oil and 1,200,000 pounds of tallow and lard.

In 1854 the **Chicago Wooden Ware Manufactory** was brought into existence by **Rosseter & Pahlman** and within a year was the greatest house of its kind in the country. Isaiah Brown established Chicago's first match factory on Wells Street and was immediately followed by Chapman & Atwood, who founded the **Eagle Match Factory**. Also, **Collins & Blachford** founded their sheet-iron and lead manufacturing facility on Clinton and Fulton Streets, and the Galena & Chicago Railroad machine shop produced the engine called the *Blackhawk*. That same year, the value of locomotive, machinery, railroad cars and iron goods produced in Chicago was $3,200,000, while the value of agricultural implements produced in Chicago was $350,000; carriages and wagons about $500,000; furniture about $300,000; sash, doors and blinds about $500,000; stoves, soap, candles, leather about $300,000; brass and copper goods about $135,000. Five thousand men were directly employed in manufacturing in Chicago.

The year 1856 saw Chicago with $7,759,400 invested in manufacturing which produced $15,515,063 worth of goods and employed 10,573. A recession in 1857 took some weak companies under, yet 12,000 tons of bar, sheet and railroad iron were produced in Chicago. This was 10.4 percent of all the bar, sheet and railroad iron produced in six western states. Because railroads and farm machinery required immense amounts of iron, Chicago began development as a heavy metals center before the Civil War.

Eber Brock Ward built the first iron works west of Pittsburgh in 1855 in Wyandotte, Michigan. Two years later he built a plant on the north branch of the Chicago River, the **Chicago Rolling Mills**. This plant was Chicago's entry into the iron manufacturing industry. It used iron ore from the newly opened Lake Superior ranges and specialized in rails. In 1865 Ward was credited with rolling the first steel produced in the United States. Four years later, Ward's plant made about one-third of the iron and steel produced in the nation.

Besides the expected rails and plows, some of Chicago's early foundries also manufactured architectural elements. For example, the **Washington Foundry and Machine Shop** of **Holmes, Pyott & Co.**, established in 1855, added some architectural iron to its many cast iron products, especially interior columns. N.S. Bouton's **Union Foundry Works** began in 1852. Later they, too, produced columns and lintels for store fronts. In 1870 there were 150 iron casting establishments in Chicago, employing some 5,312 persons.

The 1860 census showed that Illinois had approximately 3,000 manufacturing establishments, 1,000 less than Indiana and far behind the number in New York, Pennsylvania and

In 1860 Illinois had approximately 3,000 manufacturing establishments.

Ohio. This lag would not last for long as Chicago became the key non-war area manufacturing center during the War Between the States. Often new products led the list of manufactured goods. One such new product in the 1860s was pliers.

The first pair of pliers were produced in the United States in 1857 or 1861 by Mathias Klein in Chicago. Following the practice of the day, Klein established a company, **Klein Tools** of Skokie. Mathias Klein, an emigrant from Germany, was a trained locksmith-blacksmith with a specialty in wrought iron works. The first tool he made, one half of a pair of side-cutting pliers for a telegraph lineman, came about when the lineman came into his shop with broken pliers. Klein forged and finished a new half for the tool, riveted it to the first, and so produced the first pliers known to have been made in the United States.

The Civil War demonstrated the strategic value of the telegraph, whose wire repair and maintenance depended on hand tools, especially pliers. Then came the telephone and the light bulb. With them a whole new industry came to life. Railroads, too, required special tools, and Klein's forge grew into a business, a company making a respected line of tools. By 1900 Klein's company produced over 100 different types and sizes of pliers, and had become a lineman's equipment manufacturer, making such things as pole climbers, tool belts and accessories. Today, Klein Tools remains a leading manufacturer of tools and related accessories.

> The first pair of pliers produced in the United States was made in Chicago.

PACKING MEAT IN CHICAGO

Arguably the most famous industry associated with Chicago is meatpacking. It came into its own in the late 1860s, but had a long association with the city before that. Chicago's first recorded slaughterhouse, located on the north bank of the Chicago River, was operated in 1827 by Archibald Clybourne, who had a government contract to supply Fort Dearborn with meat. However, depending on the source of information, Chicago's first yard was either Myrick's, said to have opened in 1837 near what is now Madison Street and Odgen Avenue, or the Old Bull's Head, said to have opened in 1848 near what is now Cottage Grove Avenue and 29th Street. Both were taverns that provided stock pens for dealers who brought cattle to the city for trade.

In 1832 Miller & Hall established a tannery at Wolf Point and George W. Dole inaugurated the meat packing industry in Chicago. At this time slaughtering was Chicago's sole manufacturing industry. Ten years later a number of packers were thriving in Chicago. They soon cleaned out the Western country of its free-roaming live-stock, especially wild pigs, whose ancestors had come with the first white settlers, escaped and proliferated.

By 1845 Wodsworth, Dyer & Chapin were slaughtering 100 head of cattle daily, a portion being packed under contract with the United States Navy, a portion shipped to England, and the remainder for the home market. In the butchering season, November 1 to March 1 of 1845-46, they killed about 2,000 head of cattle acquired in central Illinois and Northern

Indiana. The price was then about $2.50 a hundred pounds on hoof. Also, 11,469 hogs were packed. After this came a noteworthy shift in the dominance of the hogpacking industry.

In 1850-51 Cincinnati was the hogpacking metropolis of the world, killing 334,000 hogs to Chicago's 20,000. Indianapolis packed 18,000 hogs. St. Louis, Milwaukee and Louisville were well ahead of Chicago, too, in pork production.

By 1871 Cincinnati lost its hog packing leadership to Chicago.

The season of 1858-59 saw 171,684 hogs butchered and packed in Chicago. During the same time Cincinnati processes 382,829. In 1860-61, Chicago packed 271,805 hogs, Cincinnati 443,469. A decade later, in 1871-72, Chicago packed 1,218,858 hogs, Cincinnati, 630,301. Cincinnati never again caught up.

Chicago's major hog packers during the 1860s were **A.E. Kent & Co.** (founded 1860); **Burt & Higgins** (1858); **G. & J. Stewart** (1857); **George Steel** (1843); **Holder & Priest** (1858); **J.G. Law** (1858); **Jones & Cyulbertson** (1858); **Leland & Mixer** (1859); **Louis Reichberg** (1858); **Patrick Curtiss** (1858); **Smith & Son** (1858); **Thomas Nash** (1857); and **Tobey & Booth** (1852);

After hogs came beef, for which Chicago is more famous. In 1860 the major beef packers in Chicago were **A. Brown & Co.** (founded 1853); **Cragin & Co.** (1854); **Clybourne & Co.** (1827-34); **Hayward, Bloomfield & Co.** (1850); **R.M. & O.S. Hough** (1850); **Gurdon S. Hubbard** (1834); and **Van Brunt & Watrous** (1858).

Far behind the Civil War's front lines, the upper Midwest proved ideal for cattle raising. Chicago was the most prosperous city near the war area, yet far enough away not to be threatened. Much of the meat for the Union army was prepared in its plants; in addition, a large number of cattle were shipped out of Chicago and kept close to the battle front to be slaughtered as needed.

This tremendous rise in livestock traffic soon pointed out the inefficiency of operating numerous separate yards. As a result, traders insisted that there be one large united or "union" stockyard where livestock could be concentrated and sales conducted in open competition.

Chicago's **Union Stock Yard and Transit Company** emerged in 1865 as a consolidated market to replace many of the smaller yards operating around the city's periphery. The first recorded move to establish a united stockyard came when the Chicago Pork Packers Association passed a resolution in June, 1864, calling for precisely this action. Concurrently, the nine railroads with lines running into Chicago were in the midst of negotiating the abandonment of the separate yards located on their lines; they would be most responsible for financing the construction of a new union yard.

Livestock marketing in Chicago centered around tavern yards until 1852, when the Michigan Central and Michigan Southern railroads reached Chicago. The arrival of the two

Union Stockyards by Joseph Pennel

eastern railroads revolutionized the industry. Livestock could now be shipped east year round. A stockyard with hotels, scales, rail connections for receiving and shipping, and facilities for commission men and market reports was built near the terminal of each new railroad to reach the city. Consequently, tavern yards not on the rail lines soon faded and closed, while those on along the routes prospered.

Morris, Armour and Swift were the Big Three of meat packing.

The Illinois and Michigan Canal, completed in 1848, connected the Illinois River to Lake Michigan via the south branch of the Chicago River, and opened a new waterway for shipping. To utilize this passage, several slaughter and packing houses were constructed along the south branch.

Then, in 1865, after the south side site was chosen, the land was purchased from former Mayor John Wentworth. Until a charter for a new company could be secured from the Illinois legislature, three eastern railroad officials retained title to the land. The charter was granted to the Union Stock Yard and Transit Company of Chicago on February 15, 1865. Work on the site began June 1, and on Christmas Day the yards were open for business.

Once considered almost valueless marsh, the 320 acre site, now drained and with pens constructed which accommodated 21,000 cattle, 75,000 hogs, 22,000 sheep and 200 horses, along with hotels, restaurants and an exchange, became very valuable. Resembling a miniature city, the yards were laid out in a simple grid pattern with streets and alleys. The nine railroads that had bought the lion's share of the initial stock offering constructed branch tracks to the yards and a small canal connected the yards to the river. No slaughter or packing houses were built near the yards at first since there were already well-established plants on the river two and one-half miles to the north. But in a few years, new plants were built west of the yards in what soon became known as "Packingtown."

Nelson Morris, Philip Armour and Gustavus Swift, considered the Big Three of the meat packing industry, came to Chicago between the 1850 and 1870.

Civil War contracts enabled Nelson Morris, a German who was an unorthodox trader, to build one of the first big packing plants at the stockyards. He was the first of the Chicago packers who combined efficiency with volume. Arriving in Chicago in 1854, Morris found employment with John Sherman's yards, but soon moved on to open his own business. At first he traded in disabled and dead stock; he then went into meat packing in 1859. The **Morris** plant, one of the first packing houses opened and operated at the Union Stock Yard, was to expand into an industrial community of 40 buildings occupying more than 30 acres.

Philip D. Armour, an Easterner who made his first stake building sluices in the California gold fields, is remembered as a philanthropist responsible for founding the Armour Institute, the forerunner of the Illinois Institute of Technology. He went into the pork packing business in Milwaukee in 1863. One of Armour's brothers had established a grain commission firm in Chicago, and in 1868 the firm started packing hogs under the name

Armour & Company. By 1871 Armour & Co. was the fifth largest of the 26 packers in the city, and in 1875 Philip Armour moved his own headquarters to Chicago, bringing with him Michael Cudahy, superintendent of the Milwaukee plant, who later formed his own company. In the next decade Armour's business grew to include packing as well as grain elevator and storage interests not only in the Middle West but also in the East. At the time of his death in 1901, Armour's firm owned more elevators than any other company in the world, had 50,000 employees and was exporting food worldwide.

Swift was the first to eliminate waste by manufacturing by-products.

Swift and Armour did their part

Swift & Company, incorporated in Illinois April 1, 1885, had been founded ten years earlier by Gustavus F. Swift when, in 1875, he moved his cattle buying operations to Chicago. From the start, Swift experimented with refrigerated cars in which he shipped dressed cattle east, but it was not until 1880 that technology allowed for a long distance refrigerated railroad car.

Swift's organizational talents can be traced back to 1855 when, at the age of 16 years, he borrowed $20 from his father, slaughtered and dressed a heifer, and then sold it to families in his Cape Cod, Massachusetts neighborhood. For the next seventeen years Swift established meat businesses in towns throughout Massachusetts, finally expanding to Albany and Buffalo, New York, where cattle were beginning to arrive from the West.

Once established in Chicago, the firm flourished and Swift kept moving plants closer to the source of his animal supplies until the company's second meat-packing plant opened in Kansas City in 1887. Omaha followed in 1891 and St. Louis in 1892. Swift died in 1903, leaving his firm in the hands of his seven sons. At the time, Swift & Company employed about 23,000 people.

Swift & Co. was the first to eliminate waste by manufacturing by-products which included hairbrushes, buttons, chessmen, knife handles, fertilizer, soap, perfume, glue, leather goods, surgical sutures, violin strings, photographic film, gelatin and oils.

The years immediately preceding and following World War I were extremely trying ones for Swift & Company and for the meat industry as a whole. The government was concerned about economic concentration in the industry, and the Packer's Consent Decree of February 27, 1920 was devised to keep meatpackers from moving into other closely related businesses. By this time Swift & Company had already diversified, moving into processing poultry, eggs, butter, cheese, lard, shortenings and margarine, while the livestock operations dealt in feeds and minerals for livestock and poultry, industrial oils, adhesives, wool and leather fabrication. In 1893 Cotosuet, a cooking fat made from beef suet and cottonseed oil, was a new product offered by Swift. According to the company,

Cotosuet was "the best cheap cooking fat offered to the public...a wholesome substitute for lard...unequaled for frying...excellent for shortening."

During the 1920s technological changes allowed for better processing and packaging and allowed the consumer a wider choice. Salty cured ham and heavily smoked bacon were replaced by a whole range of specialty meats, carrying some of the most famous brand names known in America, such as Swift's Premium meats, Brown 'N Serve sausages, Swift's Premium Breakfast Strips, Hostess Ham and Butterball turkeys. Swift food products, such as Swiftning shortening, Pard dog food and, later, Peter Pan peanut butter, also became household names.

Swift also processed cottonseed oil at a mill that was Cairo's chief industry in the 1930s. The seed was conveyed from the storage place by a screw to an apparatus where jets of compressed air blew away extraneous matter. The seed then entered linters, which function like cotton gins, to be stripped of fleecy fibers that escaped the teeth of the gin; the "linters" thus obtained were used in manufacturing paper, films, fabrics, batting, cellophane, lacquers and varnishes. The cleansed seed was then cracked and screened to separate the hulls from the kernels. The hulls were used as stuffing, livestock feed, and as a base for explosives. The kernels were rolled, cooked, and reduced to pulp, which was then subjected to a pressure of 4,200 pounds per square inch. The crude oil that emerged was refined and used in salad oils, shortening, oleomargarine, candles and glycerin. The caked kernels that remained were fed to livestock.

All this was reflected in the firm's prosperity which, at the time of its centennial, comprised 500 plants, employing 64,000 people. By 1971 Swift had become a major international corporation whose domestic fresh meat sales accounted for about 42 percent of total sales, with the balance coming from interests in foods, chemicals, petroleum and insurance. In 1973 Swift became **Esmark, Inc.,** the parent holding company of these diverse units. Esmark continued to develop until in 1980 its focus was on consumer and industrial chemical products, not meat.

Another important development in meat came from the **Viskase Corp.,** producers of Nojax casings, used by meat processors for imparting color and flavor to meat products such as hot dogs, ham and bologna. The casings were invented by the founder of the **Visking Co.,** Erwin O. Freund, in 1925. Production started near the Chicago stockyards and moved to the present location on West 65th Street in 1933. The company also developed the handle bag, a turkey bag with its own built-in E-Z carry handle.

Chicago's standing as a meat center was substantially boosted in 1869 by the development of the refrigerated railroad car. Using what at first appeared to be only crude ice boxes on wheels, Swift inaugurated a business which mounted in volume over the years. By 1880 the refrigerated railroad car had become very efficient. Six years later Morris, Armour, Swift and George H. Hammond & Company of Hammond, Indiana, were using some 1,500 refrigerated cars among them.

Swift processed cottonseed oil in Cairo.

Because the Great Chicago Fire of October 1871 did not come near the yards, the business of slaughter and packing was not interrupted; in fact, it continued to grow. Consequently, the city was able to maintain financial credit, and fiscal stability was restored soon after the fire. Furthermore, because so much of the economy was based on livestock, Chicago was better able than any other big American city to withstand the depression of 1873.

Pushing for advantage in the 1870s and 1880s, the packers began large-scale preparations of canned meats. The public demand for beef started the Chicago packers on establishing branch plants in such cities as Kansas City and Omaha. In East St. Louis a major stockyard developed in the adjacent community of National City.

Not content with establishing new markets in the United States alone, the Chicago packers and livestock dealers tapped a lucrative market across the Atlantic; American cattle and in particular dressed beef were shipped to England, France and Germany. By 1890, as Libby, McNeil & Libby's canning methods were perfected, the Chicago export market expanded appreciably through the shipment of compressed beef.

Moving cattle without them injuring each other with their horns was of great concern to cattle drovers, especially in the confines of the stockyards. Horn injuries were much reduced when in 1880 A.A. Haff dehorned his herd of Texas long-horns to keep them from injuring each other in the feeding pens of Hooppole (the town derived its name from its first industry, the making of barrel hoops from hickory sapling poles). Haff was promptly arrested and charged with cruelty to animals. After proving that the practice was neither cruel nor harmful, he was freed. The practice of dehorning caught on and became common by the end of the century.

By 1900 Chicago's stockyards had grown to 475 acres and had a capacity for 75,000 cattle, 50,000 sheep, 300,000 hogs and 5,000 horses. The Union Stock Yard and Transit Company itself employed 1,000 people. To make the market happen, there were 200 commission firms employing some 1,500 people. Also, there were 100 packing firms employing some 30,000 people in their packing and slaughter houses.

Probably because of the dizzying speed with which the yards had developed, working conditions and sanitation standards at the yards were poor. In 1906 Upton Sinclair wrote his famous exposé *The Jungle*. Investigations followed and eventually higher sanitation standards resulted. By the late 1890s the **Amalgamated Meat Cutters and Butcher Workers of North America** had formed a small union which grew steadily in size and influence. Eventually, in the 1930s, additional unions were organized to respond to workers' needs.

Record livestock receipts were recorded from 1910 to 1925, and the large packing houses enjoyed prosperity through the late 1920s. The Depression, however, brought a decline in meat consumption and the packers had difficulty staying in business. To compound the difficulties, a fire in 1934 gutted most of the yards. They were quickly rebuilt. Despite

The business of slaughter and packing was not interrupted by the Great Chicago Fire.

these setbacks, the packing industry began a steady return to productivity. For its 75th anniversary, in 1940, the yards could boast that since 1865 a total of 896,000,000 animals had been sold through the yards. This made Chicago the greatest stockmarket in the world. But it was to be a last gasp.

846,000,000 animals were sold in the Chicago Stock Yards between 1865 and 1940.

With America's entry into World War II the need for beef increased, but the supply was not to come through Chicago as much as other locations around the nation. These stockyards all followed the Chicago model and many of the plants had been established and were owned by Chicago's major slaughterhouses in their effort to be closer to the source.

After 1940, though, livestock receipts in Chicago began to dwindle, and during the 1950s the exodus of the major packers began. For a time, the sale and trading of livestock in the Union Stock Yard remained up, but this too began to decline. Although shipping from the yards continued and smaller firms took the place left by larger companies, in 1958 the Union Stock Yard and Transit Company concentrated operations to a small area at the south end of the yards. By 1960 all the large packing companies were gone.

Several causes may be found for the departure of the great meat packing companies. For one thing, the firms were automating and thus eliminating jobs. For another, the labor force was diminishing and many of the workers were over 40. Still, the primary reasons were technological. The eight- and ten-story buildings originally constructed were uneconomical; long one or two story assembly line buildings proved more efficient. Yet it would have cost far more to remodel these multi-storied structures than to relocate where land was less expensive. The growth of major cities on the west coast encouraged packers to set up slaughtering plants closer to the farms where the animals were raised, and the spread of the trucking industry with access to all corners of the nation offset Chicago's former advantage as a rail center. Where there were 64 stockyards throughout the country in 1929, there were 2,300 in 1959. Just as it had all started, small and local in the 1830s, by the 1960s it had come full circle. Small was again efficient, and still is.

FROM STEAK TO SOAP IT'S ALL BEEF

Among the many by-products of the stockyards was soap, and a number of meat packers produced and sold it. Soap was an easy product because its main ingredients were a natural by-product of slaughterhouses. Armour sold America Dial Soap (now headquartered in Phoenix, Arizona) and the **Armour Soap Works** began producing laundry soap in 1896, and toilet soap in 1902. Among other things, Swift & Co. produced "Swift's Washing Powder."

Because of the proximity of the slaughterhouses, many manufacturers of soap came to Chicago from elsewhere. Prominent among these was James S. Kirk, a Utica, New York soap manufacturer who moved his business to Chicago in 1859.

His first factory was located on River Street, the site of old Fort Dearborn. In 1867 he opened a new plant just north of the Chicago River at what was then 362 North Water Street, now the Equitable Building's site. This plant burned down in the Great Chicago Fire and was immediately rebuilt as a five story structure with a 182 foot chimney. The facility was described as "the largest manufactory of its kind in America." The company claimed to have an "Annual Production greater than that of any Soap maker in the WORLD" in 1880. The business produced three million pounds of soap per week, ranging from "the very finest toiletries to the more common quality." By the 1920s, as North Michigan Avenue developed, the stench of soap manufacturing was no longer appreciated there and the building was abandoned and demolished in 1929. The following year, the **James S. Kirk & Co.** was sold to **Proctor & Gamble**.

Chewing gum was a popular premium.

Probably the most famous of Chicago's soap men was William Wrigley, Jr., who came to the city to establish a soap company, but it did not fare well. So in September of 1892 Wrigley started to distribute baking powder and offered a premium, a popular advertising ploy at the time, of two packs of Lotta chewing gum (manufactured by the **Zeno Manufacturing Company**) with each half-pound purchase of Lotta baking powder. The baking powder did not sell well but the premium was in high demand, and it quickly became the product, not the premium. At the time gum came as a popular premium with products such as rugs, lamps and revolvers. By 1895 **William Wrigley & Co.** had moved to 50 Michigan (now 313 West Hubbard) and listed himself under chewing gum in the city's directory. The old soap related letter head was replaced by packages of Wrigley's Juicy Fruit and Pepsin Gum along with the words "Manufacturer of Chewing Gum."

Other Chicago soap manufacturers at the turn of the century were **Oberne, Hosick & Co.**; **Cosmo Buttermilk Soap Company**; and **N.K. Fairbank and Company** who marketed "Gold Dust Twins" brand soap.

Outside of Chicago soap was manufactured in many places. In Monmouth the **Maple City Soap Works** advertised "Self-Washing Soap;" in Rockford **G.A. Shoudy & Son** sold "Wonderful Soap." In Rock Island **Warnock & Ralston** manufactured soap and in Sycamore **E.B. Shurtleff** sold his soap.

Buttermilk Toilet Soap

FOR the Complexion.
FOR Keeping the Skin Soft.
FOR Making the Skin White.
FOR its Soothing Effect and Beneficial Feeling.

IT IS THE GRANDEST SOAP IN THE WORLD.

No Other Soap Like It.   Take No Soap in Place of It.

It Excels any Soap at 25 Cents.

If your dealer does not keep it send 12 cents for full size SAMPLE CAKE.

COSMO BUTTERMILK SOAP CO.,
84 Adams Street, CHICAGO.

Keystone Steel & Wire Company

WIRE, NOT LUMBER, FENCED THE PRAIRIE

A great westward expansion followed the Civil War, and the Great Plains became the new West. Ranchers let their cattle roam, sometimes across cultivated fields. Farmers were distressed. To protect their investments, land had to be marked by both sides. A cheap fence was the answer. But what material to use? In the East, where enclosed lands were minute in comparison, wood fences and planted hedges had sufficed, but the prairie forced whole new dimensions on the human mind, and with it wholly new costs. The opening of the plains by railroads made cattle grazing profitable because the Chicago slaughterhouses were within a few days steam powered ride from the ranch. The same railroads could also move grains to market, again in Chicago, and bring in equipment more often than not manufactured in Illinois.

The plain wire fence held no terror for cattle.

Fences of plain wire began to be used in 1850, in lieu of board fences that blew over during prairie storms. To remedy this, 142 patents had been issued to citizens of Illinois by the United States Patent Office by 1871, chiefly for claimed modifications and improvements in the use of common materials for field fences. That year, too, the Report of the United States Board of Agriculture declared the snake fence to be the "national fence, it being most largely employed in all the states." The snake fence, also known as the Virginia fence, is zigzag in plan, made of wooden rails resting across one another at an angle and occupying a strip of land twelve feet wide. In 1866 it was reported that the fences of New York state occupied 300,000 acres of land, equal to 3,000 good farms. With the rapid increase in the number and size of farms in the Midwest, especially Illinois, lumber for fence material was no longer practical and it was getting expensive. It was in the nation's interest to build a better fence and many people tried.

Wire was first patented in America as a fencing material in 1821, though at the time it was a relatively rare and costly material, being drawn by hand at a rate of fifteen to forty pounds per day. In 1874 the New York State Agricultural Society awarded a silver medal for wire fence as "cheaper and more effective for farm use than wood."

It is now estimated that three hundred and fifty thousand miles of plain galvanized iron wire were used as fencing between 1850 and 1870. It was cheap, easily transported and easily erected. But the farmers and herders were not happy with it. The fence of plain and single wire snapped when cold and sagged in heat. It held no terror for cattle, which often clambered right over it.

But a new era was dawning when on July 23, 1867 William D. Hunt of Scott County, New York obtained letters of patent for providing the "wires of a wire fence with a series of spur wheels." Others also received patents on similar ideas. Here were the foundations of, maybe, the most beneficial invention to help the prairie farmer. The idea was to attach something to the wire that would keep cattle away, and be cheap and easy to produce at the same time. Glass and spikes on top of walls had been tried, but the simple solution really rested in the novelty to shape the barb out of the fence material itself and make all parts of the fence structure repellent.

Barbed wire was just too simple a solution for some.

J.F. Glidden's barbed wire fence

J.F. Glidden of De Kalb patented just such an repellent in 1874. Glidden's elegant solution was in "coiling a short piece of wire between its ends around the fence wire," and then twisting the fence wire with another wire. Arming the steel barb with a point also helped.

Much argument followed. The idea was too simple, it was just mechanical, not an invention, some argued. Whatever, it was exactly what was needed and production soared. In the first year of production, 1874, 10,000 pounds of barbed wire were made and sold. The next year, 600,000 pounds were sold. The following year saw 2,840,000 pounds made and sold. The Glidden invented barbed wire caught on and many manufacturers of barbed wire sprang up throughout Illinois and the Midwest. The barbed-wire industry also had a home in Joliet. Among its pioneers were William Watkins, H.B. Scott, A.N. Klinefelter, John Lambert, J.R. Ashley, Fish & Connell, A.H. Shreffler, among others, and the **Lock Stitch Fence Co.** was the leading local manufacturer.

As the Prairies and the West became cattle land and mechanized farms, the pace of barbed wire production and consumption raged like a great fire. Patent infringement suits flickered up everywhere. Lawyers fanned them. For the next few years consumption of all strains of barbed wire ran at epidemic levels. In 1877, 12,863,000 pounds of barbed wire were sold; followed by 26,655,000 pounds made and sold in 1878; with 50,337,000 pounds of barbed wire made and sold the following year; 1880 saw 80,500,000 pounds of barbed wire sold. And, in 1881, 120,000,000 of barbed wire were made and sold. Within a decade of its invention, the barbed wire fence, in all its variations, had become the national fence.

Glidden put his invention to immediate use on his own farm and demonstrated its efficiency to his neighbors. In its first year the process of manufacture was crude in the extreme. The barbs were cut by hand and first a pair of pliers, then parts of an old coffee mill, were adapted into a machine for coiling them about the wire. When a piece 20 or 30 feet long had been barbed, a smooth wire was placed beside it; one pair of ends were fastened to a tree, and the other attached to the axle of a grind stone, which by turning with a crank gave it the twist. At this time, I.L. Ellwood, a De Kalb hardware and stove dealer, who had also studied the wire fence and taken out a few patents, became associated with Glidden. Their partnership was known as **Glidden & Ellwood**. Ellwood was young and had commercial experience, so he took over management of the firm. The first thing he did was move the "factory" from the farm into town. Here horses were used to do the twisting and barbs were placed on one end of the wire and then spaced as desired by hand. Now one man could do one hundred pounds per day. Initial distribution was limited to the vicinity of De Kalb.

In 1875 the company built its first shop and installed a small steam engine, which did the twisting. Glidden and P.W. Vaughan obtained a patent for some barbing and spooling devices and H.B. Sanborn and J. P. Warner were made general agents. Their territory encompassed the whole United States; their job, to introduce and sell the fence. At first sales were slow, and needing capital and credit, Glidden & Ellwood offered a full one-half interest in the patents and business for $10,000 to prominent businessmen. They were refused. But within six months business picked up and the firm felt confident enough to purchase a whole railroad car of material at one time. The following winter the shop was expanded and a 40 horsepower engine was purchased to do the twisting. By the spring of 1876, Glidden & Ellwood were manufacturing and selling a railroad car load of wire per day. At the same time the barbed wire fence was still treated with suspicion by many.

The first barbed wire ever used by a railroad was put up during the summer of 1876 by Glidden & Ellwood for the **Northwestern R.R.** The Northwestern management was very cautious and had the manufacturers agree that if the fence was unsuitable, Glidden & Ellwood would remove it at their own expense. Moreover, the test fence was to be erected on Glidden's own farm, which the railroad crossed. The great fear was that stock might be injured by the fence and Northwestern held liable. The test proved a success and Northwestern ordered hundreds of miles of barbed wire fencing. Soon over 105 railroads in America were using Glidden fencing. By the following year, Glidden & Ellwood was running day and night and could not keep up with demand.

It was under this pressure that the question of an automatic machine became acute.

In 1876 the **Washburn & Moen Manufacturing Company** of Worcester, Massachusetts noticed an increased demand for a size of wire not generally purchased in quantity and began to investigate the cause. Their inquiry led to Ellwood and the purchase of one half the stock, that is, Glidden's interest. The business now had capital and quickly assumed gigantic proportions. The company also bought up all available patents. Numerous lawsuits followed, all of them well documented and much written about.

With round-the-clock production, the need for automation was pressing. Many candidates proposed machines, but it was D.C. Stover of Freeport who came up with the best machine for putting on the Glidden barb. In short order, 50 were set up and in production. Each machine did the work of eight men. The price of labor dropped from $1.25 to 20 cents per 100 pounds. With the reduction in the cost of manufacturing the wire, the retail price of the fence dropped $7 per hundred pounds. Demand boomed. A new facility was built that included a steam driven 200 horsepower Corliss Engine. This state-of-the-art engine was 18 feet high and 42 feet long. Its drive wheel was 14 feet in diameter with a

The Northwestern Railroad was the first to try barbed wire fencings.

24 inch face, weighed 22,000 pounds and could do 72 rpm. The main drive belt, of double thick leather, was 24 inches wide, 99 feet eight inches long and weighed 750 pounds.

The invention and introduction of barb fencing in the 1870s offered a complete and satisfactory solution to a problem that had vexed human kind for centuries, taking advantage of the availability of cheap and practical steel wire in quantity and improvements in galvanizing. Other practical fencing inventions soon followed.

There was a demand for woven steel wire fences, too.

In 1889 Peter Sommer, founder of **Keystone Steel & Wire Company**, invented a hand-powered wooden machine that could weave steel wire fence. With his two sons, P.W. and John, Sommer could manufacture about 200 feet of fence in a 16 hour day. Their factory was a farm shed in Dillon, near the Mackinaw River in Southern Tazewell County. Demand was brisk, and soon a steampowered machine was built to replace the hand-powered one. In 1891 the operation was moved to a bigger barn in Tremont, closer to the main road and railroad. As word got around, dealers became interested in stocking quantities of the fence. Sommer could not keep up with demand, even though he expanded the Tremont factory three times. The same year Sommer incorporated his company as the **Keystone Woven Wire Fence Company**. The keystone-shape formed by the wire in the fence gave the company its name. In 1895 the company moved to South Peoria. When the North Western Railroad expanded its switching yards onto Keystone land, the fence maker moved to Bartonville.

In the first decade of this century, Keystone grew by leaps and bounds. The first steel mill was constructed in 1902. Then, in 1905, Keystone built a wire mill, making barbed wire and nails in addition to fencing. In 1907 the company reorganized and adopted its current name: the Keystone Steel & Wire Company.

To meet the immense post World War I demand, Keystone built a new plant, an electrically-driven rolling mill, and dug its own canal to the Illinois River. Completed in 1916, the new Bartonville plant could meet not only Keystone's needs, but could produce a surplus. Keystone went into round-the-clock operation. From its three new open hearth furnaces, the company could now provide other manufacturers with steel rods, ingots and billets. A private railroad was built to connect the new plant to the wire mill, and worker housing was erected within walking distance of the plant.

By the time Peter Sommer died, in 1924, the company occupied more than 1000 acres, and employed almost as many workers. Around 1925, some smart employee dipped the tops of the Keystone wire and fence posts in red paint, making the first "Red Brand." From now on the company's products would be instantly recognizable among the competitive field of galvanized, gray products. Keystone still manufactures the Red Brand fence.

In the 1930s, as the full impact of the Depression was being felt in Peoria, Keystone stayed busy by showing farmers how to improve the efficiency of their operations and protect themselves against drought by dividing their land with fences.

In the same decade Keystone and the famous King Ranch of Texas, one million acres in size, entered into a partnership. The Ranch needed fence, thousands of miles of fence, and Keystone had the capacity to provide it. By 1950 over 2,000 miles of fence had been sold to the King Ranch. The Texans bought so much fence that Keystone ran one machine exclusively to meet the King Ranch's needs. The King Ranch fence also became a Keystone brand name which is still available today.

Always concerned for its employees, Keystone had free life insurance, access to money for emergencies and a wage seven percent higher than the industry average by 1937. And, as part of its national advertising in the 1930s and 1940s, the company sponsored a number of radio programs, including the famous WLS Red Brand Barn Dance, broadcast live from Chicago.

Keystone of Peoria sponsored the WLS Barn Dance.

Left: Feeding scrap wire into a scrap baler at Keystone
Right: A roll of Keystone's fencing

America's entry into World War II placed an emphasis on recycling efforts in all industries. This prompted Keystone to start making all of its steel from scrap and allowed it to expand production in the time of material scarcity. The Keystone plant was large and to move materials about the firm it maintained its own railroad, which by the late 1940s ran five locomotives on more than 25 miles of track on its Bartonville site.

The two decades following World War I were the glory days for American steel. The insatiable demand for automobiles, houses, appliances, highways and sky-scrapers led to an exponential growth of the steel industry. In 1964 Keystone celebrated its 75th anniversary. Employment had climbed to 3,400 people.

The 1970s and 1980s were not easy for the American steel industry. Keystone suffered too, but employee and management concessions, combined with mill modernization, enabled the company to strengthen its position as a rod and wire supplier and to be smarter and more efficient as it faced new domestic and foreign challenges.

TIME BECOMES MONEY

The first
time lock was
used in Morris.

Although we try to believe the nineteenth century was a more ideal age, one of gentility and slower paced, the use of steam powered machines, with their soot belching smoke-stacks, affected everyone's daily life through an ever quickening pace and a growing abundance of new products. From the Civil War on, machines set the speed by which many Americans lived. As commerce increased and the pace of life quickened, clocks became an everyday need, and not just for the wealthy, but for the ordinary person, too. In 1865 the **National Watch Company** was organized in Chicago by a group of former employees of the **Walthan Company**, a Chicago watch maker. The factory was built on land in Elgin donated to the company. The first works for watches, sold to the trade in tin cases, were made here in 1866. Adopting much the same methods that Ford later used in the automotive industry, the Elgin plant, soon known as the **Elgin National Watch Company**, standardized parts and introduced a modified assembly-line whereby crafts-men ceased to be watch-makers and became watch-workers. Low prices had widened the market, and the plant began to turn out thousands of watches monthly. The Elgin Watch Company was very successful and soon two competitive firms were set up: the **Illinois Watch Company** was organized in Springfield in 1870, followed four years later by the **Rockford Watch Company**. Other clock companies followed. In Peru the Westclock Factory of **General Time Instruments Co.** covered six blocks and employed 5,000 people in the 1930s and the company had a daily production of 30,000 clocks including the Big Ben and Baby Ben alarm clocks and Westclox.

The ever growing need for more accurate time resulted, in 1909, in the Elgin Observatory being built by the Elgin Watch Company to obtain sidereal time (time determined from the stars) for the regulation of Elgin watches. From a list of 800 fixed stars, 10 or 12 were chosen nightly, and followed across the heavens. An automatic electric recording device graphed time on a revolving drum. Variations of one-thousandths of a second in the master clocks could be checked. These clocks, of the Riefler type, were mounted on a concrete pier separated from the building, in a vacuum glass case maintained at a tem-perature varying not more than one-tenth of a degree from 85° F. Secondary clocks relayed the impulses by which workers timed watches in the factory. A direct line conveyed the impulses to the Chicago office of the company in the Pure Oil Building, where they were relayed to radio stations, utility companies and other agencies requiring exact time.

Clocks also found a new application when the first time lock used in the United States was installed in May, 1874 by its inventor, James Sargent, in the door of the iron safe in the First National Bank of Morris. It worked for 40 years.

Of the many manufacturers to survive the Great Chicago Fire, very few exist today. One of the survivors was the **Tablet & Ticket Co.**, now of West Chicago, which has been in business since 1870 and an IMA member since 1898. Starting as a manufacturer of tablets and tickets, hence its name, the company has diversified into site specific directories for buildings, offices, schools, libraries, cafeterias and any place that needs public directories.

Undaunted by the Fire, a new industry began to be developed by Aaron Montgomery Ward. Ward had come to Chicago in 1868 and landed a job with what was then **Field, Palmer & Leiter**, a new and stunningly successful firm owned by Potter Palmer, Marshall Field and Levi E. Leiter. The **Marshall Field and Company.** Department store was, at its prime in the 1880s, one of the best known retail stores in the world. Marshall Field, born in 1834 near Conway, Massachusetts, started in business in Chicago in 1856 as a dry goods clerk. In 1865, together with Levi Z. Leiter, he bought an interest in Potter Palmer's Lake Street Dry goods store. In 1881, after the retirement of Field's partners, the present firm name was adopted. Over the years, Marshall Field developed many new practices and policies in department store management and invested heavily in Chicago real estate.

Montgomery Ward's catalogue was a conceptual general store.

Ward worked at Field's in sales and quickly went from earning $5 per week to $12. He soon moved on to other jobs in merchandising. On his rounds, visiting country stores by train and horse and buggy, Ward observed that prices were high and the choice of goods small. And when the farmer would complain, the storekeeper pointed out that he had to buy what the wholesaler offered at prices set by the wholesaler. The farmer's choice was to take it or leave it.

Ward considered all the angles and came up with an idea that would fundamentally change the frontier: to sell direct to country people by mail, through a mail-order store — a conceptual sort of general store. The store would buy in bulk from manufacturers and wholesalers, and pass the saving on to its customers. Farmers could order goods by mail and the store would ship their purchases to the nearest railroad station. In 1871, having finally saved enough cash, Ward started his new business, buying a small amount of goods at wholesale prices. He immediately lost it all in the Chicago Fire, but with two other friends, started over. They rented a small shipping room on North Clark Street and printed up their first "catalogue" — a one-page price list. Soon the **Montgomery Ward and Co.** warehouse sprawled along the North Branch of the river at Chicago Avenue.

A popular new item in the 1870s was ready-made clothing. Previously people had taken for granted that "store bought" clothing could not possibly fit well because no two persons had quite the same measurements. But makers of Civil War uniforms had found that if they produced different standard sizes, they could provide almost everybody with a fairly good fit. Ward was quick to see the potential in such mass-produced apparel, and devoted a whole page to it in his early catalogues. In Catalogue 13, dated Spring-Summer 1875, Ward created a stir by including one of the earliest, and certainly the strongest, pledge of consumer protection by a company. On the inside front cover appeared the statement: "We guarantee all our goods. If any of them are not satisfactory after due inspection, we will take them back, pay all expenses, and refund the money paid for them." Business boomed, and Ward could boast of how his company had greatly improved the lives of common folks by making the frontier a little more comfortable.

Eventually the company moved into manufacturing, producing such products as its own line of paints (paint was a new product in the 1870s) and farm equipment. Many of these products were exported around the world. In one case Montgomery Ward supplied a mission hospital in Korea with its lighting, heating, water supply, plumbing and arid sewage disposal plant at a total cost of $3,000 and everything arrived in perfect order.

While a mail-order catalogue could sell cars, it couldn't service them.

The company even got into the motor car business in 1912, when it announced an automobile valued at $2,500 for only $1,250 "by doing away with the expensive agency system." But the Modoc, as it was called, proved a bust, mainly because there were very few Modoc dealers. While a mail-order catalogue could sell cars, it couldn't service them. The car was withdrawn in 1914.

Over the years more trouble followed, especially competition in the form of chain stores available to anyone with a car — just about every rural American by the late 1920s. Montgomery Ward opened retail stores across the country in the 1920s, calling them "display stores" initially, because customers could inspect, but not buy merchandise. The look but don't buy attitude changed quickly to one of look and buy, and eventually the company's retail stores greatly expanded in size and number until finally, in 1985, after 113 years, the company announced its decision to discontinue its famous catalogue.

JUST LIKE A QUAKER, OATMEAL IS HONEST

As has been noted before, the Great Fire of 1871 had no lasting effect on Chicago's prominence in the business of grain storage, primarily because the milling of grain had moved out of Chicago beginning in the 1840s. But there was one great exception to this general exodus, **The Quaker Oats Company.** The company was formed as a partnership by four oatmeal pioneers who each began on independent paths, converging in Chicago in 1879, where they built a new facility at Sixteenth and Dearborn Streets in Chicago called the Imperial Mill.

The first of the pioneers, Ferdinand Schumacher, had immigrated to Akron, Ohio in the 1850s where he founded the **German Mills American Cereal Company**. Schumacher did not find it easy to convince Americans of the value of oatmeal for human consumption. Although Europeans, particularly in Germany and Scotland, had consumed oatmeal for years, it was still considered "horse feed" in America. Schumacher and other oat millers were the targets of considerable teasing from not only the general public, but the press. But Schumacher persevered and eventually became the dominant figure in the oat milling industry.

In the same year that Schumacher moved to Ohio, John Stuart immigrated from Northern Scotland to Canada, where he established an oatmeal factory known as the North Star Mills Company. Twenty years later, in 1873, Stuart and his son Robert moved from

Canada to Cedar Rapids, Iowa and started a new business called North Star Oatmeal Mill. A local resident of Cedar Rapids, George Douglas, purchased an interest in the mill, and it became known as Douglas and Stuart. The partners moved to Chicago in 1879.

The fourth pioneer, Henry Parsons Crowell, entered the oatmeal business in 1881 with the purchase of the Quaker Mill Company in Ravenna, Ohio. This company had been established in 1877 by four men, one of whom was Henry Seymour, who is credited with coining the Quaker name. The story of the name relates that Seymour was searching the encyclopedia for an image that would instill confidence in his company's product, when he spotted an article on the Quaker sect which projected values and standards of honesty, integrity and strength — all good characteristics for oatmeal, too. In 1877 he registered his trademark, a "figure of a man in Quaker garb."

Reprinted with permission of The Quaker Oats Company

A man in "Quaker garb" was America's first registered trademark for a breakfast cereal.

In 1890 the company ran a special all-Quaker-Oats train from Cedar Rapids, Iowa to Portland, Oregon, distributing samples all along the way, and a half-ounce box of Quaker Oats was placed in every mailbox in Portland. Immediately Quaker Oats was in demand in the Northwest. Other selling ideas followed, and in the process helped develop the American concept of marketing.

Entering the 20th century, The Quaker Oats Company continued its course of growth and ingenuity. In 1902 Dr. Alexander P. Anderson invented a process for puffing grains called "shot from guns." Quaker entered into an agreement with Anderson to carry on his experiments at Quaker's plant in Chicago and in 1904, at the St. Louis World's Fair, Puffed Rice was introduced to the public.

Quaker diversified in 1905 by establishing an animal feed department. Within two years this department contributed one-third of the Company's net profits. In 1916 Quaker introduced its now famous cylindrical package, the "Quaker Oats Tube." The Company ran at full capacity throughout World War I, but sales slowed dramatically after the war. Despite financial set backs, Quaker continued to be a market innovator. In 1921 it used its successful concept of consumer premiums when it offered the "Crystal Radio Set," a working radio made in the image of the Quaker tube. The same year, Quaker introduced quick cooking rolled oats (Quick Quaker Oats). Now oatmeal could be made in three to five minutes and oats could compete with just-add-milk breakfast cereals.

The next leg of expansion came in 1925, when Quaker purchased the Aunt Jemima Mills Company of St. Joseph, Missouri. And in the 1930s Quaker sought many famous Americans to tout its products, among them Home Run King, Babe Ruth, who sang the praises of Puffed Wheat and Puffed Rice in comic strips and radio commercials. Movie stars, among them Shirley Temple, Ralph Bellamy, Fred MacMurray and Bing Crosby, promoted Quaker. In her role as Aunt Jemima, Anna Robinson gave promotional demonstrations and served pancakes to visitors at Chicago's Century of Progress Exposition in 1933-34. Quaker even managed to make an important contribution to the war effort, inspite of being thought of primarily as a cereal manufacturer. During World War II, the company built a plant in Memphis, Tennessee, and produced large amounts of furfural, a by-product of oat hulls, used to make synthetic rubber. This product was widely used by the military.

Not having access to the European market allowed Quaker to focus on America, where in 1942 it purchased the **Ken-L-Ration Dog Foods** business from the Chappel Brothers of Rockford. Because it was wartime and tin was rationed, the plant's pet food production was restricted. It wasn't until 1947 that cans again became available and Ken-L-Ration dog food was available for master and dog. Immediately Quaker was a major competitor in the pet food business.

In 1946 a new Quaker Man trademark featuring the head and shoulders portrait appeared. Two years later, Aunt Jemima mixes, including cake, muffins, cookie and gingerbread, were introduced in response to the demand for ever faster, more convenient foods.

In the 1930s, Babe Ruth sang the praises of Puffed Wheat.

Reprinted with permission of The Quaker Oats Company

These greatly affected the American lifestyle, which clung to traditional foods but was increasingly eager to avoid the traditional labor. To meet the demand, Quaker introduced Quick Cooking Quaker Oats, Aunt Jemima Frozen Pancakes and Aunt Jemima Corn Bread Easy Mix, the first mix to feature a flexible plastic mixing bag and an aluminum foil baking pan directly in the box. In 1955 Quaker made advertising history with a promotion that intended to sell cereal by its sponsorship of the popular television program "Sergeant Preston of the Yukon." Inside each box of Quaker Puffed Wheat and Puffed Rice Cereal was a certificate with a serial number that entitled the owner to one square inch of land in the Yukon. Soon some 21 million square inches of the Canadian Yukon Territory were owned by Sergeant Preston fans and the promotion was a huge success. Fortunately, these fans never made any effort to develop their land holdings.

In the 1960s the demand for convenient foods was a commitment to a lifestyle and to take advantage of this, Quaker introduced two of today's flagship brands — Life and Cap'n Crunch Cereals. In 1964 Quaker introduced a hot cereal which was to become one of the company's most important brands: Instant Quaker Oatmeal. Five years later Quaker acquired Celeste Italian Foods of Rosemont, makers of Celeste Pizza.

The 1970s again saw a change in consumer lifestyles. As more women entered the work force, less time for meal preparation fueled an interest in snacks and convenience foods, but a concern also for healthy foods and a well-balanced diet. Quaker responded to this trend with the introduction of Quaker 100 percent Natural Cereal and Quaker Corn Bran — the first high-fiber cereal made from the bran of corn. Also new in the early 1970s were Aunt Jemima Frozen Toast and Aunt Jemima Frozen Pancake Batter, as well as Quaker Instant Grits. At the time, Quaker also developed a Nutrition Policy Statement which was to guide the company through the next two decades.

In the Spring of 1987 Quaker moved into its new home, the Quaker Tower, along the Chicago River.

21 million square inches of the Canadian Yukon Territory were owned by Sargent Preston fans.

ILLINOIS STEEL MAKES IT POSSIBLE

Just as the processing of grains was an important factor in Illinois' economy that eventually shifted out of state, so too did the production of iron and steel, which had made Illinois an economic powerhouse for over seven decades, move away or die. Since the 1870s steel production has, until most recently, been a major factor of northern Illinois' industrial strength. Among the earliest steel centers was Joliet, where the corner stone for its first steel mill building was laid in 1870 with appropriate ceremony. The plant began to operate in 1873. As originally planned, this entering wedge into America's heartland of steel production consisted of two blast furnaces, coke and coal-washing plants, fire brick facilities, the Bessemer mills, steel and iron rail departments and puddling mills.

From merely an iron rail mill, the plant grew into the **Bessemer Works** and the maker of steel rails. Extensive remodeling was undertaken in the 1880s when rod mills were added and additional blast furnaces, coke ovens, and other departments came on line. By the end of the decade this immense industry was rated high among the steel producing centers of the nation.

In the 1870s Joliet's mills employed 1,200 to 1,500 people, with an output of about 150,000 gross tons per annum. By 1900 there were about 3,000 employees producing approximately 1,500,000 tons. Ten years later the mills employed 4,000 to 5,000 people and created about 2,000,000 tons.

The Joliet coke ovens were built around 1900 following the most modern design of Henrich Kopper of Germany. They were the first of their type in the United States. Soon 3,000 tons of coal were being consumed per day and vast quantities of coke were also being produced. There were valuable by-products such as gas, produced by the millions of cubic feet every twenty-four hours. The gas was used to run the mills, saving on coal.

Joliet's coke ovens were the first of their type in the United States.

Closely allied to the steel mills, were the wire manufacturers. Originally there were four of these in Joliet under the control of the **American Steel & Wire Co.**, but by 1910 they were consolidated into two plants.

Other steel manufacturers also flourished in the Joliet-Chicago steel corridor. **Bliss & Laughlin**, founded as a partnership in Harvey, in 1891, was one of the first manufacturers of cold-finished steel bars in the United States. Originally confined to the manufacture of shafting, its products were distributed between Detroit and St. Louis. In 1919 the company was organized as **Bliss & Laughlin Steel Co.** Some forty years later the company became known as **AXIA**, with Bliss & Laughlin Steel Group as one of its three major operating units. Today, AXIA has its offices in Oak Brook and manufacturing facilities in many states and in a number of foreign countries.

After the Great Fire, Chicago became a center for the casting of metals, especially the production of mold steels. With more than 100 years of continuous family management, **A. Finkl & Sons Co.** has become a leader in the production of mold steels. Founded in Chicago in 1879 by Anton Finkl, a German immigrant, as a blacksmith shop, Finkl molds are now used in the production of auto and truck bodies, aircraft components, telephones, televisions, computers and appliances. Finkl has some 100 worldwide patents on steel and steel-making processes, and has achieved a number of metallurgical breakthroughs. Finkl is the only company to provide the high quality inherent in steel grades with extra-low sulfur and low, flake-free hydrogen levels and assures the center soundness of all forgings. This is attainable only through the use of proper ingot design and selection, and the use of upsetting, where necessary, along with wide die reduction. Wide dies also require extremely powerful presses — roughly double the press capacity of commonly used narrow dies.

Finkl die steel is the first and only die steel in the world to be protected by a warranty against breakage. Every heat of Finkl steel is VAD processed — a patented process developed by Finkl that permits end-point degassing and refining with closer control over gas content. Vacuum arc degassing results in a considerably cleaner steel with lower hydrogen content for greatly improved ductility. Finkl's Diamond-F has been stamped on its steel since 1920.

In 1960, at a time when energy was considered plentiful, Finkl pioneered the end of energy-wasting steam presses in the United States with the first direct, oil-powered forging presses having computer control. Today all Finkl presses are oil-hydraulic powered.

From the heat of molten steel to refrigeration, Illinois has been and continues to be a manufacturing center of primary importance to the nation. For example, Frederick W. Wolf installed the first refrigeration machine, an ice maker, in the United States into the **Wacker & Birk Brewing Co.** of Chicago. The year was 1882. Fresh ice was now available year around. Within twenty years the age old tradition of the winter ice cutting and storage for spring, summer and fall use was a memory, for all but small rural needs. Wolf had been born in Düren, Germany in 1837, studied mechanical engineering there and in 1866 immigrated to New York and then to Chicago, where from 1867 to 1875 he was in business as a consulting engineer and architect.

Wacker & Birk Brewing Co. of Chicago had the first refrigeration machine in the United States.

Seeing a future in industrial refrigeration, he acquired the rights to import the Linde ice machine, developed by Prof. Carl Linde of the University of Munich. Soon after the first success, another machine was imported and erected in the Schlitz Brewery in Milwaukee. It, too, was a success. Others followed, but the difficulty of importing the machines induced Wolf to manufacture them himself in Chicago and thus **Wolf-Linde, Inc.** was born. Until about 1960 the company manufactured compressors for industrial refrigeration. Since then, Wolf-Linde has focused exclusively on ammonia valves and fittings for large industrial refrigeration needs.

For much of the manufacturing history of Illinois, tools have been a mainstay. In 1844 Alexander Vaughan moved west to Peoria. Recognizing the need for a better way to dig post holes, Vaughan designed and patented the very first post hole auger, then moved his company to Chicago to start manufacturing. In the dirt-floored room where he set up shop for the augers, in 1869, the company soon began producing in volume. Strained finances resulting from the Great Fire of 1871 prompted the merger with the Bushnell family, owners of a hardware store behind which the shop had been located. The company was incorporated as **Vaughan & Bushnell Manufacturing Company** in 1882. Its product line had grown to include quite a variety of tools and implements for blacksmithing and shoemaking, together with chisels, punches, pincers, nippers, crate openers, star drills, planes, wrecking bars, pliers, hatchets and axes. In time, Vaughan came to specialize in the manufacturing of hammers and striking tools. Sanford S. Vaughan, Alexander's son, joined the company in 1887, just before moving to larger facilities in Chicago. He took over management in 1905 and served the company for 64 years.

Sanford Vaughan was an innovator and made many basic changes in the design of the traditional carpenter's hammer, changes which are to be found in all hammers being made today. The Bushnell family interest was purchased in 1922, the same year that Sanford's son Howard (Sr.) joined the company. It was through the coincidence of names that Howard Vaughan's attention was first drawn to the town of Bushnell as a possible

All claw
hammers follow
the Vaughan
design.

Vaughn's claw hammers and Superbar

site for a plant expansion, and manufacturing was started there in late 1940. Eventually most of the manufacturing operations were consolidated at Bushnell, with administrative headquarters and a smaller manufacturing facility in Hebron.

The company has continued its tradition of innovation. Vaughan developed the 999 style rip hammer in 1918. The extra steel behind the striking face and extra deep throat are now the industry standard for this type of hammer. Vaughan was the first hammer manufacturer to increase the sweep of the claws to enable the user to fit the claw over a 2x4. All claw hammers are now manufactured to this design.

Vaughan designed and developed the original Superbar for pulling and prying, an essential tool for both homeowner and tradesman, now copied the world over. Vaughan also developed and patented the only solid steel hammer with "shock-block." This exclusive hickory and rubber plug takes the sting out of all steel hammers.

Vaughan is now the largest employer in Bushnell and is the largest manufacturer in the world of hammers and other striking tools. It is the only company in the world that performs all the manufacturing steps necessary to transform the basic raw material of steel bars, hickory logs and fiberglass strands into finished hammers.

THE MACHINE CAME OF AGE THROUGH COAL

When the coal was mined out, the money and the people moved away.

The machine came of age in America during the 1880s and coal made it possible. Although we immediately associate Pennsylvania with coal, the first recorded discovery of the most useful of minerals in what is now the United States was made by Louis Jolliet in 1673, when he and Father Jacques Marquette reached the Indian village of Kaskaskia, which lay on the Illinois River, a few miles east of modern La Salle. What they did not know was that below an east-west line across the state at La Salle, the whole of Illinois, with the exception of the Ozark region and strips along the Mississippi and Ohio Rivers, sits upon a rich layer of coal deposits of varying thickness. Early in the State's development, coal was mined in the nearby bluffs of East St. Louis, then known as Illinoistown. The coal was freighted to the river in cars drawn by horses along wooden rails. Some historians cite this contrivance as the first railroad in Illinois. The first locomotive to burn Illinois coal successfully was converted from a wood-burner in the Illinois Central shops of Centralia. By 1868 the use of coal in locomotives had become common, not only in Illinois.

Many communities began as coal mining towns. Among them was Streator, which came into its first industry because of a veritable bed of coal was under the city. Mining began in 1872. Streator was initially called Unionville, but changed its name to honor the coal company's first president, Streator. Trenton, on United States 50, was incorporated in 1865 and became a coal boom town in 1876. Carrier Mills was a mining town named after William H. Carrier, who established a sawmill there in 1870. Coal City dates from the opening of the mines in 1875. Braceville and Garden were coal boom towns in the 1890 census. Peoria, Bartonsville, Orchard Mines and Kingston Mines were coal towns. And Carbondale is the center of the southern Illinois coal fields. Godley had 21 coal mines in operation in the 1880s. Thousands of Scotch, Irish and Welsh made up the mining population. By 1906 all the mines were closed. Only "gob-heaps" that encircle the town recall the era. Harrisburg was the focus of a serious coal boom in 1905, when 13 mines were opened. In 1940, 21 mines operated, making Saline County fifth among the coal producing counties in the state. Dowell sprang up in 1916 around the large **Kathleen Coal Company** mine. Many of the towns' heydays were flashes in the pan — when the coal was mined out, and the money and the people moved away.

In the 1930s the **Canton Central States Colliers Strip Mine**, one of four in the area, worked with 1,000 ton dipper, with a mouth of 48 feet that could scoop out earth to a depth of 40 feet. It was state of the arts for the time. During 1935, 13 mines operated in the Du Quoin region, five of them shipping 1,732,000 tons of coal to outside markets. While just outside of Du Quoin in the 1940s, one of the largest strip mines in the United States, called the **United Electric Coal Company Mine**, used an electric powered dredge.

The **Cahokia Power Plant** was, in the 1930s, the first designed expressly for the use of low-grade Illinois coal in pulverized form. Large mills reduced the coal to powder that was blown by compressed air into the fireboxes beneath 14 immense boilers. Each of the six smokestacks was 256 feet in height and 21 feet in diameter at the top. The plant consumed one ton of coal every 30 seconds.

Over the past 15 years the **Monterey Coal Co.** Mine Number 2 in Albers has turned out more than 17.4 million tons of high sulfur coal. When the last 5,600-ton trainload pulled out on December 31, 1992, Monterey Number 2 finished that year as Illinois' second highest producing mine, turning out nearly 3.1 million tons of coal. Stringent pollution controls now require coal-burning businesses to install "scrubbers" to help reduce acid rain attributed in part to Illinois' high-sulfur coal. "The Clean Air Act of 1990 created tremendous challenges for marketing of high-sulfur coal. It was obviously intended to do so. And it is doing exactly that," said Taylor Pensoneau, vice president of the Illinois Coal Association, in a recent *Chicago Tribune* quote (March 31, 1993). When Monterey Number 2 opened in 1978, it was one of about 70 mines in Illinois, which together employed 18,500 miners. In 1992 there were 39 mines, employing 10,500 miners. The decline in mines could be an indication that the fuel that drove Illinois manufacturing for most of a century may now be retiring, and giving way to perceived "cleaner" sources of energy.

In 1865 settler William Henneberry, while sinking a well, struck a vein of coal three feet wide and 70 feet down. The new coal field attracted many mining syndicates. By 1873 Braidwood had grown to 3,000 and was incorporated as a city. In 1880 the population stood at 9,000. Up to six long coal trains pulled out of town daily. 117 saloons flourished. Braidwood was in one of the major coal fields of Illinois and **Northern Illinois Coal Company** extensively strip mined there. Electricity operated the machines. The operation striped, washed and loaded 6,000 tons of coal per day.

With such an influx of miners, Braidwood served as a testing site for labor organizations and safety practices. The push came with the disastrous flooding of the Diamond Mine which in 1883 killed 74 men. Racial strife complicated the problems of labor in 1877 when blacks were brought in as miners by the operators to break a nine month strike. Out of the Braidwood field came such leaders as John Mitchell, a national labor leader; W.D. Ryan, Illinois arbitrator of mining disputes; Dan McGllaughlin, a union leader and mining executive; John H. Walker, state representative; and Anton J. Cermak, a Bohemian youth who later became mayor of Chicago and was killed in 1933 in an assassin's attempt on the life of President Franklin D. Roosevelt. Cermak worked in the mines until he was 17.

Mines had their share of labor troubles. Among the reasons for labor organizing were mining disasters such as the one that hit the Diamond Mine on February 13, 1883 or the Cherry Mine Disaster of November, 1909, when a mine fire with gas and smoke took 270 lives. Twenty miners were rescued after being entombed for eight days.

The Clean Air Act has created challenges to marketing Illinois high-sulfur coal.

Wages were another area of dispute. The most famous one being the Virden coal miner riot on October 12, 1898. Miners struck when the local company withdrew from the **Illinois Coal Operators Association** and refused to pay the rates established by that association and the miners' union. According to the Carlinville *Democrat*, the company imported 300 Southern blacks and 75 armed guards. The miners opposed the efforts of the guards to bring blacks into the mine. Ten miners and six guards were killed and about 30 wounded. To an outraged public, Governor Tanner, who had sought arbitration of the strike, declared: "These avaricious mine owners who have so far forgotten their duty to society as to bring this blot upon the fair name of our State have gone far enough... and I say now to all such and others that this is a thing of the past, that it shall not be tolerated in Illinois while I am governor." Warrants charging company officials with conspiracy to murder were drawn up but never served.

Mining brought countless workers to Illinois.

The mining centers produced a number of important labor organizers. Mount Olive was the home of English born union organizer Alexander Bailey (1866 to 1918), and "Mother" Jones (1830 to 1930), born Mary Harris in Cork, Ireland. She came to the United States at the age of five, and in 1867 became a union activist.

The **Miner's Institute** was built as a labor center by five Collinsville locals of the **United Mine Workers of America**. In the spring of 1916 their committee was assured by the Springfield district officers that a loan would be granted if 10 percent of the funds required could be raised locally and properly insured. They were, and in May, 1917 work began on the building.

Mining was just one of the industries that lured countless workers to Illinois. As the population of the state and the Midwest swelled, the need for cheap clothing and, most important, shoes was high. Traditionally each shoe had been made to fit only the foot it was to protect. But with the increase in population, the demand for shoes was greater than the ability to pay for custom work and the concern for proper fit. It was also realized that the foot was very pliable and would adapt to many approximations of foot shape. The result was shoes that could be produced cheaply and, in different standard sizes, that fit most feet. Fashion quickly replaced nature as a determinate for shoe shape, especially among women. In 1838 **Albert C. Ellithorpe and S.B. Colllins & Co.** began manufacturing boots and shoes in Chicago. By the late 1870s the factory production of shoes and boots had become common and surpassed hand made shoes in many of Chicago's leather working shops. **M.D. Wells & Co.,** of Chicago, boasted to be the "sole manufacturers for Illinois of the standard screw-fastened and saddle seam boots and shoes." **Phelps, Dodge & Palmer Co.** also of Chicago, claimed, "nothing but solid leather in tips, counters, soles & heels" for its fine sewed shoes. George E. P. Dodge, of Phelps, Dodge & Palmer Co., was, in 1893, one of the founders of the **Illinois Manufacturers' Association**, as was another shoe maker, J. E. Tilt, principal of the **J. E. Tilt Shoe Company**. By 1889 Chicago stood fifth among the nations leading 13 shoe centers.

INDUSTRIAL DISTRIBUTION IS A NEW INDUSTRY

Towns were often built around an industry.

By the mid-1880s the industrial revolution was under full steam in the United States. New technology, like the steam turbine, multiple-spindle textile machine and the automatic turret lathe, made it possible to produce products faster and more economically. Powered by these new machines, and fueled by a post-civil-war enthusiasm to put the nation "back on its feet," the American industrial movement began. And it was during this time that an entirely new industry emerged: industrial distribution.

As industrial development gained momentum and spread westward, major new industrial centers sprouted up. Pittsburgh became famous for steel, Cleveland for machine tools, Chicago for meat packing and rail transportation, and New York for importing and exporting. But in order for these new centers to specialize in their own natural and geographical resources, a faster, more efficient method of distributing industrial supplies and equipment had to be found. The day of the industrial supply distributor had arrived.

The first industrial distributors were the mill supply houses which served New England's textile and metalworking industries. Later, Midwest distributors evolved to serve the hardware and steel business. And in the west, where the Alaskan mining boom was just getting underway, distributors focused on mining equipment and supplies. By 1900 industrial supply sales had reached $75 million annually and industrial distribution was becoming big business. The nation's growth depended on it.

Among the first to recognize the importance of industrial distribution was the United States Department of Commerce. Among its early studies, the agency had taken a close look at mill supplies and defined them as "... those materials which are expended in the process of manufacture — lubricating oil, wiping pastes, belting, belt lacing, or other fasteners used in the running of machinery, files, tools, emery wheels, etc." As America's industry broadened, the need for more general types of industrial supplies quickly became evident. Seeing an opportunity to move into new markets, the mill suppliers responded by expanding their product lines to meet this demand and became the forerunner of the industrial products distributor of today.

As industrialization became the by-word of the nation, towns were built around an industry or a factory, often where neither town nor industry had existed before the other. The most famous of these is Pullman, but there were many others. Harvey was built on land bought by Chicago lumberman and capitalist Turlington W. Harvey in 1889. The site was swamp and prairie, had one small factory, a hotel and a few houses. Within two years there were several factories, new schools, churches and 5,000 inhabitants. By the 1950s Harvey was a major production center of diesel engines, highway machinery, railroad equipment, ranges and stoves.

Chicago Heights, named in 1890, was the earliest and for a time the most important steel-making community of greater Chicago. Steger, built up around the piano factory of John

V. Steger in 1892, was known as Columbia Heights until it was incorporated as a village in 1897, and John Steger was elected its first president.

In the 1890s two other firms also made pianos there and the town was known as "the Piano Center of America." In 1900 the two sold out to Steger. The peak years in piano sales were 1920-22. Then radios became popular. The **Steger Piano Company** closed its doors in 1925. The **Steger Furniture Company,** employing 700 in peak season, manufactured radio and then TV cabinets into the 1970s.

Lansing was organized in the 1860s by Dutch and German farmers. The village became an adjunct of the vast industrial area concentrated in the northwest corner of Indiana. In 1893 Posen was a polish worker's town, while Robbins was incorporated as an African-American village in 1917. Argo is a city that developed around the **Argo Corn Starch Co.** in the 1890s. And much of Calumet City was built during a real estate boom of the 1920s, even though part of the community had already been platted in 1833.

The town of Pullman was, arguably, the most important outgrowth of industry in the nation in its day. In the 1860s the Pullman car, or "sleeper,"revolutionized the railroads. The cars, developed by the cabinetmaker George M. Pullman in 1864 as long distance sleepers for the Chicago and Alton line and from 1867 on built by **Pullman Palace Car Company**, made travel from coast to coast a pleasurable experience and the new dining cars reduced travel time by eliminating the need to stop for meals. The interiors of these cars were decorated by skilled craftsmen and then furnished with plush chairs and draperies.

So successful were Pullman's railroad sleeping cars and parlor cars that by the late 1870s he needed a larger tract of land in order to expand his operations. Some years earlier, acting on the advice of his friend Colonel James H. Bowen, Pullman had purchased land along Lake Calumet, which was rapidly becoming the region's steel center. The land was cheap, and the area offered convenient transportation by both water and rail. Bowen's land transactions did not arouse the real-estate speculators, for he had long been buying in the Calumet area, whereas direct purchases by Pullman would have driven prices up. In the 1880s the Calumet region was little more than swamp, and the only settlement was a small number of farms in Kensington and Roseland, just west of Lake Calumet.

In testimony incorporated in the United States Strike Commission's Report on the Chicago Strike of June - July, 1894, Pullman explained his choice: "We decided to build, in close proximity to the shops, homes for workingmen of such character and surrounding as would prove so attractive as to cause the best class of mechanics to seek that place for employment in preference to others. We also desired to establish the place on such a basis as would exclude all baneful influences, believing that such a policy would result in the greatest measure of success ... from a commercial point of view ... Accordingly the present location of Pullman was selected. That region of the country was then sparsely populated."

Steger was known as "The Piano Center of America" in the 1890s.

Unlike other industrialists of the day, Pullman did not subscribe to the theory that if he provided source of employment, a labor force would appear, and he believed that the worker's environment influenced his output. This theory found expression in his town. And, although company towns had been built before, none had been planned along the lines proposed by Pullman. Here every building was to be both functional and beautiful, from the workers' tenements to the row houses and single family homes of managers.

In Pullman
the corporation
was
"paternal."

In 1879 Pullman commissioned Solon Beman, a young New York architect, to design the town. By April 1880, when ground was broken and the sewage system begun, Beman had completed plans for a factory, workers' homes, a town square, hotel, park, library and school, shops and a church.

Under the Pullman-Beman master plan, workers were provided with red and yellow brick dwellings which far surpassed the frame buildings found in other industrial areas of Chicago such as Back of the Yards or South Chicago. Over the next two years the town of Pullman grew so rapidly that by 1882 it was necessary to draw up plans for additional homes to accommodate the unskilled workers employed by the nearby **Allen Paper Wheel Company** and **Union Foundry Works**, companies which provided the wheels and steel dies essential to the construction of Pullman's cars. This new section became known as North Pullman. In the 1890s an area known as West Pullman became well known when Col. A.L. Conger established the **Whitman & Barnes Company** plant there. The plant, built of some five million bricks, was the largest mowing machine knife plant in the world and also the world's largest wrench manufacture. Almost as a sideline, Whitman & Barnes also manufactured twist drills.

While their environment was a vast improvement over industrial areas in Chicago, workers in suburban Pullman were reminded constantly of their indebtedness to the Pullman Company. The Rev. William H. Carwardine, pastor of the First Methodist Episcopal Church in Pullman, described the "paternalism" in his book on the Pullman strike with the words of Peter Quinon of the Pittsburgh Times: "The corporation is everything and everywhere. The corporation trims your lawn and attends to your trees;...sweeps your streets, and sends a man around to pick up every cigar stump, every bit of paper, every straw or leaf; the corporation puts two barrels in your back yard, one for ashes and one for refuse of the kitchen; ... the corporation does practically everything but sweep your room and make your bed, and the corporation expects you to enjoy it and hold your tongue."

When the effects of the panic of 1893, a severe economic downturn felt across the nation, finally began to be felt in the town, Pullman responded by cutting production and wages. His refusal to make corresponding reductions in their housing and food costs left his workers impoverished. The resulting strike of 1894 loosened Pullman's grip on the town, but it was not until 1898 that the Illinois Supreme Court ruled that the Pullman Palace Car Company had exceeded its charter by purchasing more real estate than was needed for the operation of the car works. The court also ruled that the company was not authorized to build homes for employees or to "engage in the business of renting dwellings, store rooms, market places, etc." In short, it was the opinion of the high court that had George Pullman built only the car works "individual enterprise and private capital" would have quickly provided "all necessary dwellings and tenements for the accommodation of the workmen." The effect of the court decision was to force the company to relinquish, by 1904, all holdings in the town not directly related to the operation of the car works. As quickly as Pullman had created his model community, the town skidded into industrial commonplace.

From 1905 to 1910 Pullman saw a boom as new industry located there, the Pullman car works were expanded and employment rose to more than 10,000. At the same time profound changes had occurred in the car production. Ever since Pullman established his reputation with the *Pioneer* sleeping car in 1864, all railroad cars had been made of wood. Now a change in materials "from wood to steel" was enhanced by a change in the labor force. As Pullman used more steel, cabinetmakers, gilders and polishers were replaced by riveters and crane operators. These new skills were more easily acquired than the older ones. Already by 1900 the company had reported that skilled workers made up only 40 percent of the work force. The "journeyman mechanic" was replaced by "an army of steel workers."

The stability which Pullman had sought to build into the town in 1880 was gone by 1910. And, as enterprising home owners converted the ground floor of row houses into saloons and grocery stores, Pullman took on the appearance of a working-class neighborhood, one among many in the city.

RING! RING! "HELLO?"

While the Pullman railroad car provided greater comfort to the traveler, the first telephone call on March 10, 1876, by Alexander Graham Bell, was to provide ease and mind boggling speed to comminication. A little more than a year later the telephone came to Chicago, brought by Gardiner Green Hubbard. He had six instruments and he meant to promote them. From the start he had a financial interest in the telephone.

Soon Hubbard met with General Anson Stager, the leading telegraph man in the city. Stager was a principal of the **American District Telegraph Company**, president of **Western Electric Company**, and vice president of **Western Union Telegraph Company**.

On July 2, 1877 a private line telephone service was set up between the headquarters of **N.K. Fairbanks and Company** on Dearborn Street and the firm's lard and oil factory at Blackwell and 19th Street. Everyone involved with the early telephones recognized that their usefulness was greatly restricted because they could operate only in pairs — one instrument connected directly to the other. But the development of the central exchange, almost as soon as the telephone itself was invented, solved some of this dilemma. By June of 1878, 267 interested corporate and private subscribers to the **Chicago Telephonic**

In 1878 Chicago had 267 telephone subscribers.

Exchange were talking to each other on lines furnished and maintained by Bell for a monthly rental. Financing the exchange came from Bell headquarters in Boston. By October of that year the company issued its first proper alphabetical and classified directory. It carried 291 listings.

On December 21, 1878 the **Bell Telephone Company** of Illinois was incorporated. Gardiner Hubbard, who had introduced the telephone to Chicago, became its first president.

In 1882 there were 392 telephones in Illinois outside of Chicago.

Actually this was not the first telephone exchange to be established in Chicago. That honor goes to the American District Telephone Company. This corporation had been chartered in Illinois since 1875 to provide telegraph and messenger services and opened its telephone exchange one week before Bell did. But a patent infringement suit by Bell resulted, in November, 1879, with a settlement that Western Union, parent of American District Telephone Company, would get out of the telephone business and turn its 56,000 telephones in 55 cities over to Bell in exchange for a financial settlement. Bell was now a legal monopoly until its initial patents ran out in 1893 and 1894.

Bell and American District Telephone Co. competed until 1881. Then they merged in the public interest. Wrote noted Chicago historian, Bessie Louise Pierce, "Competition between the two companies was exceedingly keen, and the subscribers to the two lines suffered an inconvenience which the consolidation eliminated." Without competition all telephones were on one system. Every phone could now talk to every other phone. People found that convenient and the phone quickly became a household item for many. In 1882 there were 2,600 phones within the city limits of Chicago; by 1890 there were 6,518; by 1900, 26,661; in 1920, 575,840, and in 1940 more than one million. This number doubled again by 1963. And in 1980 there were 2,734,837 telephones in the portion of Illinois served by Illinois Bell.

Exchanges spread throughout Illinois quickly. The Bloomington exchange opened in June, 1879; Springfield, Danville and Decatur followed in October and November. The year 1880 saw exchanges open in Joliet in March, Freeport in April, Champaign in July and Canton in December. Evanston followed in 1881. Yet in 1882 there were only 392 telephones in Illinois outside of Chicago.

In 1940 there were 415 independent telephone companies in Illinois; by 1970 costs and competition had reduced their number to 68. Today, the independent telephone company is mostly a rural phenomenon serving only a small area, but with trunk access to the nation's communication network.

Although it preceded the telephone by decades, the telegraph was slower to gain ground against its technological limitations. By the turn of the century several inventors were still attempting to replace the dots and dashes of Morse code with word messages. In 1907 a Chicago mechanical engineer, Charles Krum, financed in his efforts by Joy Morton of the **Morton Salt Company** and the **Morkrum Company**, perfected such a system. By the following year an experimental model to send printed words by wire was tested over railroad wires between Chicago and Bloomington. Within a decade the company had its own Chicago plant and in 1928 became known as the **Teletype Corporation**. In 1930 Teletype was purchased by **AT&T** to become a wholly owned subsidiary of **Western Electric**. The company later, in the 1950s, established its headquarters in Skokie.

As the use of the telephone became more common, the needs to communicate across lines arose. The switchboard soon made this possible, and coils boosted the distance it was possible to transmit a voice along a wire. And perhaps more important was the dial, which made it possible to complete a call without the intercession of an operator. Originally called "automatic telephone exchange," the first dial in Illinois was used at Fort Sheridan. This invention, by Almon B. Strowger, was manufactured in Chicago by the **Automatic Electric Co.** and the first system was introduced in La Porte, Indiana, in 1892. The first company to install the automatic system in Chicago was the **Illinois Telephone and Telegraph Company**, which operated from 1903 to 1917, when the Bell system took it over.

In 1940 there were 415 independent telephone companies in Illinois.

Other technical advances included the high-vacuum tube in 1913, manufactured at the Western Electric plant in Cicero. By 1929 the company employed 40,000 workers in manufacturing telephone equipment, audiophones, and many electrical appliances. In 1916 the condenser microphone was added to the line up and the radio telephone for airplanes received its first trials in 1917. Two years later, in 1919, Western Electric gave the desk telephone its first dial and demonstrated the first public address system at a Library Loan drive.

During World War II Western Electric produced communications gear vital to the war effort and created the most advanced radar systems. In 1950 the Bell System established microwave radio relay services for phone messages and network TV.

PUBLISH OR PERISH

Another form of communication, printing, has since well before the Declaration of Independence been a cornerstone of America rights. For much of the nation's history, printing has been thought of as an east seaboard activity. But as in so many ventures, printing, too, shifted to Illinois and specifically Chicago in the course of the nineteenth century. And in Chicago the most important printer has been **R. R. Donnelley & Sons Company**. In 1864 Richard Robert Donnelley, an established journeyman printer in Canada, joined the Chicago publishing and printing partnership of **Church and Goodman**. Six years later the company was renamed the **Lakeside Publishing and Printing Company** and was partially owned by Donnelley. In 1875 **Donnelley, Lloyd & Company** was formed as a subsidiary of Lakeside to publish softcover reprints of previously published hardcover books. The reprint series was named the Lakeside Library. Two years later, in 1877, a depressed economy forced the Lakeside Publishing and Printing Company to close its doors. Its printing equipment and materials were acquired by Donnelley, Lloyd & Co.

In 1879 R.R. Donnelley owned the company and was elected president, treasurer and director. The next year, R.R. Donnelley formed the **Chicago Directory Company** to publish the first Chicago City Directory. The Directory listed business names and addresses and was the first of many information directories to be published by Donnelley. Six years later R.R. Donnelley secured its first contract to print telephone directories for the **Chicago Telephone Company**, predecessor of **Illinois Bell**.

The Chap-Book was an innovation in selling books.

For the World's Columbian Exposition, 1893, Donnelley printed a number of guides and books, but the most noteworthy was a guide by two men who freshly abandoned the writer's circle at Harvard to write a Fair guide. It sold well and the publishing firm of **Stone & Kimball** was set up in Boston and Chicago with all the printing done by Donnelley's Lakeside Press. Stone & Kimball quickly became a very popular publisher and it can be argued that they introduced a style now known as Art Nouveau to the world, ahead of Paris by one year. Their influence was felt throughout the American publishing world when they introduced a radical new concept of selling books through a magazine called the *Chap-Book*. This collection of short essays, poems, illustrations and advertisements for Stone & Kimball's books and posters introduced a number of authors and illustrators to America, among them Henri de Touslouse-Lautrec and William Bradley. By 1904 Stone and Kimball had run out of energy and been passed by the times, and for the next twenty years the company limped along, nourished by past glories, until it went into receivership.

Hazenplug self protrait, 1896 and an 1895 Chap-Book *cover, both printed by R.R.Donnelley*

R.R. Donnelley, on the other hand, just kept expanding, adding a new plant at Plymouth Court and Polk Streets in Chicago in 1897. The same year the company commissioned artist Joseph Leyendecker to design its printer's mark, an Indian's head, to symbolize the company's pioneering spirit and its location near the first site of Chicago, Fort Dearborn.

By 1900 printing and publishing establishments in Chicago employed over 20,000 and ranked the city second only to New York in both areas, thanks in no small part to R.R. Donnelley. In 1908 Donnelley started up a new venture, an in-house apprentice school. The school helped meet the needs of the company and industry, but also was trend setting in its approach because it helped integrate the booming immigrant community into Chicago's work force. Donnelley still maintains the apprentice system for a variety of skilled crafts.

By 1900 Chicago was America's second city in printing.

Just before America's entry into World War I, Donnelley dissolved the Chicago Directory Company and set up a separate company called **Reuben H. Donnelley Corporation**, as the publisher of telephone directories. Today, the Reuben H. Donnelley Corporation is a subsidiary of **Dun & Bradstreet**. The two firms are not connected in any way, except that R.R. Donnelley prints many of the telephone directories that R.H. Donnelley publishes.

With the end of World War I, **Sears Roebuck & Company** became the catalogue giant, nudging the inventor of mail order, **Montgomery Ward**, into second place. R.R. Donnelley printed 250,000 covers and a million copies of one section of Sears' General Catalog in 1918.

Three years later, in 1921, Donnelley moved its first printing division out of state, to Crawfordsville, Indiana to produce the Indianapolis telephone directory. Today, the two-plant complex counts among the world's largest and most technologically advanced case-bound book production facilities.

In 1927 R.R. Donnelley entered the field of printing mass-circulation magazines with the production of *TIME* magazine. Having set the printing standard for the mass-circulation magazine industry, R.R. Donnelley printed *LIFE* magazine weekly, starting with its first issue in 1936. From its birth, *LIFE* documented its age and was the most important photo journalistic vehicle in the world. As the *LIFE* boom swelled with the end of World War II, R.R. Donnelley built, in 1947, the South Plant in Chicago, specifically to meet the printing, binding and shipping needs of *LIFE*. The end of the decade also saw R.R. Donnelley print *LOOK* magazine which ceased publication in 1971. The following year, 1972, *LIFE* magazine suspended regular publication, after 36 years of gracing the newstands..

During the great age of the magazine, other publishers also flourished in Illinois. One of these was the periodical publisher **Kaleb Brothers Co.**, in Mount Morris. Starting as a one room print shop in 1898, Kaleb Brothers became a modern 2 ½ acre plant in 1939, with 32 presses which printed more than 300 United States periodicals annually.

Throughout the 1950s R.R. Donnelley expanded along with the nation's craving for magazines and books. In 1956 the Willard, Ohio Division was opened to print telephone directories. Today Willard still prints six by nine inch directories for independent and Bell telephone companies, yet its primary products are books, including encyclopedias, textbooks, reference books, Bibles and trade books. Two years later construction began at Warsaw, Indiana, R.R. Donnelley's first gravure plant outside of Chicago. Today, two plants comprise the Warsaw Division, making it the largest gravure facility in America. Its catalogue and tabloid customers include J.C. Penny, Radio Shack, Land's End and L.L.

As the nation craved magazines and books, Donnelley expanded.

R.R. Donnelley & Sons Company's Goss press #2 in 1949

Bean. The following year, 1959, the Rudisill Printing Company, of Lancaster, Pennsylvania was purchased and became a division. Today, its products include catalogues, magazines and telephone directories. And in 1960 the Old Saybrook Plant was constructed to serve eastern magazine publishing markets. Today, in addition to printing magazines such as *TIME, People, Sports Illustrated, Business Week, New York* and *W,* Old Saybrook produces catalogues and newspaper inserts.

R.R. Donnelley's community involvement reached a new peak in 1965 when it became the major stockholder in the **Lakeside Bank,** whose intentions were to meet the banking needs of Chicago's Near South Side, a developing area. In 1967 R.R. Donnelley built a plant in Mattoon, whose customers include *Family Circle, Glamour, Redbook* and *Ladies Home Journal.* The same year the company rearranged its corporate structure according to products and added the Book Group. In 1968 "the world's most modern telephone directory plant" opened in Dwight to served the needs of the Midwestern telephone directory market. That year the Magazine Group was formed and the **Electronic Graphics** (EG) Division, a pioneer of computerized typesetting and related services, opened in a converted book warehouse a few blocks north of the Calumet Plant. Seven years later EG moved to the Kimball mansion on Chicago's historic Prairie Avenue. Since then, the operation has evolved into the **Directory Service Center** in Elgin; **Selectronic Services** in Lombard; and **Database Technology Services** in Willowbrook. In 1991 the company donated the Kimball and Coleman houses to the Chicago Architecture Foundation.

In 1974, the Elgin photocomposition center opened, with one of its major products being the Yellow Pages display advertising. And in 1975 a gravure printing plant was opened in Gallatin, Tennessee, to produce catalogs and newspaper inserts. Today, Gallatin's customers include K mart, *TV Guide, Guidepost* and *Modern Maturity* magazine (in 1988 *Modern Maturity* became America's number-one magazine in circulation). The following year the Dwight telephone directory plant was expanded to produced two-color classified telephone directories, an innovation in directory printing.

During the later 1970s saving natural resources became an important aspect of printing and R.R. Donnelley was among the most conscientious greens when it formed the wholly owned subsidiary called **Donnite Corp.** to manufacture pulpboard, a product made from paper waste that can be molded into furniture. Donnite Corp. was sold in 1985.

In 1977 R.R. Donnelley marked the 50th anniversary of its contractual work with Sears, Roebuck & Company, and Mattoon delivered the billionth copy of *Family Circle.* Electronics as we know them today came into their own in the course of the 1970s and R.R. Donnelley adapted them to its customers' needs immediately as they appeared. The 1970s also saw an ever increasing need for up-to-the-minute information across the United States and access to local needs were made possible by seemingly instantaneous electronic communications. In 1978 R.R. Donnelley formed the Technical Advisory Council to help evaluate and apply technological developments to the graphic arts.

In 1977
R.R. Donnelley's
plant in Mattoon
delivered its
one billionth copy
of Family Circle.

R.R. Donnelley opened its Los Angeles Division in 1978 to cover the nation's printing needs from coast-to-coast. The Los Angeles Division specialized in weekly magazines including *TIME, People, Sports Illustrated, Newsweek, Business Week* and *United States New's and World Report.* R.R. Donnelley also acquired its first foreign printer, Ben Johnson & Company Limited of York, England, a high quality magazine and catalogue printer. After a six-year hiatus, *LIFE* magazine returned in a new format for which cylinders are made in Chicago; body pages are printed in Gallatin; and covers are printed in Warsaw. Gallatin also installed the company's first web press for *TV Guide.* In 1979, the satellite transmission of *TIME* color transparencies began between Chicago and New York. This opened a new window to instantaneous publishing. Printing was now not enough; delivery directly to the end customer had to be accurate, too, and R.R. Donnelley developed computerized ZIP code presortation in 1980. This was followed in 1982 by a satellite link for R.R. Donnelley to transmit data between the UK and the United States and the development by Donnelley Direct Color Engraving (DDCE), a new system of electronic page makeup and production of gravure cylinders without film. The following year, 1983, satellite links were established at all R.R. Donnelley plants and the **Financial Printing Service Group** was created to secure the company's position in the highly competitive financial and legal printing market. The company also became the country's leading gravure tabloid printer and only printer with multiple processes for tabloid production.

In 1986 R.R. Donnelley entered into a joint venture with Philips International B.V., the Dutch electronic multinational and co-inventor of the Compact Audio Disc. The newly formed **OptImage Interactive Services Company**, headquartered in Chicago, provides studio production and related services to the authors and publishers of materials being produced for Compact Disc Interactive Systems.

In 1989 R.R. Donnelley celebrated its 125th anniversary and marked its 25th year of printing the *New Yorker* and *Sunset* magazines.

Computerized zip code presortation began in 1980.

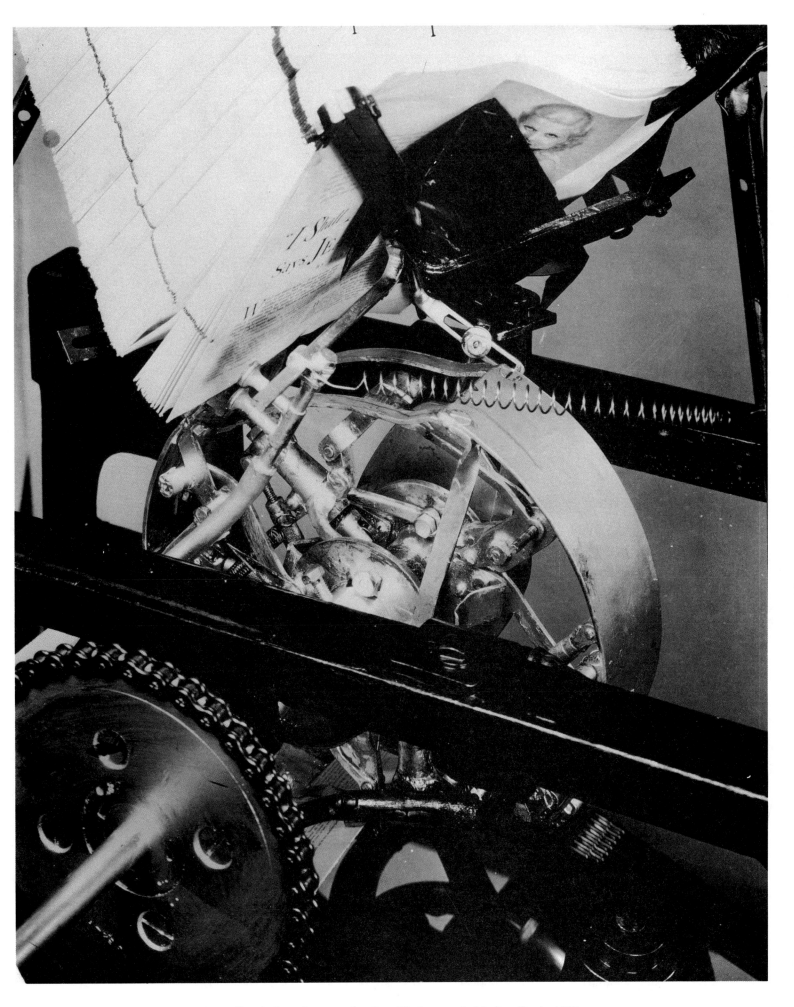

R.R.Donnelley & Sons Company has Jean Harlow on the binding line in 1936

▲

Selling popcorn in the 1890s

FUN, FOOD AND INDUSTRY

By 1890 Illinois was the third largest industrial state of the Union, with more than one fourth of the labor force engaged in manufacturing and, according to that year's national census, Chicago was first in the manufacture of agricultural implements, railroad cars, soap and candles and meat packing. Chicago was second in general railroad shops and construction work, manufacturing of clothing, cooperage works, coffee and spices, furniture, planing mill products, job printing, book publishing and tinsmith's work. Pittsburgh was Chicago's only rival in iron production.

But it was not always the production of goods or necessities that made the mark. The 1890s really got going in 1893 with the wildly successful Chicago's World's Columbian Exposition and its most famous built attraction, the Ferris Wheel. It was conceived by George Washington Gale Ferris, an engineer whose family was prominent in Galesburg. Members of the Fair Ways and Means Committee were aghast upon being presented with a proposal to build a wheel 26 stories tall. A popular magazine referred to the plans as "G.W.'s cockeyed dream." Ferris persisted while officials waffled. Finally a concession was granted July 1, 1892, only to be revoked the next day. Final approval for the project was not secured until December 10th. The fair was to open the following May 1st. The main provision of the agreement was that Ferris must secure his own funding, as the Fair's $28 million construction fund had long since been allocated. Up to this point, Ferris had already spent some $25,000 in completing the plans and specifications. By the terms of the concession, the **Ferris Wheel Company** was to construct a giant wheel which held 36 cars, each 26 feet long and 13 feet wide, to accommodate 60 passengers, or 2,160 people per trip. A trip comprised six stops in the first revolution to load before turning another full revolution without stopping. When completed the diameter of the Wheel was 250 feet, its total height was 264 feet and the total weight was 2,807,498 pounds. The structure was 30 feet wide and boasted a circumference of 825 feet. Each steel tower that supported its axle was 140 feet high, anchored in four 20x20x20-foot concrete blocks. The Wheel itself was elevated 15 feet above ground. The main axle was 32 inches in diameter and 45 feet long, and weighed 140,000 pounds, including the weight of the hubs. It was forged hollow and had a 17-inch diameter bore. The axle rested on a pair of pillow block bearings weighing 36,200 pounds each. As if the Wheel itself were not grand enough, a magnificent display of electric lights was installed. An electric plant was set up in the boiler house and electric current was transferred to the Wheel through underground wires. The tower, fence and Wheel were studded with 3,000 incandescent bulbs: 720 on the outer circle, 504 on the inner circle, 250 on the towers, 320 on the portals, 500 on the fence enclosure and additional lighting on the spokes and other points. By the time it opened to the public on June 21, 1983, with a 40-piece Iowa State Band loaded into one car, the Wheel had cost $380,000 to construct. The admission fee was 50 cents, while most other attractions cost a

> By 1890 Illinois was the third largest industrial state in the Union.

nickel. By the end of the Exposition, October 30, 1893, it had earned its entire cost back, and paid the exposition $25,000 in royalties. After the exposition the Wheel stood idle, becoming the subject of a lawsuit over the $400,000 profit, and in the spring of 1894 was dismantled and stored in a nearby railyard. The following year the Wheel was set up adjacent to Lincoln Park, in Chicago. The expected volume of riders never materialized and the Wheel suffered tremendous losses. The park closed and eventually the wheel was auctioned off for $18,000 to a junk dealer in June of 1903.

Several months later the new owners obtained a concession to operate the Wheel at the 1904 Louisiana Purchase Exposition in St. Louis, Missouri. At the Fair, the Wheel generated only a small profit and, at the Fair's conclusion, the owners abandoned the Wheel. It was sold to a wrecking company. On May 11, 1906, two 100-pound charges of dynamite reduced the once "Queen of the Midway" to a pile of scrap iron. Ferris himself had died in November of 1897, in a state of financial ruin.

Other ferris wheels were built, the thrill of the ride even moving across the Atlantic. In England, Walter B. Basset, an engineer, built four wheels all over 200 feet in diameter between 1894 and 1898 . The Riesenrad at the Prater in Vienna, built in 1896 by Basset, was his most noteworthy, and is still in operation today.

One of the two million ferris wheel riders was the Illinois inventor, William E. Sullivan of Roodhouse. Upon his return home, he began to dream of creating and marketing a portable ferris wheel. By 1897 Sullivan had moved his family to Jacksonville, home of Illinois College, founded in 1829 and, today, the oldest degree granting college in Illinois. In Jacksonville, Sullivan began trying to get parts for his Wheel built by the **Jacksonville Bridge** (later **Illinois Steel**) **Company**, but the management did not believe it could be done. They did, however, agree to rent the plant and equipment to Sullivan for 15 cents an hour. Machinist James H. Clements became interested in the project in 1899 and bought a one-third interest in it for $150.

In early 1899 Sullivan began drawing the plans for his wheel, followed quickly by the making of patterns in Crawford's Mill and the pouring of castings at the A.W. Bambrook Foundry. A contract with the Jacksonville Bridge Company was secured on March 23, 1900, and the actual construction began April 14th. On May 1212 the first Big Eli Wheel was erected in the company's yard. It stood 45 feet high, was held together by 521 bolts and had 12 phaeton-type buggy seats for passengers. A one-cylinder Davis gasoline engine powered it. Throughout the summer the wheel appeared at fairs in Illinois, Missouri and Indiana, moved from town to town in railroad boxcars and was transported to the operation site by horse-drawn wagons.

The Big Eli Wheel appeared at fairs throughout Illinois in 1900.

WHEELS STILL TURN A PROFIT

An improved model was assembled in the fall of 1901 and opened for business on October 15th in Galesburg, the birthplace of George Ferris. This wheel had 206 fewer bolts and 508 fewer pieces of steel, 1096 fewer rivets and 2872 less holes. The seats were improved and the wheel was driven by a gear. The gears did not meet with public approval and were not further developed. In 1905 Sullivan made a wheel with interchangeable parts. The new wheel was socket and pin connected. There were no bolts in the structure of the wheel. It was quick to erect, easy to operate, economical in upkeep and proved to be a money maker, too. That year, 1905, Sullivan decided to go into the business of mass-producing Big Eli Wheels. The following May, **Eli Bridge Company** was incorporated in Roodhouse. Business was brisk from the start and before the year's end, the first international sale had occurred — to the Havana Brewery Company in Cuba. Probably the most enduring international sale came in 1913 when N.E. Bharucha of Bombay, India purchased the Eli Bridge Company's 71st wheel, which is still turning a profit 80 years later. In 1919 the company built a new building in Jacksonville. It housed an assembly room large enough to erect a wheel prior to shipment. The last major improvements in the wheel during Sullivan's tenure were the introduction of the 16-seat, 55-foot high Aristocrat Wheel in November 1921, and the Baby Eli #6 Wheel in 1923. The Baby was discontinued in 1960 and was replaced by the Little Eli Wheel.

Through the Great Depression and World War II, the company remained afloat. In the post-war years business boomed. In 1950 Eli manufactured 51 wheels, the most in a single year ever. In 1954 The Scrambler, a new double-rotation ride, was introduced. It took the amusement industry by storm.

An Eli Bridge Wheel has been turning in Bombay, India since 1913.

The early days at Eli Bridge Company in Jacksonville

Craker Jack
has been eaten
since 1893

In the late 1960s W.E. Sullivan's dream of a truly portable Wheel was realized when the HY-5 began to operate directly off its transport trailer. Other trailer mounted rides followed. The Little Scrambler, a miniature version of the full-sized thrill ride, became an important attraction in 1981. In 1989 the popular Aristocrat # 16 Wheel was successfully trailer-mounted and in this configuration became known as the Eagle 16 Wheel. Standing 60 feet tall, this wheel could accommodate up to 48 passengers in its 16 seats. Almost one hundred years after W.E. Sullivan of Roodhouse rode the first Ferris Wheel, the Big Eli's Double Eagle Wheel, soaring over 60 feet above the midway and featuring facing seats that can be loaded and unloaded two seats at a time, was introduced. With it, the Eli Bridge Company of Jacksonville is poised for its second century.

What the Ferris Wheel became for rides, **Cracker Jack** became for snacks. Both were a sensation at the 1893 Fair and both are still well known. Cracker Jack was invented and first sold by F.W. Rueckheim, a Chicago popcorn vendor. The premium, the sought after prize inside each box, was added in 1912. For many years these prizes were die-cast metal. The red, white and blue color scheme of the box, which still features Sailor Jack and his dog, Bingo, were added after 1914. The colors, of course, were a patriotic gesture on the eve of war, while Sailor Jack was modeled after F.W. Rueckheim's grandson, wearing a sailor suit of the kind that had been made popular as children's formal clothing in the late 19th century by the children of the Kaiser and Czar.

POPCORN GOES TO THE MOVIES IN CHICAGO FIRST

By the 1890s the concept of snack foods was developing in the United States and popcorn was quickly becoming the nation's most popular snack. This trend was helped along greatly in 1885 when Charles Cretors founded **C. Cretors & Co.** in Chicago (the company is still in Chicago) after he devised a way to pop large quantities of corn in oil and seasoning using a cooking pan and a stirrer blade to mix the corn. The device was powered by a steam engine. Until this development, popcorn was popped in a hand held wire basket over an open flame which resulted in popcorn that was dry, burnt and not a taste sensation. With Cretors' machine, popping could be controlled, the corn didn't burn and it could be flavored as desired. He patented his corn popper in 1893. Cretor's invention eventually led to two distinct lines of popcorn machines: one for use in movie theaters and concessions and the other of industrial size poppers. Seven years after Cretor's developments, the **Dunbar Manufacturing Co., Inc.** of South Elgin invented the rotary dry popcorn machine. Popcorn became a business and a social phenomenon. Olmsted Ferris, of Galesburg and brother to the man behind the Ferris Wheel, experimented with popcorn and introduced it to England. The Prince Consort, Albert, was very interested and the prairie New Englander gave a command performance of corn-popping to Queen Victoria. The development of the corn popping machines allowed street vendors to hawk fresh popcorn and candy stores to make and sell it. Possibly the most popular context in which popcorn is eaten today is at the movies. This association began when David Wallerstein, a manager with **Balaban & Katz** in the late 1920s and later the company's president, introduced buttered popcorn as a snack to munch while watching a movie in a theatre in Chicago. With this innovation the concession stand was born. Wallerstein later introduced soft drinks, and going to the movies has not been the same since.

Shellac helps make candy shiny.

Cretors' popcorn makers turn the century

Among the food products most taken for granted is candy. It just always seems to be there and we don't really give it much thought when we consume it. But consume it we do, and in great quantities. Illinois, especially Chicago, mostly as the result of its immigrant population, transportation network, and shellac production (for coating candies as well as floors) is a natural location for the production of many nationally recognized candies.

Bradshaw - Praeger & Co. of Chicago, is one of four manufacturers of shellac in North America. The importance of the confectionery business in Chicago drew Bradshaw & Praeger to the city where it has, since 1923, supplied shellac and shellac based products to the candy, pharmaceutical, leather, hat, furniture, floor polish and ink industries.

In Bloomington a major producer of confectionery was established from the 1890s on by Paul Frank Beich, who was an Illinois Manufacturers' Association Board of Directors member from 1923-26 and President in 1927. He was Chair of the Advisory Board in 1928 - 29 and a member of the Board of Directors until he died in 1937. Beich, who was born in 1864, in Wehlau, Prussia, had studied and apprenticed for three years in the food and flavor business there, before emigrating to Bloomington upon reaching the legal age of 16. His first job was in St. Louis with the confectionery firm of **Bruce & Brown**, as a salesman. In 1888 Beich established his own company in St. Louis, **Beich-Buffe Candy Co.** Four years later Beich purchased the **Wholesale & Manufacturing Confectionery** business in Bloomington from John W. Gray, and in 1905 incorporated as **Paul F. Beich Co.**

A similar story can be told of Emil J. Brach, who by 1904 found the demand for his caramel so great that he formed a company to mass produce this single product. Ninety years later, **E.J. Brach Corporation** is the third largest company of its kind in the United States and the nation's largest maker of "general line" candies. Its red and white striped starlight mint is the top selling hard candy mint in the country and Brach's is America's top maker of seasonal candies. Always looking for new ways to present its products, Brach's introduced Pick-a-Mix in 1958. This was a new concept at the time, selling bulk wrapped candy which consumers selected themselves and bought by the pound. It has proven very successful. Brach's Chicago plant produces 1.2 million pounds of candy each day. This production is a large share of the 1991 estimated consumption of more than 21 pounds of confectionery per person.

> Brach's Chicago plant produces 1.2 million pounds of candy each day.

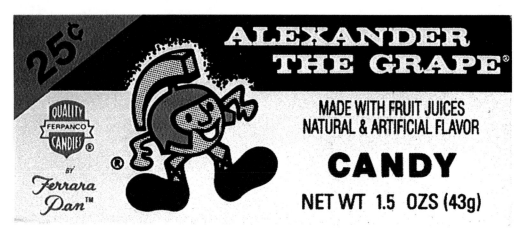

A Ferrara Pan Candy Co. treat

Ferrara Pan Candy Co. was founded in 1908 in the back of the original **Ferrara Bakery**, 2200 W. Taylor Street in Chicago, by Louis J. Buffordi and two cousins. Since then Ferrara has expanded into the largest pan candy company in the country. Its top sellers are Atomic Fireballs (a jawbreaker), Lemonheads and Red Hots. Ferrara also makes Alexander the Grape and Jawbreakers. The firm moved to Forest Park, its present location, in 1960. Today, the company stocks 13 warehouse distribution centers around the country.

The World's Columbian Exposition was planned and completed in a very short period of time and the credit for this must go to individual inventiveness. With its huge buildings and vast areas requiring paint, and not enough people or time to paint everything before opening day, the World's Columbian Exposition found its solution in an invention by Joseph Binks, a maintenance supervisor at Marshall Field's State Street store. As part of his job, he oversaw the periodic whitewashing of the subbasement walls, a tedious, time-consuming and costly chore. To ease the work, Binks invented a cold-water paint spray-ing machine. As crude as it was, it was better than hand painting. The invention was restricted to the basement use at Field's until the World's Columbian Exposition put Binks' machine to work and attracted the attention of the British import firm of Wallach Bros., Ltd, which became his primary customer for a number of years and distributed the machine in Europe and the United States. Interestingly, the machine was first used mainly by American dairy farmers, who were required by health regulations to whitewash their barns and disinfect their cattle. Soon the auto industry began to paint its cars with Binks' spray machine, and the potential became vast.

The cold-water paint sprayer began as a whitewashing device.

Binks' venture was first known as the **Star Brass Works**, located at the northeast corner of LaSalle and Lake Streets in Chicago. Later it changed its name to **Binks Spray Equipment Company**. In 1928 the company was sold to Neil Hurley and John F. Roche. It survived the Depression, World War II and the post-war boom. Today, the company is known as **Binks Manufacturing**, with offices in Franklin Park. Along the way, the company pio-neered automatic painting systems, electrostatic painting and airless spray painting. This technique uses hydraulic pressure instead of compressed air.

MANKIND CREATES HER OWN SUN

When the first World's Fair opened in London in 1854, its Crystal Palace refracted the sunlight during the day and reflected the gas lights at night. By 1893 electricity was not yet common, so it amazed everyone. For much of the nineteenth century light meant either candles, whale oil lamps or gas. In 1852 Chicago had 561 gaslight consumers. The municipality had 209 public lamps or in all 7,532 burners consuming 8,911,000 feet of gas. By the end of the century mankind had finally found its own sun — electricity — and the world changed. New light-bulb technology with improved filaments, the opening of Fisk Station in Chicago, the world's first all-steam turbine generating plant and the start of "electric shops" to sell appliances were events that have affected us greatly. On September 17, 1907 **Chicago Edison** and **Commonwealth Electric Light and Power Company** were formally consolidated to form today's **Commonwealth Edison Company**. But the story begins much earlier.

It began in 1868, when George H. Bliss and L.G. Tillotson opened a little electric shop on Clark Street. The shop burned down in the Great Chicago Fire, and Bliss continued on his own. In 1882 Bliss formed **Western Edison Light Company** with plans to prove electricity could work in office buildings in downtown Chicago. Bliss also figured that if electricity were used in offices, it would follow the user home. To set an example, the company wired its headquarters for 250 electrical lights and installed its own power station. The "gimmick" paid off. On March 28, 1887 a Chicago ordinance gave Western Edison the right to use underground wires and conductors for the transmission of electricity in an area bounded by Lake Michigan, North Avenue, Ashland Avenue and 39th Street. The franchise was turned over by Western Edison to the new Chicago Edison Company, which chose as its first service district the area bounded by Harrison, Market, Water Streets and Michigan Avenue. It made its first deliveries in August, 1887, with a total connected load in excess of 6,000 incandescent lights which in two years grew to 15,000 lights. To lure new users, Edison offered incandescent bulbs for 65 cents each. Replacements were free of charge.

To lure new users, Edison offered free replacement incandescent bulbs.

When Samuel Insull became president of Edison in 1892, he began acquiring rival companies and organizations that had wiring and underground-cable franchises. Since Chicago Edison had only a 25-year franchise and a limited territory, Insull, in 1897, incorporated as the Commonwealth Electric Light and Power Company. The new firm obtained a 50-year franchise and a larger territory. In 1898 several promotions were used to attract new customers. For a limited time the company offered to install six outlets free in unwired residences if the owners would sign a one-year contract for electrical lights. Many accepted this offer. Another promotion included selling electric fans from the back of buggies on hot days. The sales, second only to the electric iron, boosted the need for electric services in private residences. Rates that year started at 10 cents for the first 30 hours, with a minimum monthly bill of one dollar per horsepower. Meters were not installed until 1900.

In 1929 Commonwealth Edison's maximum load exceeded one million kilowatts for the first time, the millionth meter was installed and the State Line Station was placed in service with the largest unit in the world. This honor lasted until 1954. Throughout the years, the company depended on coal, gas and oil to generate electricity. A new age dawned in 1951, when the Atomic Energy Commission invited Commonwealth Edison and other major utilities to begin feasibility studies of atomic generated electricity. Four years later, in 1955, Edison announced plans to build a 180,000-kilowatt-capacity unit southwest of Chicago. The Dresden Nuclear Power Station was dedicated on October 12, 1960. It was the nation's first full-scale, privately financed nuclear power plant. Two other plants followed, giving Edison the largest nuclear generating capacity of any United States utility, about 5.1 million kilowatts. In 1981 Edison's capacity produced 27 billion kilowatt hours, or 45 percent of the company's total electrical generation.

Electricity was new in the late 19th century and electrical failures that resulted in fires were quite common. A major cause of this was the oil used in the circuit breaking fuses. Edmund O. Schweitzer and Nicholas J. Conrad, both electrical engineers with Commonwealth Edison Company, set out to develop something better. Working on their own time, they came up with a better solution in 1909, when they developed and patented their idea for a power fuse which utilized a fire extinguishing liquid, carbon tetrachloride. Commonwealth Edison and Boston Edison liked their idea and began to use it, paying $1.25

for each fuse. During 1910 Conrad produced 700-800 fuses in his home. By February 1, 1911 **Schweitzer & Conrad** were in business, having started with a borrowed $1,000. They had one employee, Ed Toman, who now produced their fuses in a tiny machine shop on the second floor of the R.J. Bennett Building, at 1774 Wilson Avenue, Chicago. Soon a one story factory was built on North Ravenswood. Over the next four decades the S&C Liquid Power Fuse was in demand, and the business prospered. The technological developments necessitated by World War II and the catch-up buying spree that followed the war helped Schweitzer & Conrad become a leader in its field and, of course, new facilities were needed. A site on Ridge Avenue in Chicago was selected. In 1992 **S&C Electric Co**. was counted among the top 75 privately held firms in Chicago.

At the end of the nineteenth century electricity seemed to be in the air everywhere and everybody was charged with ideas that could run with this new source of power. One such development happened in 1916 when J. Walter Becker, born in 1885 of immigrant German parents, developed the first commutator stones (a device for reversing the direction of an electric current). The following year Becker formed a partnership with his brother Lou and launched the **Ideal Commutator Dresser Company** of Chicago. In 1924

Becker moved his company to Sycamore and within four years the Ideal Company had become the leading manufacturer and marketer of commutator resurfacer stones and saws in the nation and its product line accommodated nearly every commutator resurfacing application in existence, from large industrial to small motor maintenance. Marketing

its product had always been a strong suit with Ideal and throughout the Depression the company diversified and sold its products by direct mail, print, market research and customer service.

In 1931 Ideal was granted the first patent for screw-on wire connectors. This achievement firmly established the firm's future growth. From 1940 to 1945 business boomed as all dry cell flashlight battery production was sent to the military, yet meter readers and others still needed lights, so Ideal manufactured rechargeable wet cell flashlight batteries. Utility companies purchased these in quantities. With the end of the war,

Ideal patented screw on wire connectors in 1931.

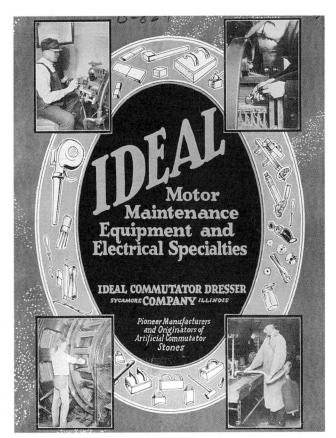

An Ideal catalogue from 1929

production of the wet cell battery ceased. In 1946 Ideal was incorporated and the following year expanded its manufacturing of wire connectors by opening a facility in Petersburg. This site was a leading manufacturer of wire connectors until it was consolidated with Ideal's De Kalb plant in 1980.

Turner Brass first made brass harnesses, saddle fittings and bicycle trim.

Another company that developed in Sycamore was Turner Brass, today a leading producer of propane powered products. In 1907 Charles Rickett decided to move the company he had bought a few years earlier in Chicago to Sycamore. The company, the **Turner Brass Works**, had been established in 1871 by E. F. Turner as a manufacturer of brass harness and saddle fittings, as well as a line of bicycle fittings and trim. Before the move to Sycamore, Rickett had become interested in gasoline fuel appliances, particularly blow torches and firepots, and purchased the patents and manufacturing rights for blow torches from the **S.S. White Dental Company.** Turner then became a known brand in the field. Over the years many related products were added, such as stoves, lanterns and heaters for the camping. In 1975 the parent company, then **Olin Corporation**, decided to withdraw from the camping industry and to sell or close the plant. Cleanweld Products, Inc. of Los Angeles saw an opportunity to expand and bought Turner. The combined facilities

Turning out brass works

made this company one of the world's largest producers of 14 and 16 ounce propane fuel cylinders and solid oxygen products for the home, farm and industry. Since 1984 Turner has been part of Cooper Industries of Houston, Texas and assigned to their tool division, CooperTools. Under this management, Turner has continued as the undisputed leader in torches, propane and high temperature fuels for heating, brazing, cutting and cooking.

FLAT BELTS ARE BETTER THAN ROPE, FINALLY

In order for machines to do what they were intended to do, the energy that drives them needs to be harnessed to them, and though the use of transmissions has been around for hundreds of years, it was not until the 1870s that flat belts finally proved to be more efficient at higher speeds than rope. The early flat belts were made either of leather or of closely woven cotton duck built up in layers and impregnated with balata, a form of rubber with low elasticity. Both balata and leather belts could be reliably spliced into continuous loops necessary for line shaft power systems. But installing either type of belt properly called for the skill of an experienced craftsman. The belt was slung over the line shaft and joined into an endless loop by one of several methods.

Leather belts were commonly joined by a process in which belt ends were shaved or skived into matching bevels, glued together, then dried for eight hours. Balata belts were joined using a similar method which involved vulcanization with heat clamps. An alternative method for leather belts, faster but not considered as good, was to lace the belt ends together with leather or gut thongs. It was said to take 60 to 90 minutes per 12-inch width of belt for an expert to complete this type of splice. As the speed of production increased, manufacturers sought better ways to reduce the time of repair and replacement.

An untold number of inventors took up this challenge. The first American patent for a rigid fastener was in 1859, while the first patent for a hinged fastener followed in 1866. Both types pioneered the concept of metal devices attached to belt ends by rivets or bolts. These concepts were refined into several distinct types of designs. Concurrent with this surge in belt drives and fasteners was a similar advance in the use of belts as conveyors. Although belt conveying first appeared with Oliver Evan's mechanized flour mill design around 1785, it was little used other than with grain milling until the late 1800s. That was when new designs of belt construction and conveyor-loading equipment developed by beltmaker Thomas Robins, Jr. proved that belt conveying was practical for heavy materials such as coal, ore and rock. This triggered a broad expansion of belt conveyor applications between 1895 and 1910.

A promising fastener design patented in 1906 by Olof N. Tevander, a plant superintendent with American Can Company in Toledo, Ohio, caught the attention of two employees of **Addressograph Company** of Chicago: George E. Purple, engineer, and Albert B. Beach, accountant and manager. Teaming up with Beach's son-in-law, Philip S. Rinaldo, a men's clothing retailer from Sioux City, Iowa, they formed the **Flexible Steel Lacing Company** to buy the Tevander patent and manufacture its design. In January, 1907 the three set up a small office and workshop in downtown Chicago at 71 West Jackson, a location adjacent to the Union League Club. The business began with a second-hand metal-forming press, a roll top-desk and a few other necessities. The original product was a hinged joint that did not employ a hinge pin. The lacing was stamped from a strip of steel with a common strip down the center. Teeth were formed on alternate sides of the

A broad expansion of belt conveyor application occurred between 1895 and 1910.

center strip. Two such pieces were meshed together so the center strips were back-to-back. The belt ends were inserted between on both sides of center strips and the teeth were driven into the belt with a hammer.

The first efficient belt fastener looked like an alligator's open jaws.

Because rawhide belt lacing was the most common method for joining transmission belts at this time, the Tevander product became known as flexible steel lacing, which gave the new company its name. The fastener worked well enough compared to others, but the splice could not be easily separated and wore out too quickly. Determined to overcome these problems, Purple, Beach and William Trout, Beach's brother-in-law and a mechanical designer for the E.P. Allis Company in Milwaukee, modified the Tevander design in late 1907. This new design was patented in 1909. At the same time other features were altered and also patented in the same year. The new tooth configuration, when viewed from the side, resembled the open jaws of an alligator — so ever since its introduction in 1909 this design has been known as Alligator lacing. As power requirements and speed advanced so did belt tension and hinge stress. To cope with this new problem the company introduce the rocker hinge pin in 1911.

In 1919 B.F. Goodrich was among the first to produce a 2-inch thick, heavy-belt conveyor for an open-pit copper mine in Chile. Preferring not to go into the fastener business, Goodrich asked Flexible Steel Lacing to help. A suitable response was conceived by George Purple and patented in 1919.

By 1921 the 14 year old company built a new plant at 4607-31 Lexington Street and employed 79 people, operated 17 presses and consumed more than 30,000 pounds of steel weekly. At about this time a whole new market opened up, the automobile fan belt and laundry "aprons." The latter were broad, flat belts that carried sheets and linens through flat-work ironing machines.

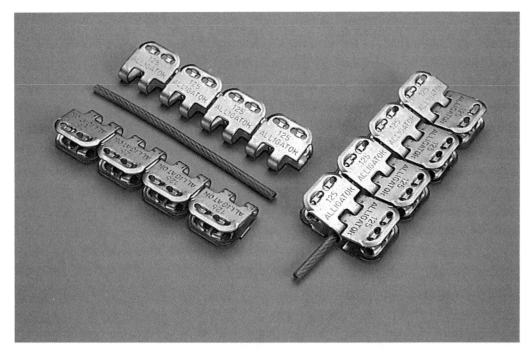

Alligator staples

In the early 1930s flat transmission belts were being replaced by V-belts, and individual motor drives had already begun replacing overhead line shafts. A number of competitive V-belt fasteners appeared in the 1930s, but virtually all either failed in service or remained too localized to compete with the national distribution of the Alligator brand. The Alligator fastener featured a link anchored at both ends by two rocker-type hinge pins using the same principle applied in George Purple's original pin design. Many variations of the basic design followed and have continued to be developed to this day.

For many years more large machines that helped make automobiles, farm equipment, refrigerators, construction equipment, and many others, were made in Rockford than in any other city in the United States. In 1905 Rockford had a population of over 32,000 and more than 250 factories, sixteen of which were furniture plants and dozens of which were supportive manufacturers such as glass works, varnish, paint and hand tools. Until 1982 Rockford was known as one of the leading machine tool manufacturing cities in the country. Today, Rockford still has many threaded fastener and screw companies serving the automotive and woodworking industries.

In 1905, Rockford had more than 250 factories.

ROCKFORD LEADS IN MACHINE TOOL MANUFACTURING

Manufacturing depends on machines and just as the product has to be manufactured, the machine, too, has to be made. As a wholly-owned subsidiary of **Textron, Inc.**, Greenlee of Rockford manufactures more than 5,000 tools and accessories for professional electricians and contractors, as well as a most extensive line of punching, pulling, bending and drill-bit product groups in the world. Among its innovative products: the Cable Run Designer, a computer software package to help electrical contractors plan cable pulls, and the 805 Fiber Optic Puller, which pulls optical fiber through conduits.

Over the years Greenlee has been an active participant of change. Before the Civil War Robert Lemuel and Ralph Stebins Greenlee, identical twins, had worked with their father to develop a barrel making machine for the Pennsylvania oil fields. But the demand there dwindled, so in 1862 the Greenlee twins moved to Chicago where there was need not only for barrels, but also for buildings and sidewalks. The Greenlees prospered. The Great Fire was a boon to the brothers. Three years afterwards the brothers developed the hollow chisel mortiser, which combined the cutting edge of a chisel with a boring bit. It literally used a round bit to cut square holes.

From this invention, and the profits it generated, came a long line of woodworking machines, ranging from a self-feeding rip saw to an entire self-contained railroad tie factory carried to the site in a freight car. The transfer machines the twins developed were among the first of their kind. They were the antecedents of the huge automated transfer lines of today's heavy industry. The Greenlees' automated processes preceded those of Henry Ford's mass production innovations. Then, in 1897, a fire destroyed the plant. The factory and its foundry were rebuilt, but the decision had already been made to relocate the business.

The firm moved to Rockford in 1904 and immediately began to expand its production of auger bits, hollow chisels and other small tools. With growing demand for both machine tools made in Chicago and the smaller tools made in Rockford, the managers of **Greenlee Bros. & Co.** decided, in 1912, to create a separate operation, **Greenlee Tool Co.**, solely for the small-tool portion of the business. This firm was run by Robert's only son, William B. Greenlee, and George Carr Purdy. Purdy saw the future of the machine tool industry was in metal, not wood, and Greenlee Bros. began moving in this direction slowly. Until the mid-1920s the company continued to developed new products for woodworking, such as the electric double-end tenoner, introduced in 1926. Then, in 1928, came the firm's entry into metalworking tools, with a line of metal hole punches for use by plumbers, construction workers and electricians. In 1930 Greenlee began the manufacture of a pipe and conduit bender, a self-contained hydraulic unit that could bend pipe up to 25 tons of ram pressure. In 1936 came a cable-puller for electrical contractors.

America's automotive industry depended on Rockford-built tools and machines.

Though the original metal hole punches are still in the firm's catalogue, the products have been adapted to meet the demands of the age. The first pipe and conduit bender has evolved into the 555SB Speed Bender, which combines updated bender technology with a digital electronic memory that allows consistent repeat bending. And Greenlee's early success with wood boring bits gave rise to to the Nail Eater line of wood bits, which can bore through nails that would dull or break ordinary bits. In 1969 **Ex-Cell-O Corporation** acquired Greenlee Tool. As part of Ex-Cell-O Corporation, Greenlee Tool was acquired by Textron in 1986.

Mattison Machine Works was founded in 1897 by Christen Mattison in Rockford to develop and design automatic equipment for manufacturers of wooden furniture, office equipment, and decorations such as table legs, porch balusters and literally hundreds of various parts which were and still are mass produced. Mattison still makes automatic wood turning machines which produce Louisville Slugger baseball bats in 12 seconds, but now they are computer controlled. They also make saws, wood sanders and molding machines, called stickers by some. In 1932 Mattison led the way to developing high production, high precision surface grinders and other metal working equipment. At the time Rockford was the nation's leader for producing production woodworking machinery equipment.

Over the years Mattison has created over 50 different high production machines, such as huge surface grinders, Planetary Production grinders and CNC corrugated roll grinders designed to produce products faster and with higher tolerances than any equipment now in production. It is noteworthy that Mattison manufactured the first woodworking equipment purchased by Henry Ford, and that without the labor saving equipment created and built in Rockford the United States automotive industry could not have grown as it did. Only Cincinnati was a close competitor to Rockford in producing high precision, high production metal working equipment.

It was in this environment that Levin Faust, an inventor and machinist, and two tool makers, Elmer Lutzhoff and Swan Anderson, each invested $500 and started the **Rockford Tool Company** to manufacture a small chuck for a furniture carving machine. The chuck sold, but not well enough to make a profit; so the three designed a new product, a furniture belt sander which became very successful. Late that same year Faust designed the first pneumatic furniture rubbing machine. It immediately became the company's main product.

In 1909 a small machine tool shop called the **Rockford Milling Machine Company** began operations in the same building as the **Rockford Tool Company**. The Company was owned by Oscar Sundstrand and his brother-in-law, Edwin Cedarleaf. A year later they were joined by Sundstrand's brother, David. By 1911 the Milling Machine Company needed more manufacturing space and moved to a new building. The next year the Rockford Tool Company moved in across the street. David Sunstrand's interests were not really in milling machines, so he invented a 10 key adding machine and in 1914 the first model was marketed. The adding machine proved so successful that a subsidiary company was formed to handle orders which then became the **Sundstrand Adding Machine Company**, with its own four story building a block north of the Milling Machine Company.

In 1926, at Hugo Olson's suggestion, the Rockford Milling Machine and Rockford Tool companies merged to form the **Sundstrand Machine Tool Company**, and Olson became its first President the following year. Hugo Olson, a bookkeeper and insurance cashier, had been associated with both companies since 1905 and 1910 respectively, as an invester, a partner and financial adviser.

In 1914 Sundstrand marketed a 10-key adding machine.

Sundstrand Aviation's first Constant Speed Drive for the Air Force's B-36 bomber in 1946

Among the new company's first orders of business was to sell the adding machine building, then the machine itself was sold to **Underwood-Elliot-Fisher**, while Sundstrand continued to manufacture it until 1933. This transaction ended the Sundstrand brothers' 20 year business partnership. Oscar remained with the adding machine business and David, its inventor, remained with the machine tool business.

Sundstrand is Rockford's single largest employer.

During the 1930s Sundstrand engineers began to investigate ways to improve the various machine tools and hand-held sanders they produced as well as more efficient ways to move parts being made by their milling machines. The solution was found in hydraulics, the use of fluids in an enclosed system. In 1932-33 the company introduced its first hydraulic machine tool: work pieces could be fed into the machine and held more precisely, thus increasing the accuracy of the metal cutting operation. A year later an entirely new application of hydraulics was introduced, a fuel pump for oil burners on home furnaces. The pumps could also be used for hydraulic feed pumps and control valves on machine tools. Variable feed pumps, high and low pressure constant volume pumps, fluid motors and hydraulic transmissions followed. Several new machine tools were introduced in 1937-1939: a hydraulic Rigidmill and an automatic lathe were two of the most successful. As the demand for feed pumps grew, fuel unit sales increased 300 percent from 1938 to 1939. During World War II Sundstrand produced machine tools to manufacture equipment such as propeller parts, shell bodies, rifle barrels, turbine blades, aircraft engine parts and pistons. Production went to two shifts and research in hydraulics was markedly expanded.

As part of this research, Swedish native Gunnar Wahlmark invented the constant speed drive (CSD) which converted the variable speed of an aircraft engine into a constant speed that could be used to drive an AC generator. It was installed on the Air Force's B-36 bomber. Later this product would make Sundstrand the predominant supplier of electrical generating systems to the world's aerospace markets. The 1950s saw Sundstrand further develop its machine tool line and refine the constant speed drive, and go international, with headquarters in France and manufacturing facilities in Sweden. By 1957 Sundstrand was listed on the New York Stock Exchange, had manufacturing facilities in Rockford, Belvidere, Ann Arbor and Denver; and employed some 5,000 people worldwide. Two years later the stockholders voted to change the name of the Company to **Sundstrand Corporation**. In the 1960s the CSD technology was applied to hydraulics with remarkable results. In 1974 the millionth hydrostatic transmission unit was manufactured. Fluid handling also came into its own in these years with the development of a pump for water injection on jet engines which could be adapted to pump virtually any fluid. Sold under the trade name of Sundyne, the high speed centrifugal pump served mainly the petrochemical industry. During the 1960s the Company diversified intensely, adding such lines as avionic systems, instruments, flight data management systems, heating and cooling transfer parts, enclosed gear drives and couplings, axial gear differentials and more. The next two decades were spent fine tuning and establishing broader markets with many more national and international manufacturing centers. Today

Sundstrand is one of the nation's top producers in its field and Rockford's largest private employer, with approximately 3,200 employees. Since its entry into the field Sundstrand has dominated the field of electric generators and controls for airlines.

One of the largest tool manufacturers in the United States is the **Illinois Tool Works (ITW)**. The company is divided into two broad categories to reflect its product mix accurately: Engineered Components, which consists of short-lead-time plastic and metal components and small assemblies, metal fasteners and adhesives, and Industrial Systems and Consumable, which is made up of systems and related consumables for packaging, data entry, measurement tools and specialty areas.

ITW got off to an interesting start when Frank W. England, a tool and die maker, Carl G. Olson, a mechanic, Paul B. Goddard, a salesman, and Oskar T. Hegg, an inspector, convinced Byron L. Smith of their abilities and the need for hobs and milling cutters made with greater precision than ever before. In March, 1912 these four Rockford men and Clyde Fiddick, a bookkeeper, each put up $1,000 and Smith contributed $10,000 to launch the partnership that would become the Illinois Tool Works. Its first home was a small loft at Huron and Franklin Streets in Chicago. By 1913 the firm employed 30 people and had moved to the St. Clair Building on East Erie Street. Meanwhile, a few blocks away, Chicago entrepreneurs Ellsworth E. Flora and J. Fremont Murphy organized the **Seal and Fastener Company** to market Flora's inventive system of steel strapping, seals and tools, making it possible to secure shipping containers without nails. Another Chicagoan, J.W. Leslie, who became the Seal and Fastener Company president in 1916, renamed the firm **Signode** from the Latin word *signum*, meaning seal, and nodus, meaning knot. In 1986 Signode merged with ITW.

In the years just before World War I, there was a great need for precision and quality machine tools. ITW fit the niche. After the Great War, ITW restructured with an emphasis on the development of new products. In 1923 a patented twisted-tooth lock washer, known as a Shakeproof fastener, put ITW in an entirely new leadership position in the manufacturing and sale of engineered metal fasteners. Creative engineering became a corporate byword.

In the 1960s ITW introduced the plastic multipack can carrier system which revolutionized the packaging industry. Today the diversity of the company's products, technologies and markets has extended worldwide.

In 1907 the **Whitney Company** of Rockford invented the hand lever punch for the sheet metal industry. In 1968 Whitney developed a punching and cutting machine for large structural steel "I" beams that led to automation with computer control steel building fabrication. Six years later Whitney invented a combination punching, plasma arc and laser cutting machine for making parts from sheet metal plate, with automatic part nesting. It has been acclaimed as the process yielding the greatest gain in productivity to ever hit the metal fabricating market.

Creative engineering became a corporate byword.

While in Rockford, the **Barber-Colman Co.** was a large producer of textile weaving equipment. Today located in Loves Park, it is still a large manufacturer of gear cutting machines. In 1918 Oscar Onsrud invented the router. Today **Onsrud Cutter, Inc.,** founded in 1925, is one of three companies in the United States manufacturing routing tools for aircraft and the only one manufacturing diamond film tooling. The company has been in Libertyville since 1946, manufacturing wood, nonferrous metal and plastic cutting tools.

In 1914, steel straping made shipping safer.

To be safely shipped, tools and machines need to be properly wrapped and metal strapping is essential for this. The **Acme Packaging Corporation**, a subsidiary of **Acme Metals Incorporated** of Riverdale, invented modern steel strapping. Until 1914 metal strapping was secured around a crate with nails. In transit the nails could loosen and the strapping fall off. But in 1914 **Acme Steel Goods Company**, predecessor of today's firm, invented a replacement for nailed-on strapping. It developed a system to wrap a continuous loop of steel strapping around a box or package, tensing the strapping so it holds the packagingtight, and then seal the strapping. Later Acme invented pneumatic tools to seal the strapping around packages more effectively and safely.

The original Maze Nail truck

Maze Nails of Peru is that area's oldest manufacturer, begining operations 145 years ago. Another longtime Peru based firm is **American Nickeloid** which has been a leader in the prefinished metals business since 1898, and more recently, in the vinyl laminates field. Today the firm is also a major local employer. The city of Peru was incorporated in 1835. Thirteen years later, in 1848, the Maze brothers established a retail lumberyard along the banks of the Illinois River. Its lumber came from Chicago on the newly completed Illinois and Michigan Canal, Peru being the western terminus. The Maze brothers bought a small barge and mules to haul grain to Chicago for the local farmers, and on their return brought white pine from the Chicago lumberyards to supply their own.

Always enterprising, the Maze brothers were not satisfied with the cedar shingle nails of iron they had to sell — they caused staining and straking — so the brothers secured a cut nail machine and started making pure zinc nails, which would never rust. At first the brothers gave these nails away to stimulate shingle sales, but word quickly spread that these were fine nails, and other lumber dealers in the area started to buy nails from Maze for resale at their own yards. In 1905 Maze was the first mill to pack nails in 5-pound chipboard boxes, as well as in wooden kegs. The next year Maze research developed a method of taking steel nails and dipping them into molten zinc to give a thick, uniform rust-resistant zinc-coating. Sales of these hot-

Pure zinc nails never rust.

dipped zinc-coated nails was so strong that the lumberyard spun off the nail making operation into its own division, known as **Maze Nails**. The zinc was purchased from **Illinois Zinc** and **M&H Zinc**, two local smelters. Coal for smelting came from local mines.

In the 1920s Maze Nails was the first firm to put ring and screw threads on nails to increase their holding ability. Today threading is done by almost all nail mills. A special feature of the Maze nails is a heavy zinc-coating which does not clog the threads on the shank. This nail drives easier than aluminum ones and is as strong as the steel ones. Maze Nails now manufactures specialty nails for world-wide distribution in its 210,000 square foot mill.

The **Dickson Weatherproof Nail Company** was founded in about 1925 or 1926 by the grandfather of the current president to manufacture lead headed roofing nails used to fasten sheet metal roofing on farm buildings. Today Dickson produces a complete line of nails and is the only remaining United States manufacturer of lead headed nails.

The **Chicago Faucet Company** was founded in 1901 by A.C. Brown, a former plumber. The new firm quickly established a reputation for high quality and for the innovative features of its products. In its early years the business was headquartered on Chicago's Clinton Street. Until 1911 most of the firm's production was devoted to supplying faucets to the **Crane Company**. During that period they also manufactured lampshades, frames, gas regulators, oil-burner nozzles, beer taps and specialty parts for other customers.

In 1913 a major breakthrough in faucet design was achieved with the introduction of the patented Quaturn faucet, which went from closed to full-open with only a quarter-turn of the handle. The faucet was also designed to close with, instead of against, the pressure of the water. Also, the operating unit was completely renewable and was interchangeable with other Chicago faucets. This standardized removable unit contained all moving and wearing parts, and made for maximum durability, ease of maintenance and economy of service. Prior to the Chicago Faucet design, repairs were expensive and required special plumber's tools. With this new innovation repairs became "as easy as changing a light bulb," which later became a company tag line.

The Royal Flushometer revolutionized the plumbing industry.

The basic operating unit — or valve cartridge — is still the backbone of the Chicago Faucet line. While it has been improved over the years, the principle and configuration on the unit has not changed. The cartridge manufactured today will fit any Chicago Faucet made since 1913. In fact, it is quite common to come across Chicago faucets that have been in continuous use for more than 50 years, which years ago prompted the use of the advertising slogan, "lasts as long as the building."

By 1961 Chicago Faucet had outgrown its plant in Chicago and moved to Des Plaines. In December, 1986 the company added a Milwaukee facility. Today the firm offers an extremely broad product line that falls into four areas: general plumbing, laboratory, food service and original equipment manufacture. Due to standardization and interchangeability of components and parts, more than 1,000 variations can be made from a particular fitting.

The inventive productivity of the first decade of the century continued up to America's entry into World War I. Of special interest to inventors was the new field of electricity and hydraulics. Though developed by William Elvis Sloan (1867-1961) in 1906, the Royal flush valve, the original product of the **Sloan Valve Company** of Chicago (today in FranklinPark) took a few years to become recognized as a major invention of the twentieth century. The Royal Flushometer revolutionized the plumbing industry when it was intro-

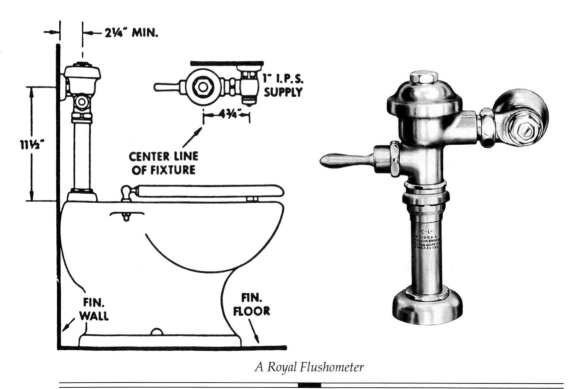

A Royal Flushometer

duced. Through intense self-education, Sloan acquired a superior knowledge of electrical circuitry and hydraulics, which ultimately led to 64 inventions. Among them were relay boosters for telegraph lines and fire safety curtains for theaters.

While there have been many refinements and improvements in component parts over the years, the working principle and fundamental hydraulic design have not changed. Today there are millions in use besides the Royal, with such names as the Star, the Crown, the Gem and the Naval.

There was some resistance to the use of valves initially because the valve was more expensive and required different plumbing than the conventional piping for toilet tanks. In his first year in business Sloan sold one valve. The next year, 1907, he sold two and in 1908 he sold 150. Initially plumbers were afraid to install flush valves because they knew nothing about them, architects would not specify them for the same reason and owners did not want to test the product in their buildings. So what to do? Sloan installed them himself whenever a building engineer would permit. Soon it became obvious that the Sloan valve was responsible for saving water, 2-4 gallons per flush, was almost maintenance free, virtually unbreakable and vandal proof, and had almost no recycling time between flushes. Once through its flushing cycle, the valve shuts off automatically, even if the handle is held down. This exclusive non-hold-open feature assures that the water economies are maintained. Over the years Sloan developed piston-type flush valves, automatic urinal flushing systems and the Act-O-Matic shower head, and has gone from being one company among some 120, to one among only four.

Initially plumbers were afraid to install flush valves.

RUMBLE SEATS MAKE HIGH SCHOOL POPULAR

For all of the nineteenth century rural inhabitants were physically isolated. Horsedrawn wagons and buggies could average about six miles per hour on mud roads; through snow drifts, heavy dust and frozen ruts they were slower. Animals also needed food and rest. A 20 mile round trip was usually an overnighter if anytime was spent at the destination. Trips were infrequent. High Schools, for example, were in town so that attending farm students would need to move into town to attend classes. Not many did. Trips to a city were rare. Though the railroad's net across the state was extensive, passenger travel was expensive. It was difficult to get to and from the stations. Layovers for connections were common. Hotels prospered, even in some small towns. The result was very limited casual travel, even for the wealthy.

The isolation of the farm was first broken by the electric railroads which flourished from 1900 to 1925. They were fast and inexpensive links between towns. By 1925 they were displaced by the automobile and scheduled passenger buses.

The automobile created the demand for hard and dry surface roads which changed the look of the country forever. After 1913 Illinois' state government began sharing the expenses of building roads. Soon road and highway building and maintenance became the major activity of state and county government. Farmers could truck products to market themselves and small towns became local, central collecting centers for farm goods. In 1923 the speed limit for motor cars in open country was set at 35 mph. And by 1927, 90 percent of downstate families owned one automobile. As a result, towns quickly became centers for social activity. High Schools became focal points. Many rural students could now attend, and did.

The first auto race in America was held in Illinois.

Illinois' road surfaces developed along with the needs of the population for quicker, dependable transportation. Oglesby's cement plant was first built in 1892 when the village was called Portland and produced **Portland Cement**, the main ingredient for construction of highways, roads, bridges, houses and dams. The cement comes from vast deposits of limestone and slate which outcrop in the Vermilion Valley. In 1902 the village sought to commemorate Jim Oglesby, Governor of Illinois, and so changed its name to his. Today the term "Portland" is generic for cement, and Oglesby, with a population of about 4,000, is almost forgotten, except for cement. The cement industry is one of the oldest large industries of America, similar to steel. For many years Dixon, along the Rock River, also had an important cement industry.

While automobile manufacturing did not become one of Chicago's most important industries, it did provide new business opportunities for ambitious enterpreneurs. Replacing the blacksmith and the livery stable, "filling stations" and auto repair shops grew up along busy streets. "Probably never before has a popular mechanical invention had such a potent influence in diverting a prominent street from its original purpose and, incidentally, influencing the development of a pertinent style of architecture as has the automobile in transmuting Michigan Boulevard in the city of Chicago, from a residence to a business street." So began an article in the Architectural Record of 1910.

By 1910 most horse traffic had disappeared from Chicago's main streets and Michigan Boulevard, as it was then known, became the longest and best automobile street of any city in the country. From 12th to 26th Street new sales offices and small factories replaced the old, fashionable residences.

Illinois has had over 160 manufacturers of automobiles in the last 100 years, but could not sustain this industry the way Michigan did. Illinois also had the first auto race in America. It was sponsored by the *Chicago Times-Harold* on Thanksgiving Day, 1895. The race was won by Frank Duryea, who drove a gas buggy from Jackson Park to Evanston and back in nine hours, a bit better than five miles an hour. Duryea and his older brother, Charles, who had a bicycle business in Peoria, feuded the rest of their lives about which one was responsible for the success of the first American automobile, which was built in Springfield, Massachusetts, where Charles' bicycles were manufactured.

ILLINOIS WAS AMERICA'S FIRST DETROIT

Another entry came from Decatur where Hieronymous A. Mueller had imported a Benz motor from Germany, reworked it, and entered his automobile (named after himself) in the Times-Harold race. His son, Oscar, took third place in the race. He built five more Muellers and planned to go into the manufacturing business, but was killed in a workshop explosion in March of 1900. Hieronymus Mueller was born in Wertheim, Germany where he learned the machinist trade in 1832. After immigrating to the United States in 1849, Mueller opened a shop in Decatur in 1857 to build guns, locks, sewing machines, clocks, in short, anything mechanical. Like many other cities in Illinois in the post Civil War years, Decatur was expanding and needed to improve its water supply system. Mueller proved to have the needed mechanical skills and was named city plumber in 1871. In 1893 Mueller incorporated his business as **H. Mueller Mfg. Company**. Mueller's skill with machines soon had him involved in the just beginning auto industry. The involvement with automobiles brought **H. Mueller and Sons** patents for a variable speed transmission, the friction disc clutch, and the spark plug, among others. His company is to this day a vital force in Decatur.

Hieronymous Mueller of Decatur patented the friction disc clutch and spark plug.

H. Mueller developed a Benz in Decatur

Since those early days Decatur has had close links to the auto industry. Paul Hiekisch at his bicycle shop turned out a steam propelled auto and George Henderson at **Wayne Sulkyettes and Road Cart Co.** designed and improved a body for automobiles. In 1916, the manufacture of automobiles actually did get underway in Decatur. The **Comet Automobile Co.,** with $3 million in capital stock, moved here from Rockford, locating its plant along the Illinois Central tracks. The firm produced six cars daily; the 50-horsepower Comet sold for $1,185. Forty Comets were shipped to Belgium in 1920, the largest single exportation of American cars up to that time. Comets were manufactured from 1917 to

1922. The Comet building was to serve the automobile industry as a parts plant for many years. **L.P. Halladay Co.** began making shock absorbers and bumpers there in 1924 and four years later **Bi-Flex Products Co.** was turning out automotive parts including starters. **Pan American Motors Corp.** came to Decatur from Chicago about the same time as Comet and began producing cars in the old **Decatur Fountain Co.** building.

At different times nine car brands were manufactured in Moline, six in Aurora.

Ten early Chicago companies built electric cars. The most successful was the Woods, which sold for as much as $4,500 and stayed on the market from 1899 to 1919. Four Illinois firms manufactured steam-powered cars, but none lasted more than three years. Starting with tiller-steered cycle cars and motor buggies and progressing through light roadsters and high-wheeled sedans with folding tops and side curtains, most of Henry Ford's Illinois rivals depended on the internal combustion engine. A few manufacturers attempted to turn out engines in their own machine shops, but most just assembled cars, with the manufacturer buying the major parts, including such engines as the Lycoming, Bristol, Continental and Knight.

The Chicago suburbs of Blue Island, Chicago Heights and Cicero had one company each, and others were scattered through northern and central Illinois. At different times nine cars were manufactured at Moline. Aurora had six car manufacturers and Decatur, Galesburg, Joliet, Peoria and Sterling each had three auto companies.

An available labor force and access to raw materials were not always prime considerations, and a compilation of Illinois-built cars lists manufacturers at Belvidere, Chrisman, Dallas City, Danville, Detroit (a Pike County community which in 1905 turned out La Petite, a two-seater with a one-cycle engine), East Chicago, Elgin, Freeport, Highland Park, Kankakee, Lanark, Lincoln, Ottawa, Plano, Rochelle, Rock Falls, Rockford, Rock Island, Springfield, Streator and Waukegan. All had one thing in common — they were unsuccessful — and some were very short lived, such as the Kirksell, which Dr. James Selkirk of Aurora planned to market for three thousand dollars. He apparently turned out one car in 1907.

Sears Roebuck & Co. had a high-wheeler available through mail-order from 1906 to 1911 at a top price of $485 for a closed coupe. Sears in 1952 briefly returned to the mail-order car business with Allstate.

At Moline, Deere and Company had its own cars in 1906 and 1907, and then in 1909 backed a well-known carriage firm in selling the Velie, which was distributed by Deere plow dealers until 1915. The Velie company began in 1902 by building carriages. Six years later the **Velie Motor Car Company** was formed and the first automobile introduced. A quality reputation was quickly formed. Velie began making its own engines in 1922 and stayed on the market another six years. In 1927 Velie purchased the Davenport, Iowa maker of the Monocoupe Airplane. The Velie Monocoupe held high ratings and was flown by many famous aviators. Another farm equipment manufacturer, **International Harvester Company,** started to make cars in Chicago in 1907, but soon shifted operations to Ohio. The Moline, made by the **Moline Plow Company,** was first produced in 1904 and in 1912 had one of the first long-stroke engines. Later it adopted the Knight sleeve-valve motor, and its successors stayed in business until 1924. The Stephens, made in Moline starting in 1916 and from 1922 to 1924 in Freeport, sold 25,000 models in its Freeport years as a competitor of the Buick in price and appearance.

An illustration of the Moline Plow Company's Columbian Exposition exhibit, 1893

The Commonwealth,
assembled
in Joilet, ultimately
became the
Checker Taxi.

The Commonwealth, which was assembled at Joliet from 1917 to 1922, ultimately became the Checker taxi. The Shaw was offered for sale in 1920-21 by **Shaw Livery Company**, which for years had operated taxicabs in Chicago. It was taken over by the **Yellow Cab Company**, controlled by John Hertz, and in 1922 the car was sold as the Ambassador. Starting in 1925 the Hertz was manufactured for self-drive rental, but in 1928 the company switched to standard makes for leasing.

Preston T. Tucker, between 1946 and 1948, provided the most spectacular failure of Illinois auto makers. With a Michigan background, he took over a World War II plant in Chicago for the production of a sedan that had engineering innovations. Charged with fraud and violation of the regulations of the securities and exchange commission, the controversial Tucker won vindication in 1950 but his financial holdings were wiped out. Only a few Tuckers came off the assembly line. But his story was glorified on the silver screen in true Hollywood fashion in a movie called "Tucker" in the 1980s starring Jeff Bridges.

HOW FAST IS "FAST"?

The automobile did not appear overnight. Its parts developed over a number of years and among the most important innovators that made the automobile possible was **Warner Electric** of South Beloit. Its history of invention, manufacturing and marketing of useful, practical motion control devices is closely associated with the automobile. Warner Electric was founded by Arthur Pratt Warner (1870-1957), an inventor of great importance with over 100 patents on file, among them, the Warner speedometer, a variant of which is still used in every automobile today, and the electric brake. In 1898 Warner was developing electric motors for use in elevators. To know how fast the elevators were going, he needed a speed indicator with a uniform scale and seized upon the magnetic principle for this purpose. His brother, Charles H. Warner, did much of the mechanical work on the first instrument produced. These were offered to General Electric, but turned down because its market seemed too limited. The device worked so well that soon many applications opened for its use and in 1904 the brothers organized the **Warner Instrument Company** for its manufacture. The first instrument, a speed indicator for industrial machinery, was called a "cut meter." Its function was to measure the speed of cutting tools in industry. Warner immediately advertised his product in *The American Machinist* , which resulted in

A. P. Warner
of South Beloit
invented
the speedometer.

THE SATURDAY EVENING POST   *January 11, 1913*

Motor Age

Model O-2
Price $145

*Automobile Show, Madison Square
Garden, New York City*

WARNER
AUTO-METER

At the Automobile Shows

THE big automobile shows are international reviews. In addition to that they are grand showdowns. Here all the real facts are before you. Here are the efforts and offerings of the world's greatest infant industry — the automobile and its accessories. Here, at your leisure, you can examine the 1913 fashions in American automobiles.

Gathered together are representatives and 1913 models of practically every prominent automobile and accessory producer in the world. Each one of these great automobile manufacturers is displaying and demonstrating what they know to be the very best they can produce —

in their respective classes. Their cars are made of the very best materials; have splendid efficient motors; strong and rugged axles; excellent bearings; quiet transmissions; sturdy steel frames; beautiful lines; handsome and graceful bodies; good tires — and in most cases — *Warner Speedometers.*

The majority of high priced cars at the big national shows are equipped with the famous Warner Speedometer — the most accurate speed and mileage indicator in the world.

Over 100,000 new 1913 cars go on the market Warner equipped.

orders from all over the world. He also applied his device to automobiles where it was found practical and fascinating. Again he advertised his device, this time with a full page ad in the *Saturday Evening Post*. In 1912 Warner exhibited his meter at the first auto show ever held in Chicago and sold the idea to several auto companies. The Overland was the first car to have an auto-meter as standard equipment; the Cadillac was second. In 1913 over 100,000 new cars went to market with Warner equipped.

The device, now called a speedometer, quickly gained fame through Warner's efforts. To show how ridiculous the ten miles per hour speed limit of New York city was, Warner built a car with a large, clearly visible speed indicator and drove around the city. He was promptly arrested for driving fifteen miles an hour, though other cars and trucks had passed him ruthlessly, but no one knew how fast "fast" was. The speed laws were quickly changed and the publicity did not hurt Warner. Meanwhile the car with the big golden speedometer was sent all over the country. Even President Teddy Roosevelt came out of the White House and asked for a ride. The successful speedometer was soon copied by competition, patents were ignored and a bitter legal struggle ensued with the **Stewart Company** in Chicago. Warner sold his company to Stewart and it was reorganized as **Stewart-Warner**, the leaders in automotive instruments. For a few years Warner continued to dabble. Not every venture was successful, but just prior to World War I, he formed the **Warner Trailer Company** which was the first to build two wheel trailers in the United States. He also designed the first tourist trailer, predecessor of recreation vehicle campers. Marshall Field applied for exclusive dealership rights in Chicago. Interest was high; 2,000 trailers were built, but orders were few and the idea was finally abandoned in favor of industrial, military and farm trailers which came into great demand. Eventually the trailer company was sold in 1929 to Fruehauf.

Ten mph
was
fast in 1912.

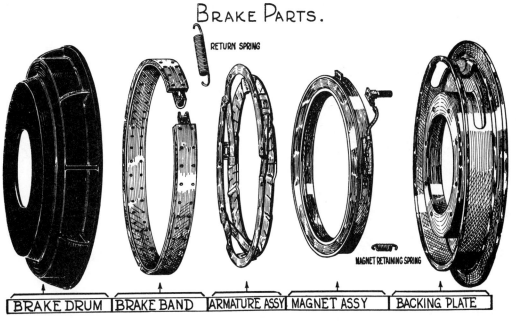

BRAKE PARTS.

RETURN SPRING

MAGNET RETAINING SPRING

| BRAKE DRUM | BRAKE BAND | ARMATURE ASSY | MAGNET ASSY | BACKING PLATE |

WARNER ELECTRIC BRAKE CORP.

In 1927 Warner organized yet another company, the **Warner Electric Brake Corporation**, based on a new brake design using electricity. It was not a good time to introduce a new product and by 1934 the business was in financial trouble. The following year a number of Beloit investors provided new capital, and the company was reorganized as **Warner Electric Brake Manufacturing**, with Warner retiring from management and returning to his vocation of making things. By 1937 his house trailer idea finally came of age, and soon the company was producing millions of trailer brakes, so that at one time more than 75 percent of all house trailers were equiped with Warner's brake. The brakes proved invaluable during World War II and production hit an all time high. After the war the company introduced its first line of electrical clutches and brakes for industrial machinery. This was the first step towards what has become the backbone of the business, products to accurately control machinery in motion. In 1950 the **Warner Electric Brake & Clutch Company** employed 295 people; in 1980, it was 2,963.

Another company that prospered along with the automobile began in 1903 when the three branches of a family consolidated and became **Maremont, Wolfson & Cohen, Inc.,** with Simon Wolfson as its president. The family business got its start in 1877 when draft notices from the Czar for men reached Lithuania. To save his son Isaac, Joseph Maremont borrowed money, closed his blacksmith shop and fled to Chicago. He vowed to bring more family members to his new home. Joseph and Isaac established a blacksmith shop and soon other members of the family began to arrive: daughters, sons-in law Simon Wolfson, Samuel Cohen and Harris Seeder, grandson Myer Maremont, and a nephew, Leo Maremont. Together and individually the industrious family opened blacksmith shops, manufactured parts for wagons and carriages and built wagons for such accounts as the **Wells Fargo Express Company**. Then, in 1903, having joined forces, the firm was successful in both the blacksmith and wagon businesses. At this time, and for the next decade, Chicago was more of a focal point of the automotive industry than Detroit. By 1914 Ford was using the Model T chassis as an undercarriage for its light trucks. Maremont designed a truck yoke, the Camelford, to help support heavier truckloads. This was the firm's entry into automotive parts.

By 1916 Maremont was producing its own springs, which with replacement parts helped the company grow markedly into the 1920s. As automobile sales plunged during the Depression, Maremont's replacement-parts business remained fairly steady. As sales fluctuated, the firm did not lay off workers, but shortened the work week. On April 10, 1933 Maremont incorporated in Illinois as **Maremont Automobile Products, Inc.** and acquisitions began with an eye towards diversification. Four years later the company acquired a muffler manufacturer. At the time each car had its own muffler design, but Maremont developed a universal shell that could be modified for a variety of leading models.

Commercial automobile production almost came to a halt during World War II. Maremont drew on muffler production techniques to design "Jerry cans" used by the military to carry water and gasoline. Maremont also opened a plant to produce heavy armor plate for ammunition carriers and Sherman tanks. After the war the president, Arnold Maremont, took great pains to improve employment opportunities for blacks and other minorities. His efforts led, in 1947, to the formation of the Illinois Fair Employment Practices Committee, followed a few years later by the hiring of the company's first female General Counsel, Jean Allard. Shortly thereafter, Maremont selected a Japanese-American, Henry Ishizuka, to be its chief financial officer. The 1950s and 1960s were a period of rapid growth and to reflect the now diversified line, the firm changed its name in 1962 to **Maremont Corporation**. A major acquisition was the **Gabriel Company**, a manufacturer of shock absorbers. Maremont began supplying its line of shock absorbers to Sears, eventually designing an exclusive line for the retailer. It was one of the great marketing successes of the 20th Century. In 1979 Maremont was acquired by Alusuisse (Swiss Aluminum Ltd.) and began operations as a separate subsidiary.

Public transportation required accurate records of fares.

FARE METERS AND TIMERS

The automobile made travel easy and commonplace. People got into the habit of riding, even when the car wasn't practical. As people began to travel more on public transport, the need to keep accurate records of fares paid on buses and trains became important. The need was met by the **Pratt and Englund Company**, incorporated on October 15, 1891 as a maker of portable fare registers. After Pratt and Englund retired, in 1895, Arthur H. Woodward became the company's president and changed the name to **International Register Co. (IRC)**.

With the purchase of the **New Haven Car Register Co**. in 1903, IRC became the leading fare register manufacturer in the United States. At the time streetcars were a primary mode of transportation and fare collecting was a growth industry. To meet demand for their fare registers, the company moved away from handcrafting each register to mass produced, interchangeable standard parts. As a result of standardization, the company became a front runner in production techniques. It also was among the first companies in the nation to introduce incentive systems, payment for overtime and company paid insurance, including both accident and death benefits. It was soon found that these practices encouraged employees to take more pride in their work and to stay with the company longer.

In 1917 Woodward invented the wind vane sight. This important invention proved to be a major contribution to America's war effort. The device allowed machine guns to fire effectively between rotating propeller blades. Also, one of the company's directors invented a bomb sight for the Navy. During World War II the company built more than million 20 mm shells, other munitions and aircraft controls.

During the 1920s the IRC developed a number of innovative machines, among them the Cutawl, a cutting machine. The company also did contract manufacturing of such items as the Checkwriter, the Stenotype and vending machines for the Automatic Canteen. From the early 1950s on, International Register manufactured the Nielsen Audimeter used for the Nielsen ratings.

During the 1930s the Company took over the marketing for Automatic Refrigerator, a Texas firm that manufactured coin-meters attached to appliances. These meters collected the daily payments, typically 25 cents, that were intended to eventually cover the purchase price of a major appliance such as refrigerator, washing machine or dryer at a time when few people could afford to make weekly payments on them. Commercial systems, such as refrigeration systems, beauty parlor equipment and electric signs, carried meters, too. It was pay as you use, much like today's laundromats or pay-per-view TV. Hundreds of thousands of coin meters were produced. They helped the hard-pressed appliance industry get through the Depression. With the end of the Depression and the start of World War II, the "meter plan" faded.

The coin-meter became the parent of many clock-actuated devices. A major break came for IRC in the late 1930s, when the Frigidaire Division of General Motors encouraged IRC to develop a line of oven and range timers for use in its products. The Inter-Matic switch was introduced in the mid-1940s. Quickly accepted by the trade for its high quality and low price, the Inter-Matic was used to control electric signs, store window lighting, apartment hall lights, stokers and oil and gas burners.

In 1952 IRC introduced its first consumer product, a kitchen timer — the Time-All. It is still in production. Sales soared, and soon a variety of switches and photo-electric controls were added for the industrial market. By 1958 the American way of life was changing fast and IRC was there with the water softener timer and pool and spa controls. An engineering department was added and much research went into the synchronous motor, one of the great achievements of that period and the basis for a large percentage of the company's products today. Two years later, in 1960, the company acquired property in Spring Grove and built a plant there, fazing out its main Chicago plant. More new products were introduced, including the Malibu low-voltage outdoor lighting line, now the company's largest single line. In the 1970s the company had severe financial problems, but turned itself around, acquired a new image and name, **Intermatic Incorporated**, and has since prospered.

AIR NEEDS CONDITIONING

The development of the American city in the 1870s introduced an innovative concept to the central urban area, the tall building. By the 1890s downtown areas of large cities began to suffer from lack of light and air because so many tall buildings had been built close together. The resulting cramped urban conditions required new solutions to age old human needs: a comfortable environment, especially inside the buildings. Up to the 1890s there had been very little concern given to the work environment. But as more and more

Coin meters helped the hard-pressed appliance industry get through the Depression.

people began to spend most of their waking hours in offices inside tall buildings, the work space had to be made more liveable. As the need arose for interior climate controls, inventors came to the fore with their products. One such inventor was William P. Powers.

In 1881 William P. Powers owned a small heating and plumbing business in Wisconsin and saw the need for temperature control of steam heat. At the time steam heat was either on or off, so rooms were either hot or cold. The idea he developed over the next decade was a regulator consisting of a diaphragm filled with a liquid that responded to temperature changes. It sold well enough for him to move to Chicago in 1891 and there found the **Powers Regulator Co.**

Powers' Regulators soon became respected and desired. In 1907 the Gold Room of the Congress Hotel in Chicago was among the first public spaces in the United States to be air conditioned and Powers provided the necessary regulators. The company's list of installations is long but of note is the Penobscot in Detroit and the Palmer House in Chicago. In the 1930s the Empire State Building, Rockefeller Center and Radio City Music Hall, for years the world's largest theater, were great challenges of climate control and Powers was able to successfully meet them. The gigantic naval hospital at Philadelphia required specialized control for operating rooms and a unique application was devised for the film drying cabinets at Warner Brothers film laboratories. When Powers celebrated its 50th anniversary in 1941, World War II was raging. The war brought its own special needs. As a result of the war, thermostats and other controls products underwent radical redesign as new technologies permitted downsizing, a key to post-war success.

The rapid development, both inside and outside America's cities throughout the 1950s, created new needs in building controls. Within the decade Powers introduced its System 320, the first practical multiplex building control and Powers stood, with Johnson Controls and Honeywell, as one of three top firms in the business. In the 1970s the computerized monitoring system made its appearance. The Powers System featured English language display format on a CRT screen. Because of the ease of extension to remote locales, the System quickly became the choice for colleges, hospitals and other installations monitoring many facilities from a central point. Until 1977 Powers was privately held. That year **Mark Controls Corporation** took the opportunity to make an advantageous purchase and the Powers Regulator Company became **MCC Powers**. Reorganized, the company spent heavily on research and development because tremendous competition was underway among the major control builders to develop the first practical, fully electronic building control system. In 1979 MCC Powers won the race when it introduced the Powers System 600. Its design was revolutionary and remarkable because it was an open ended control system — it allowed for continuous improvements to be added on. Upgrades were now possible as needed and without changing the whole system. From now on, interior spaces could be climate controlled as desired; independent room control became possible. Within two years the System was enhanced with Direct Digital Control which further extended energy management capability, reliability and performance. An offshoot of this technology was the development in 1986 of Powers Insight software for

The Golden Room
of the
Congress Hotel
in Chicago
was the first
air-conditioned
public space
in the United States.

PC and DEC-based systems. This development introduced the concept of "windowing" to the industry. A year later MCC Powers was acquired by Landis & Gyr of Zurich, Switzerland. Today Landis & Gyr Powers' systems are at work in some of the most famous buildings in America and around the world, such as the John Hancock building in Chicago, the Transamerica Pyramid in San Francisco, the Louvre in Paris and the Royal Hong Kong Jockey Club in Hong Kong.

The calorimeter made purchases to specifications possible.

PURCHASING TO SPECIFICATIONS

Besides controlling the interior environment of buildings, measuring natural things to better understand their environment became important in the 1890s. Among the leaders in this field was S.W. Parr, Professor of Chemistry at the University of Illinois, Champaign, and founder of the **Standard Calorimeter Co.**, now **Parr Instrument Co.** Parr developed a simplified calorimeter in 1899 for measuring the heating value of coal. Using granular sodium peroxide as the oxidation medium instead of the then popular compressed oxygen, Parr developed the capacity to measure things that were not easily measured at the time. Parr's calorimeters were manufactured in Urbana by the **R&V Engine Works**, operated by friends of the professor who had developed a line of small, general purpose internal combustion engines primarily for farm use. Faced with a growing engine business and a desire to locate closer to other manufacturers serving the farm machinery market, the R&V Engine Works moved to East Moline in 1911, taking with them the manufacturing operations of the **Standard Calorimeter Co.**

At about this time Parr became deeply interested in metallurgical research directed toward the development of an alloy which would resist the corrosive action of acids formed during the combustion of a fuel sample in an oxygen bomb. These investigations resulted in the formulation of a double-ternary, nickel-chromium-copper alloy which proved to be excellent for his intended purpose. With this alloy Parr was able to produce the first satisfactory oxygen combusting bomb that did not require a platinum or gold lining to resist corrosive attack. Parr's alloy, which he called "Illium" after the University of Illinois, thus became the first of many similar acid resisting alloys and stainless steels to be developed by Parr and others in later years. Production of Illium was started in 1911 by the Standard Calorimeter Co. In 1916 Parr obtained a patent covering designs for an adiabatic oxygen bomb and continued working on his calorimeter, developing one using a hot water injection procedure which became an accepted standard method for determining the calorific value of solids and liquids for many years. Parr's calorimeter, together with other fuel testing devices and procedures developed in his laboratory, made it possible for railroads, power plants and industrial fuel users to purchase coal on specification, and was a contributing factor in the development of a market for the extensive reserves of bituminous coal available in Illinois at a time when most users believed that the only useful coal had to come from Pennsylvania or West Virginia.

Today **Parr Instrument Co.**, centered in a single plant in Moline, is the leading supplier of calorimeters and other fuel testing instruments in the United States. Parr's calorimeters now fill an important need, testing not only coal, but also foodstuffs, liquid fuels, refuse, combustible waste, explosives, heat powders, rocket fuels and related propellants. They also play an important part in many studies involving chemical, physical or physiological processes in which heat generation or burning is an important factor.

Dosimetric granules were accurate.

AN ACCURATE DOSSAGE HELPS

At a time when most medicines were not produced with scientific accuracy, and were consumed as desired, thirty-year old Dr. Wallace C. Abbott began manufacturing dosimetric granules in the kitchen of the small apartment behind his People's Drug Store in Ravenswood, then a northwest suburb of Chicago. His aim was to replace untrustworthy plant extracts or "galenicals" with "arms of precision" — dosimetric granules with known accuracy. His first year of production, 1888, registered $2,000 in sales; the next year his whole family was involved in production and sales more than doubled.

Realizing that his business was local and knowing that he had a good line of products, Abbott took the bold step of placing an advertisement in a trade magazine *Medical World*, in 1891, at a cost of 25 cents, and promptly received $8 in orders. Seeing profit inadver-

Dr. Abbott's staff measures precisely.

tising, Abbott produced his first catalogue, 14 pages listing more than 150 products. At the time he had a staff of "five or six good girls." Always trying to make his product more palatable, in 1893 Abbott sugarcoated his pills by sticking dried pills on the end of a pin and dipping them into a sugary solution.

In 1893
Dr. Abbott began
to sugar coat
his pills.

Along with the most advanced Chicago companies at the time, Abbott, too, edited and then published a journal, *Alkaloidal Clinic*, which contained primarily information on the company's products. At the same time, and again up to the minute in current practices, Abbott exhorted his employees to follow his lead in riding bicycles to work and offered gold watches as Christmas presents to all employees who gave up smoking, then just becoming a fashion.

With almost a decade of business behind him, Abbott was joined by Dr. William Waugh, who edited the *Alkaloid Clinic*, which in 1898 had a circulation of 20,000 copies per month, and collaborated with Abbott in writing the *Text Book of Alkaloidal Therapeutics*, soon the standard reference on the subject. The same year a new product became popular — Abbott's Saline Laxative that "Does the Work and Never Gripes!" And in 1899 a most remarkable person joined the staff, Dr. Ephraim M. Epstein. Besides being a fine chemist, he was also a good writer who was proficient in 10 languages. The next year the business was officially incorporated in Illinois as the **Abbott Alkaloidal Company**.

By 1910 the company's customer list totaled 50,000 of the country's 130,000 physicians, plus 1,000 in Europe and 500 in Latin America, and the catalog included some 700 products. As the demand for alkaloids slackened and the War in Europe cut off America from German synthetic medicinals, Abbott began researching that market. The new direction brought with it a new name, **Abbott Laboratories**. Among its first new products was Chlorazene, a germicidal antiseptic developed by the British chemist Dr. Henry Dakin. Chlorazene achieved the same sterilization in five minutes that bichloride of mercury took seven hours to produce and was at least 50 times as effective against certain bacilli as carbolic acid. Dakin also discovered a water purifier, produced by Abbott as Halazone, that in a single four-milligram tablet could sterilize a quart of contaminated water. These were important medicines for battle victims. By 1918 Abbott Laboratories was developing the production of Barbital and Procaine.

During the roaring 1920s Abbott chemists were particularly busy. Dr. Roger Adams and Dr. Ernest H. Volwiler developed a new topical anesthetic, Butyn, that was faster-acting, more powerful, and less costly to produce than cocaine, and not addictive. Volwiler developed Neonal, a sedative that improved on the old Barbital and lead to further research into barbiturates. In 1922 Abbott acquired Dermatological Research Laboratories of Philadelphia, an organization that concentrated on organic mercurial and arsenical compounds as antisyphilitic agents. Five years later this company introduced two products, Metaphen, an organic mercury topical antiseptic, and Bismarsen, an antisyphilitic compound of arsenic and bismuth.

In 1925 all physical facilities were moved from Ravenswood to North Chicago. The old plant was sold to **G.D. Searle & Co.**, the pharmaceutical company now in Skokie which was the first in America to sell an oral contraceptive, Enovid, in 1960.

The search by Abbott for more potent sources of vitamins A and D led, in 1932, to halibut liver, which was discovered to contain from 75 to 125 times more vitamin A and 20 times more vitamin D than cod liver oil. To the great distress of children everywhere, Abbott introduced Haliver Oil and Viosterol, and became a leader in vitamins.

Again leading a trend in advertising, Abbott, in 1935, published the first issue of *What's New*, a sleek journal for physicians, with covers designed by Abbott sponsored artists. The following year Drs. Volwiler and Donalee L. Tabern introduced Pentothal, which in 1986 was the discovery that landed them in the United States Inventors Hall of Fame.

Searle was the first in America to sell an oral contraceptive.

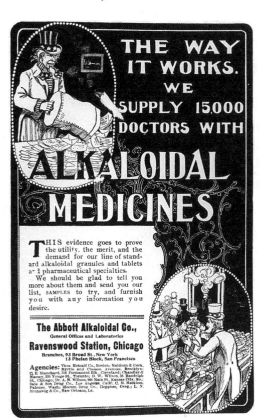

Early advertising and order forms for Abbott

Even before the United States entered World War II, Abbott began to produce dried blood plasma for the armed forces. By the war's end Abbott had processed more than 900,000 pints of dried blood. In 1941 Abbott was one of five pioneers in the United States to start the first phase of commercial penicillin production. The drug was especially difficult to produce. A breakthrough came when a new mold strain was discovered on an overripe cantaloupe in a Peoria fruit stand. In 1943 the nation's total production of penicillin was 28 pounds. Two years later, by increasing vat size and decreasing fermentation time, penicillin was ready for pharmacy distribution.

Sulfanilamide, the first of the "miracle drugs" which had been produced by Abbot since 1935, was distributed in war zones as Sterilope in envelopes which allowed the easy dusting of wounds.

The end of the World War II saw the introduction of a number of new products, including Surbex, a high potency vitamin, Venopak, the first fully disposable intravenous administration set, and Tridione, for the treatment of epilepsy.

Immediately after the war there was a boom in products, many of them civilian versions of war developments. In 1949 a total of 74 drugs, medical devices and improved variations of existing products were introduced. The next year Sucaryl, a cyclamate compound 30 times sweeter than sugar, was introduced. Within three years 150 companies sold 10 million cases of dietetic beverages and 400 food manufacturers had invaded grocery markets with Sucaryl-sweetened foods. In 1970 the U.S. Food and Drug Administration (FDA) baned the use of cyclamate sweeteners and all domestic sales of Sucaryl were discontinued. In 1951 Selsun Suspension for dandruff control was made commercially available. The next year saw the introduction of Erythrocine, an antibiotic that is still one of the safest and most effective.

By 1954 international sales accounted for about 30 percent of Abbott's total, and within three years the company developed a number of overseas plants. The one in Buenos Aires had over two acres of floor space. Closer to home, Abbott acquired a 207-acre farm near Long Grove and transformed it into an agricultural research center. And in 1959 ground was broken for an eight-story addition to the North Chicago research facility. It was dedicated in 1961. The same year 420 acres of farmland were purchased five miles northwest of the North Chicago plant. The new site became Abbott Park, the location of Abbott's world headquarters.

Throughout the 1960s Abbott consolidated its ongoing research and development of "hot" radioactive pharmaceuticals known as radiopharmaceuticals in Abbott Park. Until then, the work had been carried out at the Oak Ridge, Tennessee plant of the Atomic Energy Commission. Abbott also restructured its whole organization into six operating divisions: pharmaceuticals, hospital products, international, **Ross Laboratories**, group operations, and consumer products. Abbott also acquired the **Murine Corporation** of Chicago, a well known manufacturer of eye care products.

The next decade saw the approval of a number of new products. Three major ones were introduced in 1972: Tranxene, a tranquilizer; Ausria, a radioimmunoassay test to detect serum hepatitis; and the ABA-100 blood chemistry analyzer. Five years later Abbott developed a faster diagnostic test called Rubacell, which detects immunity for rubella (german measles). In 1978 two significant new products received FDA approval for marketing: Abbokinase for pulmonary embolism and Depakene for epilepsy. In 1982 Abbott expanded its health care line significantly with the introduction of Inpersol, which allowed patients suffering from kidney failure to administer their own dialysis treatment at home.

Sucaryl is 30 times sweeter than sugar.

By 1984 Abbott achieved the number-one position in the worldwide diagnostic market and led the domestic market in medical nutritionals. Among its innovations at this time were a diagnostic test for AIDS, the first to receive United States approval; a new therapy for prostatic cancer; a unique intravenous drug delivery system; and Vision, which allowed doctors to perform common blood tests quickly and easily in their offices. And in 1986 Abbott introduced 70 new diagnostic products, as well as the polymer-coated erythromycin of PCE. This new form of antibiotic solidifies the company's number-one position in that antibiotic's worldwide market. Then in its centennial year, 1988, the IMx immunoassay system was introduced and went on to achieve the highest new product sales in Abbott's history. The developments continue.

Cycling threw off social restraints.

NEW PRODUCTS KEEP ON ROLLING

Sometimes health can also be maintained through exercise, which at times can even be fun and have social consequences. In the second half of the nineteenth century some of the social restrictions young Americans had observed, under threat of parental reprimand, loosened as leisure time increased. Illinois manufacturers contributed to this loosening of morals in a significant way.

Roller skating was a craze in America in the 1870s that hit a high in 1884, when Levant M. Richardson of Chicago invented the ball-bearing wheel. With this single turn, the modern roller-skate made its appearance. Roller skating declined in the 1890s only to rise again by 1900. Among the leaders of this second generation was the **Chicago Roller Skate Company** founded by Ralph and Walter Ware in 1905, which is still a leader in the field today.

Even more important than the roller skate craze was the bicycle craze of the 1880s and 1890s. Among the early Chicago manufacturers of bicycles were the **Pope Manufacturing Company**, **A.G. Spaulding**, and **Schwinn**. At the time a good bicycle sold for $100, a brass kerosene lamp for $2.25, a tire repair kit for a nickel, and a spare tire for $6.50. For 25¢, **Rothchild & Company** offered a double stroke cycle bell. In the 1890s West Madison Street was known as Bicycle Row. Women frequented Bicycle Row, too, because cycling helped them take a giant step towards emancipation. Chicago's women, ready to throw off the restraints of the era, quickly related to the fetching Gibson Girl, a beautiful, self-possessed young woman who could and did join her male friend for a spin. Modishly dressed in a fetching sailor's hat, a shirtwaist with a mannish collar, leg-o'-mutton sleeves, and bloomers or divided skirts, the ladies took to the cycle.

Clothing stores produced and showed bicycle fashions. And bloomers were all the rage and controversy. Said the pro-bloomers writers in the Lake View Cycle Club's monthly magazine *The Cherry and Black* for April, 1896, "We girls are not always going to stick around the home like they did in olden times." But the old guard died slowly. In June 1895 Gyda Stephenson, a teacher at Humboldt School, put on knickers, cycled and then wore the same garb into her classroom. In the ensuing skirmish with the school board,

Stephenson made it clear that what she chose to wear while cycling or teaching was entirely her affair. Surprised by her resolute stand, the board dropped the matter.

Schwinn once built automobiles and motorcycles.

The Schwinn became the most famous bicycle. It was named after its builder, Ignaz Schwinn, who had arrived in Chicago from Germany in 1891. At the age of 29, young Schwinn had left a promising job at the Heinrich Kleyer cycle factory in Frankfurt-on-the-Main to find opportunity in America. He soon found work with Hill and Moffat, makers of the Fowler bicycle. In 1895 Schwinn joined with Adolph Arnold, a Chicago meat packer, to form a firm, **Arnold Schwinn and Company**, with manuacturing located in rental properties at Lake and Peoria Streets. Four years later they purchased the failing **March-Davis Bicycle Company**, and in 1908 Schwinn bought out his partner and built a new plant at 1718 North Kildare Avenue. Until 1905 Schwinn designed and built automobiles as well as bicycles, and from 1914 until 1930 the company was also a major motorcycle manufacturer.

During the Depression the company took the bold step of switching its production entirely to bicycles. They broke with international tradition and broadened tire tubes to two inches, and appealed to the streamlining fad of the decade with names like "aerocycle," "cycleplane" and "autocycle." A streamlined tank with a built in horn or lock enclosed the center support bar, while a large spring-supported saddle smoothed the ride. With names such as "Phantom," the Schwinn bicycle continued to be very popular after World War II.

The bicycle craze inspired a number of families in the final decade of the 19th century. Among those inspired were the Armstrong Brothers, George, James, Paul, John and Hugh, who had opened a bicycle supply store on West Washington Street in Chicago, where they provided sprockets, hubs, handlebars and most other parts and tools needed to make a bicycle turn. James was a tool maker and inventor, who in 1896 designed and built the first steam automobile to run on the streets of Chicago. One of the tools they experimented with was a tool holder. It would be the answer to the machinist's prayer. On February 28, 1893, the patent on George Armstrong's tool holder was issued. Later in that same year their tool holders were selected for use in the World's Fair machine ship. In 1985 the brothers incorporated as the **Armstrong Bros. Tool Co.** By 1903 Armstrong was manufacturing tool holders in styles and sizes suitable for every operation on the lathe, planer, shaper and slotter. It soon added the universal ratchet drills, planer jacks,

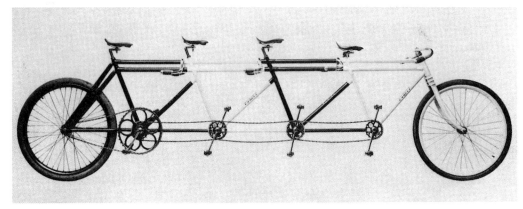

An Armstrong four seater

lathe dogs and others. Armstrong won awards, too: a gold medal at the Louisiana Purchase Exposition in St. Louis in 1904 and two first awards in 1915 at the Panama Pacific International Exposition in San Francisco. In 1910 Armstrong introduced its first "C" Clamps, the first carbon steel wrenches were made in 1917 and in the early 1920s it entered the pipe tool business with the introduction

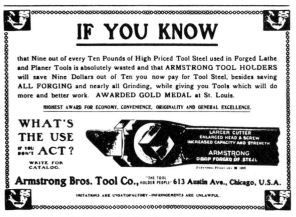

A prize winning larger cutter

Joliet was
the wallpaper
capital
of the nation.

of its first chain tongs. Business prospered and in 1960 the first significant additions of screwdrivers, punches, chisels and other hand tools were added to the line. In the late 1970s, with the broadening of the tool line, a completely rebuilt catalogue became necessary with a new numbering system — in numeric sequence to over 4,000 (the number of tools in the line). The catalogue has set an example for simplicity and order in the tool business.

ILLINOIS PAPER COVERS THE NATION

By the end of the nineteenth century America was experiencing its first flood of magazines, newspapers, and a rising desire to wrap things in colored paper and to send notes and cards home from travels or for Valentine's Day, Christmas and birthdays. This use of paper was brought on by improved printing techniques, greater leisure and more spending money, the need to be informed, changes in purchasing habits, inventiveness of advertisers and just the desire, reinforced by countless magazine articles and books on etiquette, to be current and to live and behave properly. All this required lots of paper and the production of paper was very important to Illinois. At the time, towns such as Morris and Marseilles were important paper manufacturing centers and the national craze for wallpaper was welcomed by major manufacturers of that product in Joliet. Wallpaper production seems to have started in Joliet in the late nineteenth century, but did not really gain national importance until after World War I. Documentation is not readily available for this fact, but it seems that for the years between World War I and World War II Joliet was the wallpaper capital of the nation. Of the six wallpaper mills in Joliet in those two decades, the **Joliet Wallpaper Mill**s alone produced one third of all United States wallpaper in 1939. Also of importance were the **Star Peerless Wallpaper Mills** and the **Lennon Wallpaper Company**. Both closed in the 1970s.

The last decade of the century also saw an interest in floor covering in part brought on by technological advances that allowed for mechanical weaving of carpets. To display these new products to their best advantage John H. Best designed and manufactured the first rack to hold rugs in 1892. The family-run business is still in Galva. Displays for other forms of floor covering evolved from this. **John H. Best & Sons, Inc.** is the oldest manufacturer of display racks for the floor covering industry in the country.

Another aspect of manufacturing that is related to paper but does not immediately leap to mind is paper doll production. Although Chicago was not a center of doll production, Chicago paper doll makers prospered because of the city's large printing industry. At the turn of the century newspapers regularly contained pages of cut-out dolls. In the 1910s and 1920s various manufacturing companies, such as **Swift & Co.** meat packers, sold paper doll premiums, which could be obtained for coupons or for cash.

In the same decade Jessie McCutcheon Raleigh of Chicago designed and made dolls. Though not of paper and not turned out in large quantity, they were and still are prized for their quality. **Raleigh** employed students from the Art Institute of Chicago to paint features on the doll heads molded after those of real children. She and her group of 100 employees worked in a large loft factory on Clybourn Avenue making dolls out of composition material. Each doll had movable joints connected with steel spiral springs and was dressed in fine quality clothing. During World War I, the government allowed Raleigh to remain in business probably because she aided the war effort by making prosthetic devices, and her doll business prospered, turning out 400 to 500 dolls a day in 75 different models. By the early 1920s Raleigh's business folded when European doll manufacturers, especially in Germany and Czechoslovakia, re-entered the market with less expensive products.

A SAMPLE OF SUCCESS

In the course of the nineteenth century the manufacture of clothing was a major industry for many Illinois towns outside of Chicago. When, in 1864, a woolen mill was established at Hanover, near Savanna, a whole new industry developed there. Until the 1950s the plant of the **Hanover Mills** was the center of local employment. The first entrants into the Decatur garment trade were **Race Clothing Mfg. Co.**, founded in 1891, and **Home Mfg. Co.** which began in 1895. The Race firm was the outgrowth of a clothing and drygoods store. Charles A. Allison, a businessman and banker, started Home Mfg. Co., making garments in the attic of his home — hence the name. "Home Made" became a widely known trademark and a trusted concept for quality.

For fine clothing and main line clothing requirements, there is no better known manufacturer than the Chicago firm of **Hart Schaffner & Marx**. The Hart brothers, Harry and Max, sons of German immigrants who had arrived in the United States in 1858, opened a retail clothing store with the sum of $2,700 saved from the money they had earned working for other retailers on Chicago's State Street. Harry and Max Hart were evidently successful, for in 1875 they opened a second store on Clark Street. As business increased, Harry and Max Hart began to have suits made for their two stores. These suits began to be bought by stores in other Illinois cities. At about the same time, Levi Abt and Marcus Marx, two brothers-in-law, joined the Hart brothers and the partnership of **Hart, Abt & Marx** was formed in 1879. Since the demand for ready-made clothing was increasing and the completion of the transcontinental railroad in 1869 had made Chicago a major transportation

"Home Made" was a trademark first, then a trusted concept.

Hart Schaffner and Marx suited every man

center, the wholesale business was a natural development for the young entrepreneurs. Their business soon became much larger than the volume in their own retail stores. Hart, Abt & Marx prospered. But persuading men to abandon their custom tailors and purchase ready made clothing was still not easy. By the end of 1887 Abt decided to leave the firm. And by a fortuitous chance, Joseph Schaffner, a cousin, joined the company to form Hart, Schaffner & Marx. Schaffner was to have a profound effect on the company.

One bright
Hart Schaffner & Marx
salesman
hit upon the idea
of selling
with swatches.

Born in 1848 in Reedsburg, Ohio to German immigrant parents, Joseph Schaffner's first job was counting and candling eggs in a country store. He moved to Cleveland and then on to Chicago, where he was eventually employed as a bookkeeper in a wholesale drygoods establishment. After seventeen years with this firm, he resigned and was ready to go into the mortgage business in St. Paul, when by chance he ran into his friends and distant cousins, Harry and Max Hart. They invited him to join the firm. And so, at the age of forty, began the real career of Joseph Schaffner in a partnership that was to give the clothing industry the creativity, dignity and respect that it had never before possessed. Many of his ideas, ideals and principles have survived. He made Hart Schaffner & Marx a market-driven company before this phrase came into the American business vocabulary.

In 1887 the Hart Schaffner & Marx salesmen went "on the road," nattily turned out in a silk topper, spats and walking stick, with as many as twenty wardrobe trunks to hold their sample garments. This, while guaranteeing a grand entrance, made traveling cumbersome. One bright Hart Schaffner & Marx salesman hit upon the idea of selling with swatches clipped from mill purchases. His first season was so successful that his colleagues quickly adopted what was then a revolutionary idea.

Not only did this make buying and selling much easier, it proved to be a great impetus to the expansion of style, fabrics and models. At about this time the "one price policy" was adopted by Hart Schaffner & Marx, which made the salesmen real representatives, since their price was the same as the owners'. Both concepts were firsts in the industry and a clear identification of the integrity of the firm.

Perhaps it was this keen understanding and awareness of the company and the people in it that led to Schaffner's determination to tell the rest of the world about the company. About 1897 Schaffner, with the support of his partners, took $5,000 of the firm's profits to launch the first men's clothing advertising effort. National advertising was unheard of in the apparel industry at the time, so naturally competitors were amused and amazed that the young firm would squander its assets so.

It took a few years, but the truth became evident. And as Schaffner put it, "Advertising increased our volume; volume has enabled us to increase our value-giving, both by lower prices and by putting more quality into the goods. Advertising has been, and is, an economy." It still is.

Hart Schaffner & Marx used advertising to announce another first, their "guaranteed all wool" policy in 1900, a remarkable assurance at a time when fabrics were rarely identified in garments and many were notoriously shoddy. The dapper fellow visiting the Chicago

Columbia World's Exposition to ogle Little Egypt or ride the Ferris Wheel favored wor-
steds and serge, followed by "clays" (a twill weave), cheviots and tweedy fabrics for his
wool coat, fancy vest and patterned trousers.

In 1906 Hart Schaffner & Marx was the first company to introduce proportioned suits
with "basic body" types. From then on short, tall, thin and stout suits joined the swelling
ranks of regular sizes bearing the Hart Schaffner & Marx label recognized nationally,
thanks to the consistent advertising promotions which included double page spreads in
such major magazines as the *Saturday Evening Post*, *Harper's Magazine*, *Collier's* and *Munsey's
Magazine*. Artists were commissioned to show clothing in a natural situation and eventually famous illustrators such as Samuel Nelson Abbott and Edward Penfield produced
life-art for Hart Schaffner & Marx ads, posters and style books. During these formative
years of the men's garment industry, when newspapers and magazines gave little exposure to men's fashions, Hart Schaffner & Marx produced seasonal style books which were
sold to consumers through national ads. Hart Schaffner & Marx style books were started
around 1898, and by 1925 had reached a distribution of several million. The idea was not
original, but innovative for the clothing industry, having already been used by the book
trade in the *Chap Books* and related posters produced by Stone & Kimball of Chicago from
1894 on. Retailers were encouraged to purchase quantities of Hart Schaffner & Marx
booklets to distribute to their own customers. Retailers also received posters featuring the
style book covers, which also appeared in national ads, to put in their windows. They also
received point of interest displays and sales training in order to help the customer better.
At the time the idea of helping the retailer in a direct way to move the merchandise sold
him was considered a very advanced marketing concept and was widely copied.

> Making a coat required 150 separate operations.

The labor that made all this advancement possible is another important story. As did the
other large manufacturers of men's clothing in Chicago, including the **House of
Kuppenheimer**, founded in 1876 as a retail store, the **Scotch Woolen Mills**, **Royal Tailors**, and **Society Brand**, Hart Schaffner & Marx contracted orders to sweatshops, most of
which were located in tenements employing an average of fifteen persons per shop. The
designing and cutting were done in a factory. The cut cloth was packed in bundles and
delivered to these shops where a series of specialized machine operators did the sewing.
Basters loosely stitched the unsewn pieces and removed the threads from sewn ones. The
garment went to the buttonholer; went on to the finisher, and finally came back to the
presser at the factory. The making of a coat required 150 separate operations. By 1905 the
company had purchased 48 sweatshops to bring production under its direct supervision.

WORKING CONDITIONS BECOME MORE HUMANE

By 1910 the men's clothing industry had become Chicago's largest employer — even
larger than the stockyards — with a workforce of 38,000. Sixty-five percent of these
clothing workers were foreign born, with another 32 percent having foreign born parents.
The two largest ethnic groups were Polish Catholics and Bohemians, with substantial

numbers of Italians and Eastern European Jews also working in the industry. Approximately half of these workers were women.

Employers furnishing information to the Immigration Commission of 1910 explained that, "To a certain extent immigrants have been employed in the clothing trades of Chicago, because of their peculiar skill. This is especially true of the Bohemians, who are considered the best coat makers in the world; of the Scandinavians, who are the best workers on pants and vests; and of the Italians, who are the best hand sewers. The chief explanation ... given by manufacturers... that American employees are not available was that ... the Americans had a very marked prejudice against the business and refused to work at it."

Working conditions were improved, but proved far from satisfactory. Hannah Shapiro, who was working in Hart Schaffner & Marx Shop No. 5, announced she could no longer accept a mere 3 ¾ cents to sew a pocket into a pair of men's trousers. Sixteen other young women joined her and walked out to start the Chicago Garment Worker's Strike of 1910 on September 22nd.

The strike spread to almost all Chicago apparel manufacturers and cut production in half. The Harts and Joseph Schaffner were shocked. They had prided themselves on the modern, sanitary conditions of their shops as compared to the rest of the industry. It became apparent that physical surroundings alone could not correct the problem, that a process had to be set up to handle workers grievances on a continual basis. It was, and Joseph Schaffner became a leader in the difficult and delicate negotiations with the striking workers. A settlement was reached on January 14, 1911 providing for collective bargaining and arbitration, which recognized the union with terms previously unheard of in the apparel industry. As part of the settlement, a Board of Arbitration was created. Two great lawyers, Clarence Darrow for the union and Carl Meyer for the company, were part of the Board of Arbitrators. The agreement was so advanced that other Chicago clothing companies would not agree to it for seven years. It later became the model for many other industries across the country. As a result of the agreement, Hart Schaffner & Marx abolished homework and dealing with contract sweat shops. It established centralized production under one roof. The company pioneered the use of safety equipment in apparel plants. The installation of fire escapes and periodic fire drills was so unusual in 1912 that the event received widespread press coverage.

From the ranks of Hart Schaffner & Marx workers came Jacob Potofsky, who started as a pocket maker, and became one of the founders of the **Amalgamated Clothing Workers of America**, and Sidney Hillman, who became head of the Amalgamated Clothing Workers and in 1935 split with the American Federation of Labor (AFL) to found the Congress of Industrial Organizations (CIO). At the Hart Schaffner & Marx 50th Anniversary celebration in 1937 he was a keynote speaker.

World War I brought many changes to the garment industry. Because of the war, colorfast dyes could no longer be obtained from Germany. Hart Schaffner & Marx worked with

Collective bargaining and arbitration are recognized by the apparel industry.

leading chemical companies to develop them in the United States. In the process it established the first fabric testing laboratory operated by a clothing manufacturer in this country. In 1917 the company made history by introducing the world's first tropical-weight wool suit, the famous "Dixie Weave." Summer was now a time for suits, too. That year the United States entered the Great War and patriotism was the theme of advertising and daily life. After the war the ready-made men's clothing specialty store flourished and the firm decided to expand its operation by going back to its retailing roots. Hart Schaffner & Marx began to acquire stores, beginning with the 1926 purchase of Wallach's, the famous New York City specialty store, closely followed by the purchase of **Baskin** in Chicago. From 1929 to 1931 some 19 other stores were acquired. Today retail operations are an integral part of the company, with almost 450 stores.

In 1936 Hart Schaffner & Marx caused quite a stir in the industry by introducing the zipper in pants. At the time it was considered radical and a somewhat dangerous move. In 1937 the company celebrated its 50th Anniversary with speeches and advertisements to retailers featuring Henry Fonda as a model. Business boomed, and then came Pearl Harbor. Patriotism, this time with women in the WACS and WAVES and in factories as well as men, became the theme in advertising. In the later 1940s demand for suits soared. Padded shoulders and pleated pants were out and slim, trim lines of the natural shoulder suit, the most radical change in men's clothing in more than 20 years, was in.

In 1949 Hart Schaffner & Marx again pioneered in marketing, this time by signing a lease for a store in a new suburban shopping center. Others clothing retailers followed. The mass migrations to the suburbs across America proved it a savvy move.

Hart Schaffner & Marx introduced the first Dacron polyester and wool suit and revolutionized the industry in 1953. It was also the first clothing manufacturer to use nylon-wool and Orlon acrylic-wool blends for lighter-weight clothing.

The next year, in 1954, **Society Brand Clothes** was acquired. Since 1902 Society Brand had become synonymous with fine quality and fashion and had been the first to introduce the raglan shoulder coat as well as hook closure trousers. In 1964 the **Hickey-Freeman Company** was purchased. Established in 1899 and at first making topcoats which sold for $7.50 and $10, the company soon developed a reputation for hand tailored quality clothing, which it still has.

In 1967 Hart Schaffner & Marx made another major manufacturing acquisition, **Jaymar-Ruby** and its Sansabelt Slacks. Jaymar-Ruby evolved out of the overalls made by J.M. Ruby, in Michigan City since 1920. By 1931 the company was a major force in the production of quality slacks at a value price. Then, in the 1950s, two Frenchmen brought their waistband invention to Michigan City and the rest is history.

Over the past 25 years Hart Schaffner & Marx has prospered and broadly diversified its clothing lines, entering the women's apparel field in 1981 with the purchase of **Country Miss** and its 80 Old Mill outlets and in 1982, **Kuppenheimer**, the direct-to-consumer retail

Zippers were considered radical and dangerous when they replaced buttons on men's pants.

manufacturer of its own suits and sportcoats, and which has over 100 outlets. In 1983 **Hartmarx Corporation** became the new corporate name and Hart Schaffner & Marx is now a subsidiary.

Other garment manufacturers were also very important in their particular field of manufacturing. One of these, in Decatur, was the **Osgood-Heiner Mfg. Co.**, later **Osgood & Sons**, which began in 1900 and specialized in wash dresses. In 1930 some 2,000 men and women were employed in the garment industry, turning out 10,000 garments daily and giving Decatur a wide reputation as a dress supplier. There were only 800 employed in 1955 and three years later only 300. The plant closed in 1976.

Bear Brand Hosiery began in Bucyrus, Ohio when Dr. William Pope became interested in knitting machines and founded the Franz and Pope Knitting Machine Company. Franz and Pope developed for the first time a method of raising and lowering the needle for toe and heel power, an operation previously done by hand. In 1876 Franz and Pope won a prize at the Philadelphia Centennial for the most advanced knitting machines.

In 1893, visiting at the Chicago's Columbian World's Fair, Dr. Pope's son, Henry Pope Sr., found Chicago so impressive that he borrowed $400, bought a few sock machines from his father, moved to Chicago and founded the **Paramount Knitting Co.**, soon renamed the **Bear Brand Hosiery Co.** Since its beginning the company has led in the development of new technological improvements in hosiery production and in the pursuit of new methods of marketing and distribution. In the 1960s the Bear Brand operated five mills. The company plant at Kankakee was established in 1897 and was the firm's first constructed knitting mill. In the 1960s the Kankakee mill finished 750,000 dozen pair of ladies' nylons and 1,200,000 dozen pair of men's socks annually.

Bear Brand introduced "Resil'yarn," a yarn produced on standard spinning machines with special attachments. During its creation, staple yarn, both natural and synthetic, are spun around a tiny core of elastomeric stretch yarns. This spinning process produces yarn that has an evenness of tension providing a consistent and accurate stretch. As a result, socks made of Resil'yarn do not cut or bind, and do not shrink in the laundry. The properties of Resil'yarn made it ideal for home furnishings, industrial applications, medical uses, as well as other aspects of the apparel industry.

"Double-Knee Hose" was the product of **Alexander Westbay & Co.**, which started in 1883 in a four-story plant. The hose was manufactured exclusively in Decatur, as the firm held the only patented machines. The plant, which employed about 100 persons, closed in 1892 after producing millions of pairs of hose, mittens and leggings.

> "Double-Knee Hose" was exclusively manufactured in Decatur.

ZIP

Arguably the most important invention relating to clothing came sometime around 1891 when Whitcomb L. Judson, a Chicago mechanical engineer, came up with an arrangement of hooks and eyes with a sliding clasp for hooking and unhooking them automatically.

Judson called it a "clasp locker and unlocker for shoes." It was an ingenious replacement for boot-laces and the grandparent of the zipper. Two years later he patented the device and exhibited it at the Chicago World's Columbia Exhibition.

In 1894 Judson and Col. Lewis Walker, a lawyer form Meadville, Pennsylvania organized the **Universal Fastener Co.,** but the original design proved impractical, so Judson patented an improved version in 1896 and hired a firm of engineers and machinists to design and build machinery to mass-produce it. The hired machinists produced a series of machines that did not work and Judson came up with a series of improved fasteners until he finally hit one that his company could manufacture successfully.

It was called the C-Curity, and it was peddled door-to-door for use in skirt plackets and trouser flies. Despite the catchy name, the C-Curity had an unfortunate tendency to pop open, which produced in the public mind considerable cynicism about the new-fangled fasteners.

In 1906 the company, by then reorganized as the **Automatic Hook and Eye Co.,** hired an engineer named Gideon Sundback, who developed yet another kind of placket fastener, the Plako, which didn't pop open quite as often as the C-Curity. But it still wasn't the zipper. In 1913 Automatic Hook and Eye, on the verge of bankruptcy, was reorganized by Walker as the **Hookless Fastener Co.** and patented yet another of Sundback's designs, this time one that worked.

This one was the zipper much as we know it. The Navy used it in windproof flight suits. It was used in moneybelts, tobacco pouches and gloves. In 1923 B.F. Goodrich introduced galoshes that featured hookless fasteners and were marketed successfully as "Zipper Boots." But the public still remained zipper shy. Then Elsa Schiaparelli introduced them into her line and, according to her biographer, by 1935 they were everywhere in her collection, even on hats and evening gowns. "In scarlet they ran the length of the front of a dressing gown in white brocaded satin... They fastened shoulder seams. When zipped up, the dress was informal, when unzipped it was appropriate for lunch or tea. The Schiaparelli Zipper Back [was zipped] up for dinner and down for formal occasions." They sold like mad.

In 1892 Milton Florsheim and his father, Sigmund, started the **Florsheim Shoe Company** in Chicago. They promptly set about to revolutionize the world of men's footwear with some very modern concepts. At the time all men's shoes carried the name of the retailer, not the manufacturer. The maker had no incentive toward quality or consistency. By deciding to put his name on shoes, Milton Florsheim, in essence, created the concept of brand-name footwear. To ensure quality craftsmanship he began manufacturing shoes in his own Chicago factory at Adams and Clinton Streets at the turn of the century. As former shoe jobbers working the north side of Chicago, the Florsheims understood what retailers and customers were looking for in men's shoes, as well as how to make fine footwear. Florsheim's second move to establish the Florsheim name was to provide retailers carrying his footwear with an outdoor sign. The Florsheim name appeared on

> The zipper began as an ingenious boot lace replacement.

storefronts in hundreds of towns across America, establishing the wide recognition the name now enjoys.

Following his success in merchandising the Florsheim name with manufacturing, signage and salesmen, Milton Florsheim proved his marketing sense with a masterstroke: in the early 1900s he opened the first Florsheim retail store, located at One North LaSalle Street

Milton Florsheim created the concept of brand-name footwear.

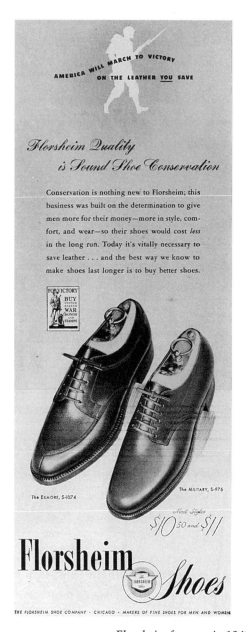

Florsheim for men in 1942 and for women in 1946

in downtown Chicago. Soon Florsheim retail stores opened on prime corners in the downtown areas of every major metropolitan center in the country. With the advent of shopping centers, Florsheim Shoe Shops became a cornerstone of every major mall in America.

The high-top was the look in men's shoes at the turn of the century. Florsheim was the first manufacturer of lower-quarter shoes, the low tops that revolutionized the look of men's shoes and became a standard. The company's next breakthrough was the genuine moccasin, which required the training of an army of craftsmen in the handsewing of leather. These craftsmen became so proficient they averaged 20 pairs per day.

And in the late 1960s, when European boots dominated the men's fashion scene and American shoemakers claimed the technique for making such footwear was impossible to master, Florsheim techniques soon made the company the number one maker of dress boots in the country.

Florsheim had one of the finest manufacturing centers in the United States.

When the original plant became too small in the 1940s, a new one was built across the street. Florsheim's dedication to forward-looking facilities was echoed when the building was hailed by architectural societies as one of the finest manufacturing centers in the United States. In March, 1953 Florsheim became a division of the **International Shoe Company**, now known as **Interco, Inc.**

BAKING TOOLS

The manufacturers that have survived the test of time have been managed very well, often making important contributions within their area of production and many have since grown into major corporations. A major contributor to the food industry has been the **Weidenmiller Company** of Itasca. For almost a century they have been meeting the needs of the baking industry by providing tooling and machinery. The company originated in 1903 when August Weidenmiller left his position, one he had held since the late 1880s, as superintendent of the engraving department of **Croname Plate and Engraving Company**, Chicago.

Die for a biscuit

In 1919, at the age of 14, his son, Edward A. Weidenmiller, began learning the trade from his father, working part-time. Two years later, Ed's older brother, Emil, joined the company, bringing his expertise as a steel stamp engraver.

Originally the company hand-made all die engravings. The first mechanical engraving machine, a pantograph, was purchased from George Gorton Machine Company in Racine, Wisconsin in 1914. This facilitated the mass production of hand embossing dies and steel stamps until 1924, when a small aluminum foundry was started in a garage to produce cast aluminum sugar wafer plates for the baking industry, primarily for Nabisco. During 1927 the two sons built a three-story building on Chicago's North side and the company

Mass production
of cookies
was helped by
cast dies.

became known as the **Weidenmiller Bros. Foundry**. The first floor housed a brass, bronze and aluminum foundry; the second, the machine and engraving shop and the third was leased to an electroplating company.

During the first quarter of the 20th Century, development of cylindrical Rotary Moulder die machines brought about the need for Uniformity Engraved die rolls. Weidenmiller Company purchased its first Gorton 3-Z machine in 1928 to make brass sugar wafer plate patterns and in 1933 converted it so the Company could produce brass rotary die rolls. Late that same year Ed and Emil separated as partners in business. While Emil took over the foundry, Edward headed the machine and engraving shop.

The next year, 1934, the Edward Weidenmiller Company engineered its own Rotary Moulder machine "head" to operate in conjunction with conventional stamping cutters. A prototype was then built and sold to Wortz Biscuit in Fort Smith, Arkansas. The use of Rotary Moulders increased during the 1930s and was curtailed early in the 1940s due to the war. After World War II the use of rotary machines increased markedly. In 1940 the company moved to 3628 Lincoln Avenue and in 1946 was incorporated in Illinois as the **Edward Weidenmiller Company**, Inc. That same year, the company purchased land in Morton Grove and in the following year constructed a plant there.

During the late 1940s the biscuit industry, which traditionally made hard sweet goods on embossing and stamping cutters, began experimenting with producing them on Rotary Machines. Increased knowledge of dough formulation enabled bakeries to manufacture base cakes such as Oreo, Social Tea, Arrowroot cookies and animal crackers on Rotary Machines. Today more than 8,000 designs, shapes and configurations are catalogued.

The 1950s earmarked the coming of Wire Cut machines into many bakeries. Weidenmiller was again instrumental in pioneering the first United States "heavy duty" Wire Cut machine for soft doughs. The year 1970 saw the introduction of steel side frame versus cast iron for the Rotary and Wire Cut machines. The same year a jackpot sales order for two 52" wide Heavy Duty Rotary Molders from **Quaker Oats Petfood Division** set the stage for the firm's establishment into the petfood market. From 1973 to 1978 **Lance Corporation** employed Weidenmiller's new Rotary Cutter units and eventually purchased six of them to increase their production capabilities. The machine building program was well underway.

In 1987 the company relocated into a modern factory in Elk Grove Village and five years later moved its facilities to DuPage from Cook County primarily to reduce the real estate tax bite. Today Weidenmiller is the number one die roll engraver in the cookie, cracker, hard candy, snack and pet food markets. Other related product areas included dies for pizzas, ethnic and specialty flat breads. The Company also serves the hard goods industrial/commercial markets with, for instance, floor mat and textured embossing rolls. The Company's Machinery Manufacturing Division produces snack food forming machinery and systems.

Among the giants of food processing, and arguably among the most interesting of these companies, was Beatrice. Despite a growing demand for fresh milk, butter and cream in the rapidly expanding eastern cities, business failures were common among the dairies and creameries in the Midwest during the 1890s. The problem as George Everett Haskell, a native of Nebraska, saw it, was the uncoordinated handling and marketing of their products. To make matters even more difficult, most farmers concentrated on grain crops, considering dairying only a marginal sideline. And since each farm wife had her own recipe for butter, product quality differed considerably from family to family. Standardized quality was only a dream. Other difficulties were the size of the independent creameries,

> Weidenmiller is the number one die roll engraver for cookies, crackers, hard candy and pet food.

too small to command reasonable freight rates, and seasonal production, with half the annual milk output coming in the three warmest months of the year.

Haskell's plan was to coordinate the flow of dairy products from farmer to consumer. Essentially this made local dairies and creameries more than mere processors of milk products, they now became central marketing agents. Each dairy in the network would make a uniform product which, if enough of it was made, would be economical to store, handle and ship.

Beatrice made local dairies and creameries central marketing agents.

In 1894 Haskell took his savings and joined them with those of his friend, William W. Bosworth, to form the firm of **Haskell & Bosworth**. They began in Fremont, Nebraska and soon bought a defunct operation of the Fremont Butter and Egg Company in nearby Beatrice, Nebraska, leasing the Beatrice Creamery Company's plant and opening a new branch in Lincoln. At first the new company did little more than follow the traditional butter-collecting system. But soon the firm began reblending the farm churned butter at its plant. Fresh water flushed out excess salt and buttermilk, creating a uniform consistency, color and sweetness acceptable in any market. Packed in 60-pound tubs, it then was shipped in refrigerated railroad cars to New York, Chicago and other large distribution centers. The partners also began collecting fresh cream and making their own butter. Conveniently located cream-separation stations let farmers deliver their milk without excess travel. Later, separators were sold directly to the farmers, who paid for them on the installment plan from cream sales revenues. Between 1895 and 1905 Haskell & Bosworth sold 50,000 such separators.

This innovation had an immediate revolutionary effect. It made dairying profitable. Farmers saw the results and enlarged their herds and improved its management. As the cream supply increased, Haskell & Boswell expanded its distribution. The **Beatrice Creamery Co.** was incorporated in 1898. (It became **Beatrice Foods Co.** in 1946.) All churning operations were concentrated in a large new plant at Lincoln. In 1899 Bosworth withdrew from the partnership, which was then consolidated as Beatrice Creamery and its success continued. In its first year Beatrice Creamery sold 940,000 pounds of Lincoln Brand Separator Creamery Butter and more than 350 cream-separation stations were shipped to the Lincoln plant. The problem of seasonal production was resolved with cold-storage warehouses. Quickly the company expanded both the number of its plant sites and the scope of its operations. Creameries were built in Chicago, Oklahoma City and Pueblo, Colorado. Other companies, among them Lincoln Ice and Storage Company in Lincoln, Nebraska and Chicago's **Fox River Butter Company**, were acquired. An ice cream plant opened in Topeka in 1907, three years after ice cream cones had conquered the nation at the St. Louis Exposition. By 1910 the company was operating nine creameries and three ice plants, and had sales offices across the nation.

Needing nationally centralized headquarters, Beatrice moved to Chicago in 1913 and began planning the giant structure, still standing, on South State Street. Opened in 1917, the new building's top floor accommodated the corporate offices. Creamery operations were on another entire floor. The second floor, adjacent to the elevated right-of-way of the St. Charles Air Line Railroad, contained indoor siding capable of holding 20 railroad cars at once. In all, the warehouse could hold 3,500 railroad carloads of refrigerated foodstuffs.

Haskell died in 1919, and vice-president William Ferguson succeeded him, retiring in 1928. Then followed Clinton H. Haskell, a nephew. Under his direction a surge in corporate growth ensued that even the Depression could not slow. Marketing opportunities in the East sparked a construction boom: a modern creamery in Brooklyn, ice cream plants in Baltimore and Washington, and a milk and ice cream facility in Pittsburgh. The company had only four milk plants in 1919. Three years later it had 32. Between 1927 and 1932 Beatrice's milk processing leaped from less than one million gallons to 27 million, while ice cream production went from 1.5 million to 9.5 million gallons per year. By this time the trade name *Meadow Gold*, which had been coined by employees of the Topeka creamery in 1901, had become a nationwide household name and so the country's first national retail brand name for butter. During the 1930s the public began to demand clean, sanitary, table-ready products available under the same brand name, and Beatrice met the demand with new technology and distribution methods. In 1931 Beatrice introduced the Vogt continuous freezing process and almost overnight the traditionally produced 40 gallon batches of ice cream were obsolete. The new process reduced cost and ice cream went from being a pricy delicacy to a common dessert. Beatrice was also one of the first companies to package butter in sealed one-pound cartons and to pasteurize churning cream on a large scale. By 1952 Beatrice was a very diversified company, with connections to most aspects of the convenient food industry. LaChoy Oriental foods, Clark candy, Gebhardt and Rosarita Mexican foods, Fisher Nuts, Martha White convenience corn meal and biscuit mixes, Tropicana orange juice and soft drink bottling operations made up Beatrice's product lines.

Manufacturing companies making machinery used in the food business also fit neatly into this merger pattern. Among these were Taylor soft ice cream freezers, Market Forge cooking equipment, Bloomfield restaurant equipment and Wells commercial cookers. Other companies also came into the fold, such as Samsonite luggage and furniture, Stiffel lamps, Melnor lawn and garden tools and **Culligan Water Systems** equipment, to name but a few. Special chemical companies also contributed to Beatrice's diversification. Among these was **Stahl Finish** and other suppliers of finishes for the apparel industry; also specialty ink, paint, waterproofing and high-technology plastic molding firms. By the early 1980s Beatrice owned or had substantial interest in nearly 200 plants and branches in dozens of countries outside the United States.

Beatrice packaged butter in sealed one-pound cartons.

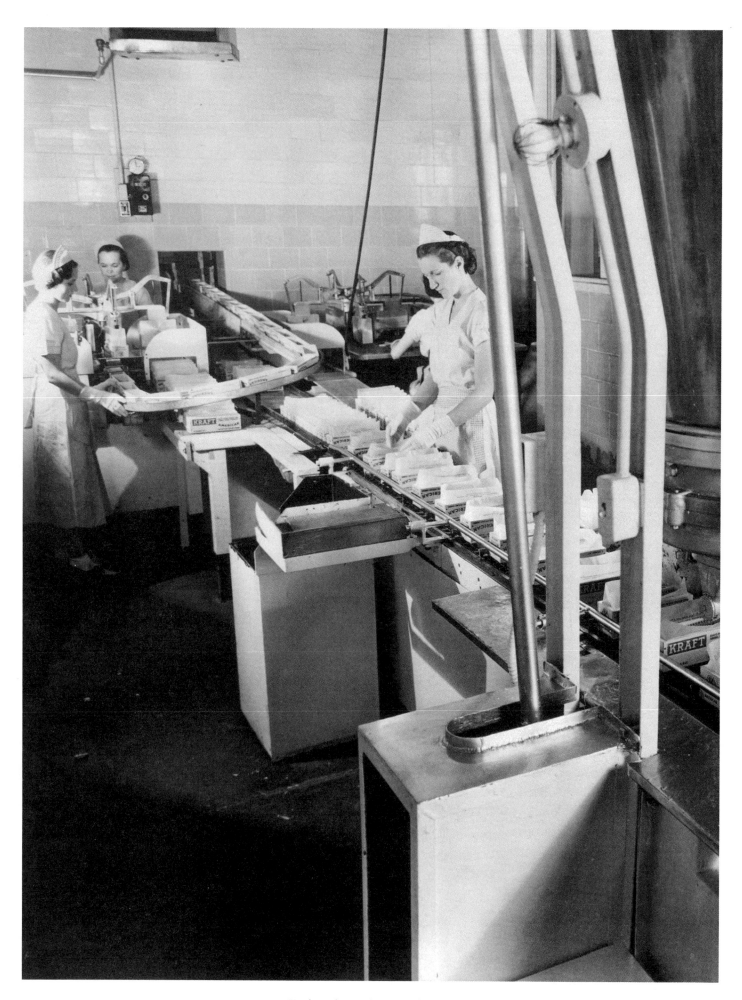

Kraft packages cheese in the 1930s

MANUFACTURING GROWTH

The 1920s and 1930s were marked by some developments that would have long-range consequences for manufacturing. First, in 1921, new immigration laws limited what had been a continuing source of skilled technical labor emigrating from Germany, Italy, Scandinavia and the old Austro-Hungarian Empire. Second, the introduction of modernistic styles and of new materials such as chromed iron, stainless steel and initial forms of plastic began to bring about fundamental changes in demand and production techniques. Third, factories which had operated with a single motor powering entire lines by belt drive were converting to individual motors for each station; and cities across the United States were converting from DC to AC. Other changes were also underway that would affect American life for the coming decades. Among these were new sources of protein: the soybean and hybrid corn.

Possibly the most important new grain of the 20th century was the soybean, which had been introduced into Illinois from Manchuria during World War I, but did not gain much notice until the early 1920s. Within the decade Illinois was producing more soybeans than all other states combined, and Wenona was its major soybean growing center.

In the Orient, where meatless diets were commonplace, the soybean had been a staple for many centuries. But in the United States it was a strange, new, experimental legume growing within a pod on a bushy plant. As soon as soybeans were shown to be profitable, farmers, whose fate and fortune had for more than a century depended on such tried-and-true crops as corn, wheat and oats, became interested. Especially in the Illinois flatlands, farmers were becoming increasingly aware of the virtues of rotating crops. Corn farmers, in particular, many of whom had intensively corned their farms to death, were eager to tap any new crop that was easy to maintain. Soybeans were an answer. They were high yielding and not susceptible to such blights as bugs, weeds and diseases in an era prior to the development of chemical fertilizers, herbicides and insecticides.

Central Illinois farmers had created some of their own problems. The farmers' reluctance to rotate crops during World War I, when corn prices rose to all-time highs, resulted in ever smaller yields per acre. In the 1918-1922 period, many affected farmers told tales of woe to Gene Staley and his colleagues when the farmers dropped in at the Staley plant in Decatur, where their corn was the one and only raw material the plant needed. At about the same time literature began to appear indicating "several Illinois farm-related groups" and "an Illinois processor" were ready to give guarantees to provide a market for "all the beans grown on 50,000 acres" in the Illinois Corn Belt. The "Illinois processor" was the **A.E. Staley Manufacturing Company** of Decatur, and the man behind it all was Augustus

Soybeans
were an
answer.

Eugene Staley, Sr., the ever-restless, ever-inquisitive, ever-innovative founder of the company. He was motivated by the pure and simple desire to achieve profit and growth through corporate diversification. He also felt that soybeans needed advocacy.

As news about soybeans spread, the knowledge that they were an unprecedented source of protein for animal feedstocks, and also for humans, received a wide hearing. Soybean meal and oil, the two principal derivatives, were initially produced on a small scale in the United States in 1911 through a crushing process in Seattle, Washington, using beans imported from Manchuria. American-grown beans were initially processed on an even smaller scale in 1915 by several cottonseed oil mills in North Carolina.

Decatur was "The Soybean Capitol of the World."

It's all from corn

Staley's corn syrup

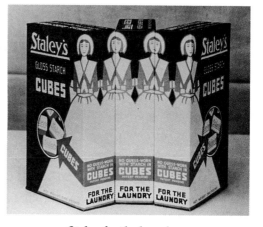

Staley for the laundry

Corn refining by the "wet milling" process would continue to be the principal line of activity at Decatur, but Gene Staley insisted that soybeans be given a fair deal, and in 1922 he declared, "The day will come when our plant will process more soybeans than corn." It did in 1950, when Staley handled 50 railroad carloads of soybeans daily, while he handled only 30 carloads of corn. That year the Staley Company boasted, "We are the world's largest in soybeans and Number Two in corn. It takes 3,500 acres to grow enough soybeans to keep us operating for a single day." The company also had the largest conveyor belt in the world in 1957.

Gene Staley made his money in cornstarch, but his love was football. In January, 1920 Gene Staley heard of a man named George Halas, who was class of '17 at the University of

Illinois where he had studied engineering and played football, basketball and baseball. He was employed at the time as a bridge engineer for the Chicago Burlington & Quincy Railroad. Staley asked his general superintendent to meet Halas in Chicago He did, and Halas moved to Decatur to organize a football team. In less than nine months professional football was born. On Sunday, October 3, 1920, more than 2,000 local fans turned out to see the Decatur Staleys play the Moline Tractors. The Staleys won 20 to 0. By the end of the season the Decatur Staleys proclaimed themselves world champions, yet the bottom line in the corporate accounting department showed a loss. Staley loved his team but Decatur didn't have the space it needed and the 1921 Depression, a left over from imbalance of World War I, held him back financially. He transferred the team to Halas who moved it to Chicago. There Halas made a deal with William Veeck, Sr., president of the P.K. Wrigley-owned Chicago Cubs baseball team. In 1922 the Bears came out running.

Decatur boasted that it was "The Soybean Capital of the World," and became the host to such organizations as: Soy City Bank & Trust Company, Soy Capital Electric Inc., Soy City Electric Supply Co., Soy City Marine Inc., Soy City Motel, Soy City Tire & Retreading Inc., Soy City Towing Co., Soyland Power Cooperative Inc., Soyland Service Center, Inc. and a radio station, WSOY. Besides soybeans, Decatur should also be remembered as the home of R.R. Montgomery, who invented the fly-swatter in 1900.

As soybeans began to show their potential to Illinois farmers, corn, that old American farm war-horse, also came under investigation. In 1925 Lester Pfister of El Paso was convinced by Henry Wallace, an Iowa farm editor and later Secretary of Agriculture, that a satisfactory hybrid of corn could be developed. For the next ten years Pfister inter-mingled various corn pollens until by inbreeding and crossbreeding he produced high-yield corn. He began to market his seed corn in 1935. The nearby **Funk Brothers Seed Farms** were the initial source for this new seed. The farms covered 22,000 acres in the 1930s. A hybrid corn that is chinch-bug resistant was an important development of the farms. Since 1928 the Funk Brothers have also been soybean seed producers.

Today corn is consumed in many ways, most of which we don't think of or know about. The **J.R. Short Milling Co.** of Kankakee has introduced a line of products from corn which go into many types of food, including breakfast cereals. They also produce an enzyme bleaching cereal flour from soybeans.

In the United States, Argo has been a synonym for corn starch for about 100 years. That Argo is also the name of a town, next to Summit, a company town, is generally not known. The ancient Egyptians, Greeks and Romans were adept at using starches, but it was not until Marco Polo or one of his contemporaries opened trade routes to China that the knowledge of starch brought back from there became important to Europe. These early starches were based on wheat or rice, but as demand increased other sources were sought and, in 1717, S. Newton of England was granted a patent for the manufacture of starch from potatoes, a food also not native to Europe. The English brought the idea of potato starch to New England and by the Revolutionary War numerous small potato and

Lester Pfister of El Paso developed hybrid corn.

wet starch manufacturers were operating along the eastern coast. As demand grew, again new sources of starch were sought, this time it was corn, another native American crop. In 1844 Thomas Kingsford, then employed by Wm. Colgate Company, built the first corn starch factory in Jersey City, New Jersey. Over the next 50 years the wet milling industry grew in leaps and bounds. Competition was fierce and soon two monopolies emerged, the Glucose Trust and the Starch Trust.

Argo is a corn starch and a town.

In 1899 E.T. Bedford, a director of Standard Oil Company, and his son Fred began to look at the glucose industry as a business opportunity for Fred. At the time the glucose industry was the biggest and most mismanaged of the conglomerates. Bedford and son formed the New York Glucose Company which, by 1902, had a new plant in Edgewater, New Jersey. The Glucose Trust saw New York Glucose as a threat, but failed in its attempt to gain control of it. In 1906 the stockholders of the Glucose Trust revolted, threw out the management and requested that E.T. Bedford take over. The total grind of the new organization, **Corn Products Refining Company** , was 140,000 bushels a day, with plants in Edgewater, New Jersey; Granite City, Waukegan, Chicago and Pekin; Davenport, Iowa; and Oswego, New York. After surveying the facilities, only two were found modern and efficient, the remainder too old to be even remodeled. A new plant had to be built. For the plant to work properly, the perfect site had to have corn, coal and sulfur supplies nearby, as well as an abundant supply of water and good transportation. These needs were met by the newly completed Illinois Canal and Archer Road, the former Indian Trail, southwest of Chicago, near Summit. The site was name Argo, perhaps after a recently acquired plant in Nebraska that made starch under the Argo brand name.

A birdseye view of the Argo plant in the 1950s

The Argo plant was constructed in four units, each capable of grinding 15,000 bushels per day. The first bushel of grind went through the plant on March 28, 1910 and the average weekly grind for the first year was 8,875 bushels per day. The second unit was completed in 1912. By 1916 all four units were integrated and production was approaching 60,000 bushels a day. Each building, of steel and concrete, was a self-contained unit spaced a suitable distance from its neighbor to minimize the effect of a fire or explosion, a common occurrence in grinding mills at the time. A maze of tunnels, each one wide enough for six workers to walk abreast, carried materials between building and housed the necessary piping.

Originally starch came in lumps as large as walnuts and was sold in large packages, mostly 40 pound boxes. The lumps and quantity were a result of manufacturing. Raw, damp starch leaving the production cylinders was broken with sledges into pieces that could pass through a grating with 6"x6" openings. The pieces were dried in trays on cars in warm rooms. While drying, they would crack. Leaving the trays, they would go through another breaker that further reduced the lumps and then over a sieve to remove the small lumps. These small lumps were reduced to powder and sent through the cycle again. One day some unsung genius packed these small lumps of starch into one pound packages for domestic use. The industry was changed forever. At first demand was low and only a few women would fill a few boxes, then as demand increased so did the number of box filling women until mechanization replaced them. This starch was called Argo and became the name for domestic laundry starch worldwide.

> For decades, the CPC plant was the largest corn refinery in the world.

In the 1930s and 1940s the Corn Products Company Plant in Argo was the largest corn refinery in the world. It employed 1,700 at capacity. Many of the plants by-products were used in the manufacture of candy, beer, chewing tobacco, mucilage, fireworks, ink, and stationary. By 1984 there were over 90 buildings on the Argo site, and the plant was grinding approximately 50,000,000 bushels of corn each year. But this was not enough to meet demand and a new plant was started, Argo II. The first phase of construction included a new refinery and production facilities for HFCS II, a dextrose unit, and an all new infrastructure for utilities. This phase was completed and in operation within the year. Two years later a new power house, a wet starch unit and an expansion of HFCS I production was finished. By the late 1980s Argo was the flagship of CPC's Corn Refining Division, today known as **Corn Products, a Unit of CPC International Inc.**, grinding some 60,000,000 bushels of corn each year.

The **International Agricultural Corporation (IAC)** began in 1909, when Thomas Meadows, a pioneer in the new United States phosphate mining business, sought to sell American farmers the same inexpensive fertilizers that had helped European countries achieve a dramatic increase in agricultural output. Along with Waldemar Schmidtmann, an Austrian, Meadows started IAC with several tracts of phosphate-bearing land in Tennessee and a collection of small mines and fertilizer plants. Surviving various difficulties, the company, in 1929, developed a flotation process that achieved dramatic increases in phosphate mining efficiency. The development gave IAC the stamina needed to survive the Depression and to increase growth. In 1939 IAC was the nation's leading producer of phosphate rock and began mining potash at its new operation near Carlsbad, New Mexico. By the 1960s the company had changed its name to **International Minerals & Chemical Corporation (IMC)** with headquarters in Northbrook. Also in the 1960s, IMC overcame previously impossible underground mining problems to open the world's richest potash deposit in Saskatchewan, Canada. Today the company has a global network of fertilizer, mining, animal products and chemicals.

The ready availability of steel and tin from Chicago's mills helped business take off for Chicago's two big can manufacturers, **Continental Can Company** and **American Can Company**. By 1924, 3.5 million cases of 24 one-pound cans were being produced for the food industry alone. Companies like **Libby, McNeill and Libby, Inc.** (whose main packing plant was in Blue Island) began to wean consumers from the greengrocer, the butcher and butter-and-egg man with long lasting, canned foods. Canning was very important to Chicago's 96 meat packers, 25 canned food producers, 26 picklers, 13 preserve makers, 11 evaporated milk companies and one egg canner.

In the 1920s almost the entire onion set crop of America was produced around South Holland.

ILLINOIS' BROOM CORN SWEEPS THE NATION

While many food manufacturers and processors were located in Chicago, others were very near the fields and orchards where the produce was raised. Mendota was an important canning center, shipping more than four million cans of corn annually in the 1930s. Rochelle was a peas, corn, pumpkins and a major asparagus growing area, where the **Asparagus Company** operated 1,500 acres and a cannery in the 1930s. Another large cannery was run by Del Monte there and in De Kalb, for corn and tomatoes.

The broom corn belt extends from Arcola on the north to Neoga in the south. Broom production is still important to this region. **Libman Co.**, a broom manufacturer in Arcola since 1931, was founded in Chicago in 1898 by William Libman's grandfather. Libman is treasurer of the company.

Flora was the headquarters of the **Egyptian Seed Growers Exchange**, a cooperative of the redtop grass seed growers of southern Illinois. While Fulton had more than 12 acres of prairie soil under glass, producing thousands of baskets of tomatoes and boxes of cucumbers annually, South Holland was the heart of the truck farming described by Edna Ferber in *So Big*. The chief product of the community was raising onion sets (onions less than one inch in diameter), raised from seed, stored all winter and then sold to commercial growers. The work was done by Italians and Polish women. In the 1920s almost the entire onion set crop of America was produced in this area.

For most of the 20th Century, Pana has been a rose growing town depending on local coal to steam heat its 102 greenhouses, which in the 1930s shipped 15,000,000 cut roses annually. Near Du Quoin were the Maple Lawn Gardens, a 60 acre tract of narcissuses, daffodils and peonies. Beardstown was, in the 1930s, an important watermelon and cantaloupe exporting center. Jerseyville shipped much of the apple crop of Calhoun County because there was no railroad from the center of production, Hardin. New Burnside, in the Illinois Ozarks, was the center of a fruit growing region for which the United States Weather Bureau maintained a reporting station.

CHEESE, BEES AND BUTTONS

Illinois did not have a shortage of dairy farming either. Highland was settled predominantly by the Swiss and by 1831 had quickly developed an important dairy products industry. In 1884 John Mayenard brought a new process for preserving milk from Switzerland and established a factory there. After a strike in 1920, the factory was closed and production moved to St. Louis. In Harvard, in 1939, the Starline Model Dairy Farm featured an all steel barn and a horizontal silo that had no post supports. The futuristic structure of the barn served as a symbol of promise for the industy. The farm also developed and tested dairy equipment.

Elgin began to ship milk to Chicago in 1852 and soon processed a growing surplus into cheese and butter. The city's importance as a dairy center was greatly enhanced by Gail Borden, who in his youth had begun experimenting with condensed foods. After experiencing a stormy sea voyage, during which he noted that the cows did not give milk, **Borden** focused on condensed milk. He soon had a factory going in Elgin. By 1875 it was condensing the milk from a thousand cows. The main plant, erected in 1911, was one of the largest malted milk and dried milk producers in the United States by 1940.

The booming dairy trade in Elgin resulted, in 1872, in the formation of a local Board of Trade, which until 1912 served as the Midwest's milk marketing center. The Board was an important factor in setting the national prices of butter and cheese. The peak for cheese was 1883, when board members marketed 12,500,000 pounds; in 1911 they reached a butter high with sales of 57,000,000 pounds. During World War I the Food Administration requested the Board to suspend operations as butter was considered a non-essential product. After the Armistice it was not reorganized. By the 1930s Elgin no longer manufactured butter.

The best known and largest of the dairy and cheese companies to develop in Illinois is Kraft. James L. Kraft, born 1874 at Fort Erie, Ontario and died in 1953 in Chicago, was a Canadian immigrant who revolutionized the packaging and merchandising of cheese and cheese products. Kraft moved to Chicago in 1903 and soon started selling cheese he bought from wholesalers. By the end of the first year he was $3,000 in debt. Americans at the time did not consume much cheese. He perservered and in 1909 incorporated his business as **J.L. Kraft & Bros. Co.** In 1911 he became a United States citizen. In 1916 he patented a method for making pasteurized process cheese, a product that could be shipped long distances without spoilage. Six million pounds of this processed cheese were bought by the United States Government during World War I. Business boomed. Soon Kraft bought other companies such as the Phenix Cheese Corporation in 1928. Philadelphia Brand cream cheese was one of their leading products.

By the end of 1929 Kraft owned 50 subsidiaries with operations in Canada, Australia, England and Germany. In 1930 the company became a subsidiary of **National Dairy Products Corporation** which was renamed **Kraftco Corporation** in 1969 and **Kraft, Inc.** in

Elgin was
the Midwest's
dairy center.

Legend has it that Max Crosset developed Miracle Whip in Salem.

A Kraft line in 1943

1976. In 1980 it became **Dart & Kraft**, which, six years later split into two companies: Kraft, Inc. and **Premark International**. In 1988 Kraft became a subsidiary of Philip Morris Companies. Kraft introduced Miracle Whip Salad Dressing in 1933, a product, according to legend, developed by Max Crosset and served in his cafe at 312 East Main Steet in Salem. He is said to have sold the recipe to Kraft in 1931 for $300. No records of this acquisition have turned up in Kraft's archives, while a body of evidence exists that Miracle Whip was an internal development. Kraft macaroni and cheese dinners followed in 1936, and Parkay margarine in 1937.

Kraft was among the first to advertise in consumer journals and was an early promoter of full-color advertisements in national magazines, especially *Good Housekeeping* and *Ladies Home Journal*. In 1933 Kraft sponsored a two-hour musical and variety radio program, the "Kraft Musical Revue," which became the "Kraft Music Hall." In 1947 "Kraft Television Theatre" premiered on WNBT-TV in New York. In 1972 the Kraftco offices moved to Glenview from New York City, while Chicago based **Kraft Foods** moved to Glenview about 10 years later.

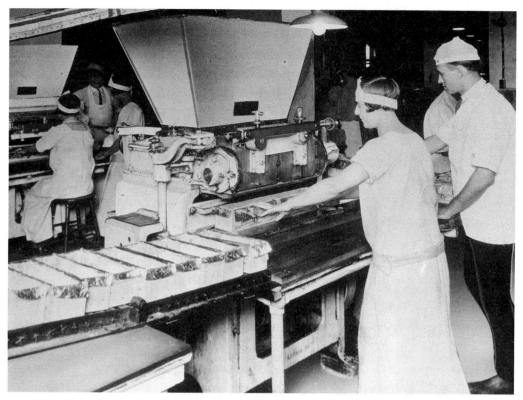

Kraft's Rush Street, Chicago plant in the 1920s.

Mississippi river shells made buttons, pearls and pavement.

In fields where cows roam, bees find nectar. Bee keeping has been an important Illinois business for more than a century. The **Dadant** company in Hamilton invented the reinforced sheet of honeycomb bee foundation which enables beekeepers to remove honey quickly and efficiently through high speed centrifugal extracting machinery. Dadant is also the publisher of the *American Bee Journal*, the fourth oldest continually published magazine in the United States.

While we often mention the birds and the bees, few nice things are said about fish, yet commercial fishing was once of great importance to Illinois. Not long ago, as recently as the 1930s, Beardstown was a center of commercial fishing and clamming. Liverpool, near Peoria on the Illinois River, served as a commercial fishing port, while Bernadotte, on the Spoon River, had a fishing business and packing plant. A century before, in the 1840s, Havana recorded daily fish catches of 100,000 pounds from the Illinois River. This trend seems to have continued down to our own century, when in 1906, 1907 and 1908 the Illinois River at Havana was second in importance only to the Columbia River with its salmon as a freshwater commercial fishing river in the United States.

Before plastics were common and other substitutes were not adequate, molluscs were the favored raw material for button manufacturers. The principal business of Oquawka, seat of Henderson County, in the 1930s was the manufacture of pearl button blanks from Mississippi River mussels shells. Shells were so abundant that crushed ones were used to surface the local streets. In the same decade Andalusia's only industry was the manufacture of pearl buttons from Mississippi clam shells. Across the state Brookport, on the Ohio

River, had a mussel shell button factory as its principal industry in 1939. While Mount Carmel, on the Wabash River, had a lucrative mussel industry from 1900 into the 1930s. Over $1 million worth of fresh water pearls were found there during these three decades.

ILLINOIS STAMPS AND FORGES STEEL

Once upon a time, Chicago made 17 percent of the nations steel in 41 furnaces.

From the time of the Civil War to about the First World War most of the nation's steel production had been used to make railroads and then equipment, especially farm machinery. But by the end of the 1920s, 16.5 percent of the country's steel output was going into structures and only 6.5 percent into manufacturing of agricultural machinery. Chicago was a leader in both areas.

In 1924 the Federal Trade Commission made a decision that was of critical importance to the Chicago steel industry. It struck down a pricing mechanism known as "Pittsburgh Plus" which pegged all steel to the base price in Pittsburgh plus the cost of shipping that steel from wherever it was made. Therefore, even though Chicago's steelmaking costs were 10 to 15 percent less than Pittsburgh's because of Chicago's proximity to the raw materials needed to make steel, Chicago could offer no price advantage to western buyers, only quicker deliveries. The 1924 FTC ruling changed all that. Within a year after the ruling the results were clear: Chicago surpassed the eastern steelmaker's production, and 25 steel processors rushed to build factories in the Calumet region .

As a result, the nation's steel production was 51.4 million tons in 1928, half the world's output; up more than 40 million tons since 1900. Chicago was making 17 percent of the United States total at the time in 41 furnaces. Significant contributions to the nation's steel production were also made by other iron and steel centers in Illinois, especially in the East St. Louis area.

In 1891 William F. Niedringhaus, a St. Louis industrialist, bought 3,000 acres in Granite City. Later that year Niedringhaus and his son George selected a plant site for his **National Enameling and Stamping Co.** The plant and many two-family flats were constructed in 1892. Shortly afterwards a rolling-mill was added. In 1893 the **American Steel Foundry** was established. **Granite City Steel Works** and the **Commonweal Steel Mills** also settled in Granite City, which became an industrial boom town until the steel slump of 1907 closed the plant for a few years.

Madison, like Granite City, was also a product of the steel industry. A group of St. Louis industrialists, spurred mainly by the high cost of bringing coal into St. Louis over Eads Bridge, formed the Madison Land Syndicate in 1887 and promoted the construction of the Merchant Bridge in 1890. The **American Car and Foundry Co.** built a plant on the site in Madison in 1891. It and a few flimsy houses were incorporated into a village the same year, and a place called Venice was developed around a railyard at the foot of Merchant Bridge. Brooklyn, organized in 1874 and dependent on the steel industry, railroad switch yard and stock yards, is the oldest and was the largest all African-American town in Illinois for two decades, from 1930 to 1950.

Michelmann Steel Construction Co. of Quincy was founded in 1865 as a boiler maker. The company switched to the fabrication of steel about 1900. Since then it has been in the business of structural and miscellaneous steel fabrication. In Barrington Carl von Malmborg developed a metal formula that simulated gold and had the strength of steel. For a time it was used for tableware, vases and similar decorative products.

Michelmann Steel Construction Company of Quincy has been in business since 1865.

When Joseph T. Ryerson (1813-1883) came to Chicago in 1842 as an agent for Pittsburgh iron interests, he found little competition for his products. Realizing the need for iron products in the city, he soon organized his own iron works and quickly ventured into other enterprises. Today, known as **Joseph T. Ryerson and Son Inc.**, the company is the largest steel service center in the country. Since 1908 Ryerson has had four plants and an administrative center in Chicago. Nationally it has 30 facilities and 4,000 employees.

In 1895, at the age of 20, Axel N. Lindberg, born into one of the metalworking families that had already made Sweden famous, emigrated to the United States. He first went to work for a manufacturer of laundry machines in Chicago as a apprentice machinist and odd-job man, then joined another company as a blacksmith. Here he learned the technique of forging tools and of hardening them by heat. Twenty-seven years later, at the age of 47, Lindberg, with his son LeRoy, went into business for himself in the rear second floor at 413 North Carpenter Street in Chicago. He purchased four furnaces, quenching tanks, benches, a desk, a typewriter and a sign that read "Lindberg Steel Treating Company." Since that start in 1922 **Lindberg Corporation,** as it has been known since 1967, has become a leader in heat-treating plants, offering a broad range of essential metallurgical processes and technical services to the metal using and metal-working industries. In the 1980s Lindberg was the largest commercial heat-treating firm in the world.

MANUFACTURING FITS TOWNS LIKE A GLOVE

In the 1920s and 1930s Hartford, north of East St. Louis, existed solely because of the **International Shoe Company** tannery established here in 1915. This large processing facility could process 27,500 hides in a week, with each hide going through 110 steps before it could be used as shoe leather. Casey was an oil boom town in the 1930s and became, when the oil ran out by 1939, a shoe producing center, as were Mattoon and Flora. Effingham served them all by manufacturing heels.

When the assembly line became predominant in many industries in the 1920s, gloves became an important everyday accessory for many workers. Beardstown and Effingham became important glove manufacturing centers then, and they continue to be so with the **Illinois Glove Co.** plants. And the **Boss Manufacturing Co.**, started in 1898 as a manufacturer of work gloves in Kewanee, has since expanded into sports and garden gloves, boots, rainwear and a variety of industrial safety products.

Other small towns, like Flora, in Clay County, or Carmi, seat of White County, found the manufacture of underwear important to their economy for much of this century. With the rapid growth from the 1890s to the 1930s of fraternal organizations that required special uniforms and paraphernalia for lodge ceremonies, or costumes for vaudeville and circus performers, or banners and such for all occasions, the leading manufacturer in the nation was and still seems to be the **De Moulin Brothers & Co.** of Greenville.

In the 1920s and 1930s plastic was new.

WARP WRAPS UP AMERICA

Sheet glass had been around for well over 1000 years before plastic in sheet form was introduced. Called "the greatest scientific invention known ... for poultrymen, gardeners, farmers, at one eighth the cost of glass," Harold Warp, founder **Warp Brothers,** introduced his new product, Flex-O-Glass, in an ad on December 4, 1924. He may have believed in it, but couldn't have imagined how much his plastic products would change the way America and the world is wrapped. In the 1920s and 30s plastic was new, and Chicago had the honor of being one of birthplaces.

Noticing that the family gathered more eggs in the new chicken coop that faced south, and that the little chicks seemed healthier there, Harold Warp experimented with flour sack cloth saturated with wax as a window material. The defused light seemed to be kind to the chickens, while conventional clear glass was harsh. He expanded his experiments to plants by building a type of hotbed and found that plants liked the defused light, too. Thus Flex-O-Glass was conceived in Minden, Nebraska, but manufactured from the start in Chicago because Warp, then 20 years old, knew his business would depend on mail order sales. Chicago was the place for that. Warp's unbreakable product had a cloth base and was touted to withstand hail, rail and all kinds of weather, while it radiated the sun's heat most readily by transmitting ultra-violet light. But Warp did not know this scientific fact at the time.

Later it would be realized that Warp's experiments on the family farm with growing chicks had established the fact that the ultra-violet, actinic rays in sunshine were essential to the sustenance of animal life and growth and that his Flex-O-Glass was the first product made expressly for this purpose. Ever vigilant against fraudulent claims, various state experimental stations and government testing laboratories sought to verify the claims made by Warp. The Iowa State Experimental Station and the United States Bureau of Standards could not believe their own results and ran the test again, with the results again confirming Warp's claims. The test results were published and greatly helped Warp's struggling business.

By 1930 he had 3,000 dealers for his product. But the first machine to make Flex-O-Glass was built by Warp himself and pulled with a Ford crank. And to find his product under an alphabetic listing meant looking for it under "window glass substitute," because the word plastic was not yet in the vocabulary. In the 1920s glass substitutes were sheet Mica commonly called Isinglass, for little windows in hard coal heaters; Nitro-Cellulose commonly called Celluloid, for buggy and automobile side curtain windows; and Phenolic Bakelite, for transparent pipe stems and ignition parts. Two years after the introduction of Flex-O-Glass, DuPont introduced cellophane, and it was not until 1939 that Rohm & Haas introduced Plexiglas into the United States and agreed "not to use the word Plexiglas on any product especially intended, designed, manufactured or sold for use as a substitute for glass in poultry or other animal houses of all kinds, greenhouses, hotbeds or health rooms." The same year DuPont announced that Dr. W.H. Caruthers had discovered Nylon.

In 1933 Harold Warp developed Red Viotex, that when tacked over window openings, neutralized the color of blood to prevent cannibalism among chicks and pigs. For about five years the product sold, and then the reason for the cannibalism was discovered. It seems that the removal of the hulls from oats, a popular practice at the time, before feeding the chicks and pigs also removed certain ingredients such as furfural which the chicks and pigs needed. Lacking it, they turned on each other. This discovery made Red Viotex unnecessary. Various other Flex-O-Glass products followed, and in 1935 a highly versatile 12 inch steel interlocking fence, marketed as Flexo Fencinettes, was introduced. The wartime restrictions placed on steel after 1942 put an end to its production. In 1938 an open mesh of cotton cords between two layers of clear cellulose acetate butyrate was introduced as Glass-O-Net. The next year the same mesh was made of wire and sold as Wyr-O-Glass and, just before World War II, Warp introduced plastic screen, but could not get a patent on it because the patent office claimed it was merely a substitute for wire screening.

In 1954, after years of experimental work with various types of extrusion dies, Warp introduced to the hardware and building trade the very first wide polyethylene film, "Warp's Coverall." The first ad for it ran as the back cover of the June 10, 1954 *Prairie Farmer*. That year also saw the introduction of the first plastic floor runner.

> Red Viotex helped reduce piggy cannibalism.

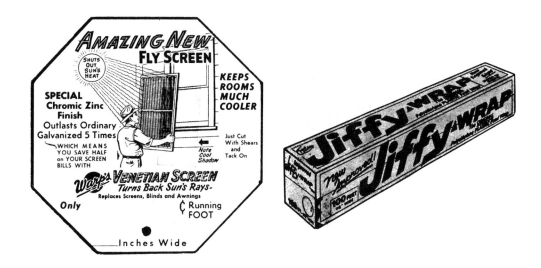

Warp took plastics to new lengths.

The following year the first film for skin-packaging or shrinkpack, now known as shrinkwrap was introduced as Flex-O-Film, Poly-Wrap and Warp-Wrap. It is hard believe that it took over six months of hard selling before the first order came in for this material, when today it is so common. In 1956 Warp introduced the first Polyethylene food wrap under the trade name Jiffy-Wrap. Later they introduced bags on continuous rolls. The variety and inventiveness of Warp's products, all created as solutions to some of life's simple problems, is truly phenomenal.

From the time he started in business, Harold Warp had been a believer in advertising; first in farm magazines and then in the 1930s on radio by starting the Flex-O-Glass Barn Dance Programs in cooperation with **Johnson's Aladdin Lamp Company** and Keystone Red Brand Fence. At the end of the radio age, WLS in Chicago honored the company for its 25 year sponsorship, which had heard the likes of Gene Autrey, Pat Butrum, George Gobel, Roy Rogers, Minnie Pearl, Lulu Bell and Scotty sing the praises of Flex-O-Glass.

Ployethylene film wrap for food was a hard sell.

TOMMY'S TEA ROOM AND GUN SHOP

Possibly the most famous aspect of the 1920s in Chicago, and the one that always raises the most interest among foreign visitors, are the gangsters that rat-tat-tatted their way into the world's image of the city. For a time legislated morality had its way. And as is usual when laws dictate morals, the underbelly of society flourished. The Prohibition caused about 250,000 workers to be unemployed in industries related to alcoholic beverages and the state lost an estimated $750,000,000 in taxes for the years prohibition was in effect. Taxes on tea, munitions and Tommy Guns did not make up these lost revenues.

Among the many developments of this era was bullet resistant glass. Beginning in 1922, the Prohibition and resulting changes in social behavior introduced law enforcement and the public to a level of violence to which they were not accustomed, and they clamored for protection.

One such group that was subject to an extraordinary amount of violence was the Chicago Police Department, who ordered bullet resisting windshields for its cars from the **Progressive Windshield Co.** No doubt the often wild tommy-gun assisted escapades on the streets of Chicago by the likes of the Capone gang and others was an influence in this purchasing decision. Progressive Windshield was begun in 1912 by Bernard Carsten as a manufacturer of windshields for cars and trucks. At the time windscreens, as they were called, were not original equipment that came with the automobile of your choice.

Just as the running of booze affected the Chicago Police Department, some Union leaders felt threatened by running their membership, and they decided to purchase bullet resisting windows for their offices as well as cashier areas where dues were paid. The demand generated by these two customers, and others that followed, was enough for Carsten to realize there was a future in protective glass. He changed the name of his company to **Chicago Bullet Proof Equipment Co. (CBP)** in 1928 to more aptly describe the company's line of products.

During the Depression, when many banks were reduced to currency exchange or local check cashing stations, CBP began manufacturing bullet resisting cages for these new facilities. These cages were the models of the present day modular guard enclosures and ticket booths that incorporate bullet resistant wall panels, transaction windows and doors. The high insurance rates charged currency exchange owners not equipped with bullet resisting equipment also spurred demand.

Chicago's police sought protection behind glass.

Chicago Bullet Proof could have saved the pane

The 1970s saw another major market open for CBP when the Nuclear Regulatory Commission instituted regulations concerning the security of nuclear power plants. To meet these regulations, CBP increased its product line to include Modular Guard Enclosures and bullet resisting/fire resisting doors and frames. In 1987 CBP became part of the **Florence Corporation** and entered a new

A modern bullet proof exchange

market that included convenience stores and service stations. Five years later, in 1992, Florence sold CBP and another subsidiary to Francis J. Sazama, Jr., who has since expanded the market internationally. Today Chicago Bullet Proof Equipment Co. is the leading designer, manufacturer and marketer of bullet resisting products in the United States.

Cut crystal was an important business in Chicago.

Another glass product, and one that counts among the least known industries in Illinois, is crystal cutting. This industry came into being in the 1880s at the hands of highly skilled Europeans, and Chicago was its center then.

Many materials became scarce with America's entry into World War I. Among them was glass, whose production slowed significantly because the government needed lead, a key ingredient of prismatic glass, for the war effort. Unable to get the necessary materials, many glass manufacturers and subsequently many glass cutting firms were forced out of business. The survivors turned their attention to producing less costly glass which flooded the market throughout the 1920s. By 1932 all lead crystal cutting firms, except for the Parsches', had closed in Chicago. **F.X. Parsche & Son Co.** was established in 1876 and produced cut crystal until about 1952. Parsche was a Bohemian whose firm hit its peak in 1905 when it employed 50 cutters.

Among the leaders in the field were **Pitkin & Brooks,** who were in business for about 50 years, from 1871 to about 1923. The enterprise was founded in Chicago by Edward Hand Pitkin and Jonathan William Brooks, and quickly became one of the largest wholesale and retail dealers in china and glassware in the country. Pitkin & Brooks manufactured its own cut and engraved glassware from the mid-1880s on, and by 1906 much of its cut glass was produced in two Chicago factories and a branch factory in Chicago Heights.

In its catalogue Pitkin & Books illustrate more than 300 different vases and serving pieces in 17 different patterns, often in three price ranges. An exquisite Pitkin & Brooks grade "Plymouth Pattern" punch bowl supported on a graceful pedestal base cost $175, or nearly four months' wages when figured at the average 1906 manufacturing scale of 17.5 cents per hour. At this price very few people could afford to buy a complete dinner service or decorate their homes extensively with cut glass. The second and third price range were more affordable and often imitated the first range but without the attention to detail and quality of cut.

Another Chicago cut crystal producer was **Monarch Cut Glass Company**, established in 1901 by Richard Emil, Otto Heinz, Edward E. and Frank Kotwitz. By 1905 the factory had outgrown its Chicago facilities and moved west to St. Charles. There the firm employed an average of 80 to 100 cutters. The **Central Cut Glass Company** began with five cutters when it was founded 1906 by Herman T. Roseen and Andrew Swanson, both immigrant Swedish glassworkers. Ten years later the firm employed 200 cutters.

The UNO-VEN Company's modern 153,000 barrel-per-day refinery, Romeoville — story on page 233

Courtesy of Michael Fitzsimmons, Decorative Arts, Chicago

Teco-Ware made Terra Cotta Illinois famous — story on page 24

Hot-rolled strip steel is coiled at Acme Steel Company, Riverdale — story on page 108

Ardco's frost free freezers — story on page 210

Remaking the original Weber grill — story on page 209

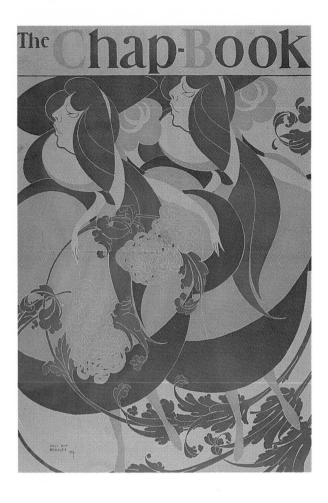
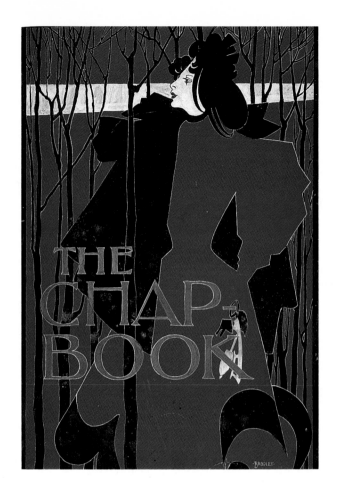
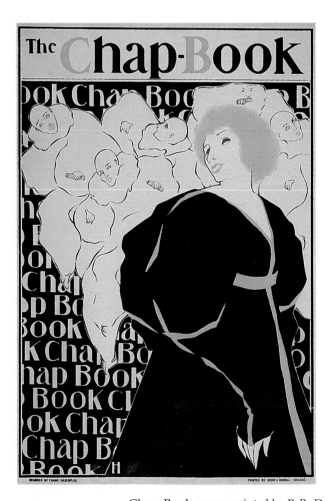

Chap-Book *covers printed by R.R. Donnelley for Stone & Kimball — story on page 84*

Courtesy of the Newberry Library

Deere marks its progress — story on page 37

Pfanstiehl is about chemistry, too — story on page 162

Videojet Systems' air knife blows away excess moisture — story on page 228

MacLean-Fogg's new truck wheel fastening system — story on page 221

Eli Bridge keeps on turning — story on page 93

Hart Schaffner and Marx ads were signs of the times — story on page 130

INDEPENDENCE FROM FOREIGN PRODUCTION

The use of stencils was very common in the eighteenth and nineteenth centuries, especially for repeating patterns on walls or ceramics. To use a stencil in printing was also known, but the application in a manufacturing context had to wait until certain developments had occurred in the 1920s. In 1920 John W. Marsh and his two sons, Walt and E.J., established **Marsh Shipping Services, Inc.** in Belleville. Two years later the company was renamed the **Marsh Stencil Machine Company** because the Marshes, with a handful of employees, had gotten out of the shipping business and into the manufacture of hand-operated stencil cutting machines, stencil oilboards, inks and brushes. In 1925 the company launched its products in Europe,

American modern inventiveness surpassed Europe in most everything.

too. As business grew the company expanded accordingly and took advantage of technological developments such as electrically operated stencil machines, which they were among the first to use. Renamed **Marsh Company** in 1987, the firm has been a leading manufacturer of a line of electronic microprocessor driven ink jet printers, such as the "Unicorn," a small LCP ink jet printer that has become the industry's standard. Marsh now presides over an array of innovative products protected by over 40 United States trademarks, 60 United States patents, 50 foreign trademarks and some 10 foreign patents.

One of the most important outcomes of World War I for the American economy was independence from foreign production of materials important to the United States. The shift away from Europe and towards self reliance showed Americans to be very inventive in things modern and they soon surpassed Europe in most everything. Many of the firms founded in the early 1920s around a certain industry or product are still with us, as is the product. Post war independence affected many industries, especially in the production of chemicals. In 1919 Carl Pfanstiehl, with the encouragement and help of the Federal Government, established **Pfanstiehl Laboratories**, dedicated to chemical independence in bio-chemical research and production of sugar chemical materials that had, until the war cut America off, only been available from Germany. Chemistry helped put Pfanstiehl in business, but it was not his only enterprise. Almost simultaneously Pfanstiehl established three other companies; chemical, metallurgical and detergent, each representing an interest of his and each in Waukegan.

As a high school student in Highland Park, Pfanstiehl traveled to England where he became fascinated by an x-ray machine. Returning to school he built a copy of this machine in his spare time for the Highland Park hospital. It was the first x-ray diagnostic machine in the nation and its maintenance was done by Carl Pfanstiehl after school.

A Highland Park high school student builds the first X-ray diagnostic machine in the United States.

Between 1919 and 1954 Pfanstiehl Laboratories prospered and for a time was owned by the **Babson Bros.** In 1954 Pfanstiehl became an independent company with headquarters in Waukegan. Today Pfanstiehl is the foremost corporation specializing in carbohydrate chemistry in the world and probably the only one of its kind in the United States. Typical areas of production are pharmaceutical intermediates, bulk finished pharmaceuticals, diagnostic chemicals, anti-viral compounds for treatments in areas such as cancer and AIDS, the bulk production of fine chemicals, industrial formulations ranging from ingredients for metal cleaners and bottle washing compounds to customer proprietary formulations used in concrete admixtures and in micronutrients for agricultural applications.

Pfanstiehl Chemical, the second branch, was also founded in 1919. It was set up as a metallurgical specialty producer of phonograph items such as needles and tone arms. It, too, became independent in 1954, and to this day produces not only needles and tone arms, but also video, telephone, audio components for computer use and auto stereos.

The third member of the trio, **Fansteel Inc.**, which changed the spelling of its name to differentiate it from the other two, was also founded in 1919. Fansteel is now located in North Chicago and manufactures spacecraft components, aerospace pressure vessels, castings, formed wire parts, metal cutting and coal mining tools.

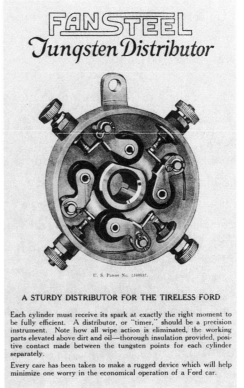

Fansteel's early ads

Among the many technical innovations of the 1920s was the first modern oil seal, patented in 1927 and manufactured in Chicago by **C.R. Industries**. Metal bellows seals manufactured by this same firm were used on the Apollo Space Craft. C.R. Industries now manufactures Elastomeic oil seals. These are considered a precision rubber product, but are not manufactured by most rubber companies.

Other sealing devices were developed by **White Cap, Inc.** of Downers Grove. This firm began in 1926 on Goose Island in Chicago. By 1930 White Cap had introduced vapor vacuum machinery that automated the sealing operation for applying metal closures to glass containers. From now on a jar could be vacuum packed just like a can. In 1956 White Cap introduced the "Twist-Off" lug, now a mainstay of the closure market.

In 1939 waxed paper came in rolls, finally.

As sealing things became more important, storage of the sealant became a concern, as did ease of access. To this end Nicholas Marcalus, founder of the **Marcal Paper Mills** of Chicago, invented a new way to package waxed paper. He started manufacturing his waxed paper products in 1939, at a time when waxed paper was the primary means of wrapping food for storage and was only available in waxed sheets, which stuck together in hot weather and in steamy kitchens. The invention, now the most obvious way to package paper, was a way to roll waxed paper on a paperboard tube and package it in a serrated dispenser box. Today **Marcal Chicago Division** (now a division of Marcal Paper Mills of Elmwood Park, New Jersey) produces roll wax, interfold waxed and baker tissue, waxed sandwich bags, doctor examination roll paper, kraft lunch bags and specialty printed waxed food wraps. The manufacture of these types of products is limited to about half a dozen companies in the United States.

"THAT SOMETHING EXTRA WAS SERVICE"

In the early 1920s there were some 80 sand and gravel companies operating in Chicago, and a company named **Material Services** ranked last. Having been founded just after the close of World War I by Sol and Henry Crown, it was a firm which owned no sources of raw material and had only a single distribution point, a 50 by 100 foot lot on North Crawford Avenue, and has since grown to be the largest producer and distributor of building materials in the Midwest. Recalling those early years, Henry Crown told an interviewer: "We started on the premise that our building material was really no different than any competitor's, so we had to provide something extra. That extra was better service...." One example will suffice. One Saturday evening in 1925, Crown was at the theater when the show was suddenly stopped and he was paged from the stage. Wacker Drive was then being built and the workers had run into water when sinking a caisson. Crown recalled years later, "that water hole had to be plugged right away and they needed sand and gravel to make the concrete plug it. I went out to our yard in that darned tuxedo, loaded a truck from a big hopper, and drove it to the project. It did the job, too."

Since that time concrete has been the mainstay of Material Service's business. Its bright red and yellow mixer trucks are a familiar sight in Chicago. The firm also maintains a fleet of barges and towboats, and operates a number of sand and gravel pits and stone quarries. Among these is the mammoth Thornton Quarry, the largest commercial limestone quarry in the world. It has been operated by Material Services since 1938 and has been producing stone since the last century. In 1960 Material Service merged with **General Dynamics Corporation**, one of the largest defense contractors in the world.

Thornton Quarry is the largest commercial limestone quarry in the world.

When the Merchandise Mart opened as the world's largest building in 1929, most of the floor forming had been done by Ceco, an innovative company founded by C. Louis Meyer in 1912 as the Concrete Engineering Company in Omaha. Seven years earlier, in 1922, the Ceco method had already been tested in Chicago on the Tribune Tower. Meyer developed a removable and reusable steel form to replace the traditional tile forms to form and support poured-in-place reinforced concrete-joist floors. His forms supplanted the forms previously left in the structure, which added to the weight of the building.

Meyer's innovation brought wide versatility to concrete as a building material and helped to extend its applications. In 1937 the company built a major plant and office in Cicero, and adopted the name **Ceco Steel Products Corporation**. Nine years later the corporate headquarters were transfered from Omaha to Cicero. To indicate its wide range of activities, six divisions and five subsidiaries, the firm eventually dropped "Steel Products" from its name and became the **Ceco Corporation**.

Among the many applications of Ceco's technology a few stand out: the Nebraska State Capitol, 1922; the Golden Gate Bridge in San Francisco, 1937; the United States Air Force Academy at Colorado Springs, 1959; the 70 story Peachtree Center Plaza in Atlanta, 1975; the New Orleans Superdome, 1975; Cincinnati's Riverfront Stadium, 1977; and in Chicago, 900 North Michigan, 1989. In 1980 the corporate headquarters were moved to a reinforced concrete structure, showcasing Ceco technology, in Oak Brook.

TO DO MORE WORK AT LESS COST...

After the United States stock market crash in the autumn of 1929 — echoed, and in some cases foreshadowed, by similar financial collapses around the world — it seemed to many that America had hit its industrial end and would not recover. But when **Caterpillar Corporation** of Peoria introduced the Diesel Sixty tractor in 1931, the company had something to make a depression-wracked world sit up and take notice. Just when customers had their backs to the wall because of the lack of work and their own operating costs, Caterpillar's diesel crawler gave them a dramatically effective tool to take the offensive — to do more work at less cost.

The Caterpillar diesel engine didn't just appear overnight. It was the fruit of years of patient research and testing. At the time there were those who thought it foolish to pour money into technology that was by many considered "exotic." Early diesel engines were slow in speed and extremely heavy in relation to the power they produced. Until the 1920s diesels were used almost exclusively in stationary and marine installations.

Caterpillar's experience with diesel engines predated the company's formation, which occured in 1925 when C.L. Best Tractor Co. merged with Holt Company, both of California. In 1889 Daniel Best had brought out his first steam traction engine. His Best Steam Harvester, patented in 1889, was a milestone in mechanized agriculture. Within two years more than 25 of the machines had been sold, but high costs kept it out of the hands of all but the most prosperous farmers. **Holt Manufacturing Company** had been incorporated in 1892 to manufacture combines, steam harvesters and steam traction engines. To increase the traction engine's area of contact with the ground, Benjamin Holt hit upon the idea of replacing wheels with tracks. Tracks were not a new idea — in fact, by the turn of the century well over 100 patents had been granted in the United States, England and France for track-type mechanisms. Holt, a successful company, could afford to build and test prototypes under working conditions. The company's metallurgical experience was of particular significance in building workable tracks. The first Holt track-type tractor was tested on November 24, 1904 and pronounced "a decided success." Soon after the test the Caterpillar trademark was coined by Holt. In 1909 Holt bought the East Peoria factory of the **Colean Manufacturing Company**, one of the many United States tractor manufacturers that failed to make the transition from steam to gasoline in the first decade of the century.

The first Peoria-built tractor, a 45 horsepower, two-speed model, was completed and demonstrated to Julius Funk of Bloomington. The tractor performed well and Funk bought it. Others did too, and **Holt Caterpillar Company** grew.

In 1904, the first Holt track-type tractor was a "decided success."

An early Caterpillar tractor

CATERPILLAR HELPS TANKS CRAWL IN WAR

Caterpillar track-type tractors won gold medals in Russia.

War tends to adapt technology to its own purposes faster than could ever be accomplished during peacetime. The discovery that crawler tractors were effective as hauling units for artillery and supplies under battle conditions was a gradual process. It began before World War I with isolated tests by European militaries. Probably the first and best look at the tractor's military potential was taken by the Hungarian Leo Steiner when he thought of using Holt's Caterpillar to work the difficult soil of his estates. By 1912 he had assumed the Holt agency for Austria-Hungary and Germany. The Holt's performance attracted the attention of the Austrian military. Tests proved successful and in 1913 Steiner was ordered to procure as many Holt tractors as possible. The outbreak of war caused Holt to decline the order and Steiner was ordered to manufacture crawlers. He lacked the engineering drawings, know-how and manufacturing capacity; yet he set to work. Eventually about 20 German tanks may have seen action in the war.

The English, too, became interested and in September, 1914 Holt engineers were sent to England. The British War Department in turn sent an officer to East Peoria. Earlier that year Lieutenant Colonel Ernest Swinton of the British Army conceived of an armored "machine gun destroyer" which was soon embodied as an armed, armored crawler. As military haulers, about 10,000 Holt tractors, mostly built in East Peoria, went into action for the Allies.

By 1929 the factory in East Peoria had 25 acres under roof, more than double its space of just four years before. Caterpillar was in fairly good health when the Depression hit because of exports. In particular, sales to the U.S.S.R. had proven a successful business. Holt tractors had been used in Russia in pre-Revolution times. In May, 1913 at St. Petersburg, the Imperial Automobile Club under the patronage of Czar Nicholas II held an exhibition and plowing contest to help celebrate the 300th anniversary of the Romanov dynasty. A Holt Caterpillar track-type tractor won gold medals, prompting the Russian army to buy machines for testing. After the Revolution the press to mechanize agriculture and collectivize farms into 20,000 to 400,000 acres throughout the country proved a boon to Caterpillar. The tractors were so successful that in the fall of 1929 an order was placed for 1,350 tractors. Other orders soon followed.

By late 1929 production had been combined to a new factory in East Peoria, Building HH. Corporate headquarters moved there soon after, as did the new Research Division. And from this new Research group came some of the most significant developments in Caterpillar's history.

Not long after Caterpillar was formed in 1925, company engineers began work on adapting the diesel for crawler use. After much research, "Cat" engineers decided they would have to design their own engine. It arrived in September, 1931. The first two Diesel Sixty tractors were ready; others followed off the assembly line in East Peoria. Another job now was to educate the users, many of whom were overzealous about the advantages of diesel. While fuel problems were relatively easy to correct, problems with lubricating oil were not. By the mid-1930s, with the help of an oil company, certain oil additives had been identified and oil companies began to market lubricants incorporating these ingredients as "suitable for use in Caterpillar diesels." The compounded lubricating oils used today in virtually all internal combustion engines are a direct outgrowth of this research. In 1933 Caterpillar's diesel production exceeded that of the entire United States in the preceding year. Within a few more years Caterpillar was among the world's largest producers of diesel power — and had the world's only moving assembly line for diesel engines.

By early 1933 Caterpillar had a completely new product line to sell — every model of tractor, engine and road machinery had been redesigned since 1930. The company's products even had a new color scheme. Beginning in 1932 the gray-with-red-trim colors carried by Holt were replaced with Caterpillar's soon-to-be-famous "Hi-Way Yellow."

Entry of the United States into World War II added urgency to a project Caterpillar had been working on since July of 1941: to convert gasoline-powered radial airplane engines to the diesel cycle for use in tanks. By January, 1942 a prototype radial diesel was ready. Within a month a subsidiary, the **Caterpillar Military Engine Company,** had been formed to manufacture 1,000 of the new RD-1820 engines per month. Decatur was chosen for the plant site. Also, in the spring of 1942 the company formed a Special Products Division to coordinate production of various military items. Among these were tank transmissions and final drives, shells and bomb fuses, howitzer carriages, fuel injection equipment, special machine tools and fixtures, and high speed and armored versions of standard track-type tractors.

In 1933 Caterpillar's diesel production exceeded that of the entire United States in the preceding year.

Caterpillar diesels in the 1930s

To relieve a shortage of aluminum cylinder head castings, the company set up an aluminum foundry at the East Peoria Plant. Completed in 1943, it was one of the most efficient aluminum foundries in the United States. Because of the man shortage, almost 85 percent of the employees working there were women. Production improvements developed in this foundry were adopted by the entire United States aluminum casting industry.

Almost 85 percent of Caterpillar's aluminum foundry employees were women.

In the years immediately following World War II, one of the biggest problems Caterpillar faced was getting enough product to customers. There was no post-war sales slump for the company as there had been following World War I. In the United States customers had been "making do" with obsolete equipment for years, building up demand. And the destruction in Europe and Asia called for construction equipment, too. By 1946 a major effort got underway to expand the East Peoria Plant by 50 percent. The important addition was a large new diesel engine factory, opened in 1947 as Building KK. Four new diesel engine models were introduced in 1949, followed in 1950 with two tractors, the DW20 and DW21.

In 1949 a completely new plant was begun near Joliet. Upon its completion in 1951, its products were scrapers, wagons, blades, rippers and controls. Beginning in 1953 a new plant was built in Decatur, which went into operation by mid-1955, manufacturing wheel tractors and motor graders. The next year a plant was opened in Aurora to produce D2 and D4 tractors and several models in the company's new line of Traxcavator loaders. During this decade Caterpillar also expanded internationally, opening subsidiaries in Australia, Brazil, the United Kingdom and Canada.

The 1960s saw massive changes that affected attitudes, expectations and life-styles of much of the world's population. Tens of thousand of miles of roads were built throughout the world; bigger airport runways to accommodate jets were needed, as was more energy, more water, more mining. In the United States the interstate road building program went into high gear and Caterpillar kept pace by introducing new product lines, such as a pipeline layer, off-highway trucks and front-end loaders. This decade also saw new subsidiaries and assembly plants in France, Mexico, South Africa, Belgium, Switzerland, Singapore, Hong Kong and Japan. Long the world leader in construction equipment, Caterpillar was now also seriously pursuing more of the materials handling equipment business.

In mid-1969 Caterpillar started on one of the largest development programs it had ever undertaken, the 3400 family of engines. Four years later, with Building BB nearing completion at Mossville, near Peoria, a 3046 engine was built in East Peoria. Early in 1974 production shifted to Building BB — then the most modern engine manufacturing factory in the world. It was designed solely to produce the 3400 family. Meanwhile, in 1972-73, the 3300 family of heavy-duty engines was introduced. Also in 1973, the remanufacture of used truck engines on an exchange basis was begun. This made Caterpillar the first United States producer of mid-range diesel truck engines to establish its own captive facility devoted exclusively to remanufacturing. Caterpillar resells the engines through the company's parts distribution system. In 1977 a plant in Pontiac began manufacturing fuel system components. Two years later a second major foundry opened at Mapleton, near Peoria, to increase capacity to produce engine blocks and heads. The success of the 1970s paved the way for expansion in the 1980s. In 1987 General Motors selected the 3116 as the only diesel option in a new line of medium-duty trucks; Navistar International Corporation selected Caterpillar as a major fuel system component supplier; and in October, 1988 the 3176 heavy duty diesel truck engine was unveiled by the Engine Division. Using electronics to control the engine, the 3176 set new standards in performance, economy and low emissions — a combination essential for truck engines of the 1990s.

American Flyer trains became very popular by the 1930s.

TOYS ARE MADE BY ADULTS

Just as big machines reworked the face of the earth, small ones replicated them and made them docile. For many, the 1920s and 1930s was the great age of toys, with Illinois standing at the center of their production. For example, the inventor of the American Flyer trains was William F. Hafner, a native Chicagoan and son of a soda fountain manufacturer. Born in 1870, Hafner, after a number of starts, established **Hafner and Company** in 1900 on Indiana and Kingsbury Streets, where he manufactured a clockwork swing and a windup toy auto. By 1904 Hafner's windup car was being produced in three body styles. Sales went very well and he added a new line of black cast-iron clockwork toy train engines. The accompanying tin railroad cars were lithographed by the **American Can Company**'s Homewood plant.

In January, 1907 Hafner, in partnership with William Ogden Coleman, landed a $15,000 order from Steinfield Brothers, New York Wholesalers, for four types of cast-iron trains. The new line was named American Flyer, and within a year Montgomery Ward was

Models copy the real thing

selling large numbers. In 1914 the Hafner and Coleman partnership ended. Hafner formed his third toy firm, called **Hafner Manufacturing Company**, while Coleman continued to head **American Flyer**. Hafner trains were bought out in 1951. By the 1930s Chicago's American Flyer had become one of America's two largest toy train manufacturers. To compete with Lionel trains of New York and others, American Flyer broadened their range. Following the lead of others, they began making electric trains in 1918 and in 1925 they added other gauges. In the 1930s they also produced an O gauge replica in cast aluminum of the Chicago, Burlington & Quincy's streamlined, diesel-powered Zephyr. Although sales suffered during the Depression, Flyer's Halsted Street factory in the Bridgeport neighborhood lasted until 1938, when A.C. Gilbert (of Erector set fame) bought them out and moved the company to New Haven, Connecticut. In 1966 American Flyer trains passed into history.

Many children wanted to play with cars that looked like the ones their parents were driving, and toy manufacturers soon produced Model Ts. **Structo Manufacturing Company** of Freeport was one of the important producers of toy cars at this time. Founded by Louis Strohacker in 1908, the company first began to market erector-set type construction toys. In 1923, however, Strohacker sold his patent and dies to A.C. Gilbert and devoted all of his energies to toy mechanical vehicles. In 1918 Strohacker had marketed a new toy concept: bolt-together metal cars in kit form, powered by a strong clockwork motor. The motors were wound by a separate hand crank like a real car of the 1920s; gears allowed the child to shift his orange and black roadster through three forward speeds. By 1921 Structo kits included trucks and tractors on the same principal. For the next 40 years the company prospered. Then in 1975 it was sold to the Ertl Company of Dyersville, Iowa, a major toy manufacturer specializing in farm machinery toys.

A giant of the American steel toy industry also made giant toys. This innovative company was Fred Lundhal's **Moline Pressed Steel Company** of East Moline, whose Buddy "L" toys were named for Fred's son. The company began in 1910 by producing steel trucks and farm machinery parts for the growing Illinois industry. In 1920 Fred Lundhal designed a large toy truck as a present for his son. It was constructed of steel from the company's scrap pile and weighed in at nine pounds of steel on a red, two foot long chassis with 4 ½ inch aluminum wheels. On his next birthday Buddy received a dump truck and his father saw a business opportunity. With orders from the famed new York toy store, F.A.O. Schwarz, and Chicago's Marshall Field's, Buddy "L" toys were introduced to the public in September, 1921. They were an immediate success. After the next year's annual New York toy trade show, the company's products were being handled by more than 300 jobbers and dealers. By 1925 the company was producing more than 200,000 large and expensive (at $5 and $10 apiece) steel toys a year. The Buddy "L" line did not survive the Depression and in 1942 the trade name was purchased by a New York manufacturer of wooden toys. The name still appears today.

The **Arcade Manufacturing Company** was founded in Freeport in 1895. It produced a broad line of hardware. In 1913 a young lawyer, Isaac Gassman, married Florence Munn,

Buddy "L" toys were sold at Marshall Field's.

whose father was company secretary. In 1919 Gassman succeeded him in his position and added to it the role of sales manager. Gassman hit on a novel scheme. He approached Chicago's **Yellow Cab Manufacturing Company** in 1921 seeking permission to market a faithful cast-iron replica of their cab. In turn, they would be able to use the toy in their advertising. Arcade made replicas of Fords, Chrysler Airflows, McCormick-Deering and International Harvester farm equipment, Mach and White trucks, among others. They also made castiron doll furniture, such as Thor washing machines, Hotpoint appliances and Crane bathroom fixtures. In 1927 Arcade built a new factory in Freeport. In 1933 they produced the most popular souvenir of the Century of Progress Exhibition, the white and blue tractor-trailer vehicle. Like most metal toy makers, they halted production due to restrictions on the use of raw materials during World War II, and shortly after the war they were sold to Rockwell Manufacturing of Pittsburgh. In the 1950s Arcade metal toys gave way to plastic ones.

The major toy manufacturer of the age was **Tootsietoys**. At the Columbian World's Exposition Charles O. Dowst, publisher of the trade paper *National Laundry Journal*, saw a new machine known as the Linotype, which cast lines of type from hot metal. By the turn of the century **Dowst and Company** was casting on a Linotype-like die casting machine a wide variety of charms and novelties for candy stores and prizes for Chicago's **Cracker Jack Company**. In 1911 Dowst produced the the world's first die-cast miniature toy car, and within a few years the company had become a giant maker of tiny toys. Dowst's second car was a faithfully reproduced Model T Ford and from then on Tootsietoys, like Arcade's toys, were intended to look real. In 1927 Tootsietoy introduced replicas of General Motor cars and in 1928 Henry Ford allowed Dowst to produce a two inch toy of Ford's new Model A, which came on the market that same year. In 1932 and 1933 the **Mack Truck Company** and the makers of Graham Paige automobiles actually subsidized development of Tootsietoy models of their trucks and cars. Creative management and low prices allowed Tootsie to thrive in the Depression, survive the war years, and continue on.

Blocks have had a large place in Chicago's toy industry. Even though we might not know the names of all the designers of blocks, children of all ages know their inventions. Charles H. Pajeau, of Evanston, and John Lloyd Wright, of Oak Park, are probably the best known wooden toy inventors in the nation. In 1912 Pajeau, then a tombstone manufacturer, moved to Evanston from New England and two years later developed Tinkertoys, an ingenious improvement on the discarded thread spools and sticks children had played with for ages past. Tinkertoy spools had eight holes around the edge and one through the center to fit quarter-inch diameter rods of several lengths. An endless variety of buildings, constructions and machines could be created. Pajeau went to the New York toy fair of 1914 to promote his product. While there, he persuaded a local druggist to put some Tinkertoy windmills with paper blades in his window. A fan supplied the wind, the blades turned, and Tinkertoys stopped traffic.

For a few years Pajeau ran a one-man, one-room shop; then in 1919 he took a partner and expanded. During the 1920s Pajeau's **Toy Tinkers Company** of Evanston introduced a

In 1911 Dowst produced the world's first die-cast miniature toy car.

variety of toys, but none came close to Tinkertoys. In the 1930s Tinkertoys got competition from another Illinois company, **W.R. Benjamin Co.** of Granite City. W.R. Benjamin patented a Tinkertoys look alike in 1937 and 1939 under the brand name Makit. Their slogan ran "Makit Toys of Today, Train Engineers of Tomorrow," but Makit never got the renown of Tinkertoys. By their fiftieth anniversary in 1964, over 55 million sets had been produced and were selling at a rate of two million annually. Purchased by **A.G. Spaulding** in 1952, it later became a part of **Questor Corporation**, but Tinkertoys have never lost their appeal and are still being made.

The other inventive toy was thought up by John Lloyd Wright, son of the architect, Frank Lloyd Wright. Wright's notched redwood logs were first marketed in 1918 by his own **Red Square Toy Company**. He soon developed a whole line of "unbreakable" and "safe" wooden toys, and changed the name of the company to the **John Lloyd Wright Toy Company**. By the early 1920s his involvement in the company's products had diminished to the point that he only held stock. The company was sold to Playskool in 1943.

Most small toy makers have not survived the ups and downs of the 20th Century, and either went out of business or were absorbed by other toy makers, such as Chicago's enormous **Playskool Corporation**. The Playskool Institute, as the company was first called, had been formed by two Wisconsin school teachers in the early 1920s, who were interested in improving wooden toys for pre-schoolers. By 1930 it was absorbed into Chicago's **Thornecraft, Inc.;** then in 1938 acquired by the Joseph Lumber Company, and in 1968 by the Milton Bradley Co. Each owner recognized the value of the Playskool name and retained it.

ELECTRIC ACTION HELPS ORGANS AND FURNITURE

Just as with the manufacture of toys, Illinois' role in the production of major musical instruments is important, but has not been readily recognized. Yet the **Wicks Organ Company** of Highland is counted among the finest organ manufacturers in the world. Wicks has been producing pipe organs since 1906, and in 1914 gained international attention in the musical world by developing a direct electric action pipe organ. This device greatly simplified the operation and maintenance of an organ. It was patented in 1922 by John F. Wick.

As in all manufacturing that involves the assembly of parts, the need to maintain consistency in the individual pieces is very imporant, so from its beginning Wicks has manufactured all its own parts. The founder of the firm, John Wick, an organist, built his first organ in the late 1800s on the second floor of a jewel store in Highland. That instrument still plays today. Originally installed in St. Paul's Catholic Church in Highland, it was later moved to St. Anthony's Church in Lively Grove. In the early 1970s the organ was repurchased and returned to the factory. There it was cleaned and repaired and then donated to the university museum at Southern Illinois University in Carbondale. Wick

Wicks developed a direct electric action pipe organ.

and his brothers, Adolph and Louis, continued building pipe organs, incorporating as the **Wicks Pipe Organ Company** in 1906. By 1910 electropneumatic action was becoming a popular replacement for mechanical action. But the Wick brothers believed it possible to make the organ action entirely electric and eliminate perishable materials, specifically leather. They began working on the idea in 1914 and produced an electric-action organ by year's end. It took some doing to perfect the small copper and steel magnetic device that replaces the wood and leather of pneumatic systems. The device was patented in 1922 and improvements on it were again patented in 1929. A modern variant of it is still manufactured.

Chicago made
one-fifth
of America's
furniture, then.

The console department at Wicks Pipe Organ Company in the 1920s

That Chicago was the nation's lumber port for much of the nineteenth century has been much publicized, but that at the same time and for long afterwards it was also a major furniture manufacturing center remains less well known. In 1924 a survey conducted by the Chicago Association of Commerce revealed that there were 294 furniture factories located in Chicago, with a total of 15,715 employees. Of these firms, 49 made upholstered furniture, including 35 who made davenport (sofa) beds (named after a Boston upholsterer) and seven who made this item exclusively; 21 manufactured metal furniture; 19 made office furniture; 20 turned out case goods and dining-room furniture; and 65 made novelty furniture. In addition, 16 factories created rattan and reed goods, eight made chairs, seven manufactured tables and 13 made only parlor frames.

Throughout the 1920s the output of Chicago's furniture factories soared, keeping pace with a building boom that filled the city's, as well as the nation's, downtowns with new skyscrapers and encircled them with new residential, institutional and commercial buildings. In all, Chicago's furniture manufacturers turned out as much as one-fifth of the furniture made in the United States and at least 14 buildings of various sizes stood along

Michigan and Wabash Avenues, housing samples of furniture made by factories located in a crescent formed around the lake by Wisconsin, Illinois, Indiana and Michigan.

Although a few of the firms employed between 300 and 1,000 workers, the industry as a whole was still composed of a large number of small companies. Many were family owned and operated by a team of brothers, or by more than one generation, such as **S. Karpen & Bros., Fenske Bros.** and the **Kroehler Manufacturing Co.** As in the previous century, the majority of the factory owners and most of the workers were foreign born. While most of the woodworkers were German, others had come from Italy, Lithuania, Holland and Scandinavia. The upholsterers included large numbers of Poles, Scandinavians, Bohemians and Germans. In contrast to earlier decades, a growing number of women could be found in the ranks of the semiskilled and skilled, performing such tasks as assembling, upholstering and finishing.

In the larger factories assembly-line procedures allowed the use of numerous semiskilled and unskilled workers. Furniture sales reached a peak in 1927. Of all American furniture workers, those working in Illinois were the highest paid. During the Great Depression many of Chicago's furniture makers went out of business, others managed to survive by reducing their workforce, cutting wages and modifying their product lines.

During the 1920s the popularity of bridge playing, cocktails, the radio and phonograph, curios, magazines and babies led to the production of countless card tables, cocktail tables, hostess carts, console cabinets, curio cabinets, magazine racks and baby cribs. In 1941 Chicago outranked all other cities in total pieces of furniture produced; some three million, that is, some 11,500 items each working day.

Many of the items were sold to large volume dealers such as Sears, Roebuck & Co., Montgomery Ward & Co., **Spiegel** and the **Hartman Furniture & Carpet Co.** By buying large quantities, the mail-order firms were able to offer the furniture at prices lower than those charged by retailers for similar pieces. Direct shipping also reduced the cost of overhead and handling since customers paid the freight charges and unpacked the furniture themselves.

By the mid-1920s several factories making wooden furniture had located in the new Central Manufacturing District (CMD) developed on Chicago's Near-South side. Among them was the **Martin Polakow Corporation**, a large producer of "occasional" furniture, who by 1927 was shipping 3,000 pieces of furniture per day. There was also the **Milano Furniture Company**, with its slogan of "Rain or shine, a daily new design."

Metal had been used to make furniture in Chicago as early as the 1890s by **A. H. Andrews & Co.**, the **Royal Metal Manufacturing Co.** and the **Tonk Manufacturing Co.** However, it was not until the 1920s that the **W.H. Howell Company** began to produce steel furniture in stylish shapes suitable for use indoors as well as in the garden. The Howell Company had a factory in Geneva from 1924 to 1935, and in St. Charles from 1936 to about 1979, with showrooms in Chicago.

The Howell line underwent a drastic change in 1929, when the company's owners first saw tubular chairs designed by Ludwig Mies van der Rohe and Marcel Breuer. Importing samples of the chairs from Germany, Howell employees adapted the design for production by the firm. Within a year a series of chairs, armchairs and settees had been created, with tubular steel frames chrome-plated for indoor use and enameled for outdoor use. These Howell products "can probably be regarded as the important beginnings for tubular steel furniture in America," Murray Moxley, former vice-president of the company, said. The use of tubular steel furniture in 87 percent of the exhibition buildings at the 1933 World's Fair, the Century of Progress, promoted the acceptance of metal furniture by the American public and helped establish it as an essential element of the modern interior.

Patent number 701,839 belongs to the first glassine window envelope.

MORE PAPER

Another important development occurred to the Central Manufacturing District when in 1938 the **Stone Container Corporation**, a leader in the field of corrugated packaging, made a deal with the CMD and a local architect, A. Epstein, who was developing a new industrial center in the Crawford Avenue area. The Stones bought land at 42nd Place and Keeler Avenue for 50 cents per square foot and contracted to erect a 150,000 square foot building solely for the manufacture of corrugated containers. Stone Container began operations in a shared one-room office as **J.H. Stone & Sons** in late 1926, under the guidance of Joseph H. Stone, who worked for a paper company in Chicago selling paper and boxboard. His oldest son, Norman H. Stone, worked for a firm that sold paper, twine, tissue, tape and used and new boxes. By 1927 the company was established and grew as a packaging supplier. Five years later Stone expanded outside Illinois. They bought raw materials suppliers and expanded aggressively over the next 30 years, developing along with the ever increasing container market. Along the way a number of important corrugated products were developed, including Super Stone Cor, to meet higher warehouse stacking needs; Stone-A-Matic, a corrugated container that becomes an instant box without tape; and industrial skin packaging machines and materials.

Another company that focused on paper was the **Continental Envelope Corporation**, founded in Chicago in 1936. And it should not be forgotten that Americus F. Callahan, of Chicago, was awarded patent number 701,839 on June 10, 1902 for the first "outlook" or window envelope. In the 1930s the glassine window envelope became a standard business tool and established the **Regenstein Company of Chicago** as the nation's leader in envelope production.

While paper was the backbone of the office, the office secretary became one of the most important individuals in the firm because of her skill with machines, especially the typewriter. The **Woodstock Typewriter Co.** was the largest manufacturer in Woodstock in 1939. And in Chicago, the **Oliver Typewriter Co.** had its own building downtown, at 159 North Dearborn.

At the same time as the American office began to develop, the consumption of paper publishers in the Chicago found paper dolls in great demand and turned them out by the millions. At that time the **Merrill Publishing Company** was the most successful paper doll company in America. Marion Merrill started the company in 1934, joining forces with **Regensteiner Printing and Publishing Company** of Chicago. By 1944 Merrill was the second largest publisher of children's books in the nation. Capitalizing on the American fascination with Hollywood's stars like Bette Davis, Jeanette McDonald and Vivian Leigh, the company stayed in business until 1956.

Treated water
steams better.
Conditioned water
heats better.

BOILER SCALE REQUIRES SCRUBBER

Along with the development of the high rise building in Chicago came a number of technical problems, many of which were solved there. The elevator, though not invented in Chicago, was definitely perfected here. It made tall buildings accessible. The revolving door, also only perfected here, helped control the airflow within a building, which in turn kept the elevator doors from reacting to drafts by opening when there was no cab to step into. Other developments occurred in heating and cooling, especially boiler maintenance and general water treatment, which the National Aluminate Company helped perfect.

Nalco was officially established in 1928 as **National Aluminate Corporation**, but its story began in 1922 when Herbert A. Kern, of **Chicago Chemical Company,** and P. Wilson Evans, of **Aluminate Sales Corporation,** first met. Both firms were selling sodium aluminate; Chicago Chemical to industrial plants for boiler feedwater treatment, and Aluminate Sales to railroads for treatment of water used in steam locomotives.

Kern had organized Chicago Chemical in 1920, marketing a product called Colline to plants in the Chicago area. In trying to extend sales to other parts of the Midwest, he and his associates discovered that while Colline was very effective on Chicago water, it was not a universally applicable product. He went on to find that a compound called sodium aluminate, a liquid variant which he patented, was far more effective than Colline on many types of water.

About the same time, Evans discovered the benefits of sodium aluminate. He too had a patent on a liquid form and had established Aluminate Sales in 1922, selling his solution primarily to railroads for steam locomotive boiler feedwater treatment. Kern sought out Evans as a possible supplier to meet the needs of his water treatment business and, in 1928, they formed National Aluminum Corporation, better known as Nalco. The same year, Nalco helped organize a small venture in Texas known as Visco Products Company. The firm sold an additive for drilling mud (which is a mixture of clay and water used in the drilling of oil wells). This product helped establish Nalco in the oil industry, which eventually became its biggest customer.

In 1930 Nalco bought Paige-Jones Chemical Company of New York and with it acquired the equipment and rights to supply water treatment chemicals in convenient and easy to feed ball briquette form. The result was a large increase in its water treatment business. Two years later, Nalco went international by establishing Alfloc, Ltd. in England. In 1937 National Aluminate undertook a major expansion. A new building, housing offices and laboratories, was built on the company owned site in the Chicago Clearing Industrial District. The building was one of the first large, windowless, air conditioned facilities in the country.

During World War II National Aluminate was classified as an essential industry. A second plant was built in Chicago at the request of the government to produce catalysts required in the production of high-octane aviation fuel. The postwar boom saw the replacement of steam locomotives with diesel and virtually eliminated half of Nalco's business. "Finding a customer need and filling it" became the corporate theme. New water chemistry solutions were found and the company gained a strong reputation in Europe. In April of 1959 the corporation changed its name officially from National Aluminate Corporation to **Nalco Chemical Company**. By now the company had become a leading supplier of specialized chemicals and technology, selling, in addition to water treatment, process chemicals for the paper making, oil refining, steel and metal working industries.

At about the same time advanced polymer technology began to play an important role in helping Nalco maintain leadership in water chemistry and point the way in the emerging field of waste management and pollution control. During the 1960s new plants were built or enlarged in Illinois, Louisiana, Texas, California, Georgia and New Jersey. International expansion brought subsidiaries and affiliates in Austria, Brazil, Chile, Colombia, Finland, France, Holland, Japan, the Philippines, Sweden, Saudi Arabia, Taiwan and South Africa.

In 1980 additional construction and expansion focused on a 147 acre site in Naperville and business opportunities were developed in the People's Republic of China, while subsidiaries or affiliates were established in Argentina, Ecuador and Hong Kong. New manufacturing plants were constructed in Italy, Spain, France, Colombia, Venezuela and Singapore. During the 1980s Nalco was considered the world leader in industrial water treatment and other specialty chemicals that improve operating efficiencies and minimize energy consumption in water, waste and process systems.

Streator became a major glass producing center by 1900.

SILICA RULES

The first half of the1930s is remembered as the Great Depression. By January, 1933 more than 1,500,000 of the 3,184,875 gainful workers in the state as a whole and nearly 850,000, almost half of the gainful workers in Chicago, were unemployed. But at the same time, the production of American glass at the industrial level emerged as a strong industry, with Illinois as one of the leaders. Streator, where beds of siliceous sand used in the manufacture of glass were easily available, as were quantities of coal, already had a small glass bottle works in 1873. The city became a major glass producing center by 1900. Nearby, in

Ottawa, the **Libby-Owens-Ford Glass Factory** used the local St. Peter sandstone, a superior glass sand, to produce the finest window glass manufactured in the United States, while another local plant produced more than 1.5 million "Mibs" and "Shooters" per day in the 1930s. In Alton, the **Owens-Illinois Glass Factory** claimed to be the largest bottle-producing factory in the world. Each of its glass blowing machines had 10,000 moving parts.

In Ottawa more than 1.5 million "Mibs" and "Shooters" were produced per day in 1930.

Wedron Silica's innovative storage silos in the 1930s.

Wedron Silica is one of the nation's major producers of premium quality round grain silica sand, mined from the St. Peter's sandstone formation in the Ottawa area. For over a century Wedron's principal markets have been the glass industry, foundries, hydraulic fracturing and abrasives, with additional sales to the construction, filtration and specialty markets. Crude sand was first mined in 1890 by the **Garden City Sand Co.** In 1894 the land was sold in its entirety to the **Wedron White Sand Company**. Additional sand was acquired from **Keen Kleener Manufacturing** of Ottawa, a producer of cleansers and abrasives. In 1916 **Wedron Silica Company**, a corporation, was acquired as an independent holding of the **Chicago Brick Company**.

In the late nineteenth century the actual mining process was quite complicated. First the overburden had to be removed from the area to be mined. A narrow gauge steam railway was used. The sand was mined by pick axe and shovel and then transported by mule or horse-drawn wagons to the production site, where it was loaded into hand sewn burlap bags made by local women before it was hauled onto rail cars.

The first grinding mills were installed in 1925 for grinding silica sand into silica flour. **Wedron Silica Company** soon became one of the country's largest producers of silica flour. This process was discontinued in 1983 so that Wedron could concentrate exclusively on the production of whole grain sand. By 1927 hydraulic mining was being used at Wedron. It was the idea of an employee who did not patent it. In the early 1930s two round storage silos of common brick, supplied by the Chicago Brick Company, were built. Each had a capacity of 500 tons. These silos were the first of their type in the United States and continued in use until 1983, when they were replaced by a new loading system. During the 1940s United States foundries and arsenals needed much sand, and Wedron, to attract more labor, built company housing.

Since the late 1960s Wedron has had a very lively history, one that mirrors American industrial strategy as a whole. In 1969 Wedron merged with **Del Monte Properties,** forming **WSC,** and growing from one to five plants. Another name change came in 1977, when Del Monte became **Pebble Beach Corporation** with WSC as a subsidiary. One year later Twentieth Century Fox purchased Pebble Beach Corporation and all of Wedron Silica's holdings. In 1979 Martin Marietta Corporation purchased Wedron Silica Division from Twentieth Century Fox, which brought their total number of plants in the Industrial Sand Division to 12. Then, in 1983, Martin Marietta divested all of its holdings in the Industrial Sand Division with the exception of Wedron. The next year Best Sand Company of Chardon, Ohio and the Wedron management group entered into an agreement to purchase the sand plant from Martin Marietta. At the time of the purchase Wedron had just completed a major expansion and modernization to increase efficiency. In 1986 the holdings of Wedron and **Best Sand Company** were merged into a new company called **Fairmont Minerals Limited.**

From the 1930s on Illinois has also been a center for the production of fine porcelain. When Austin Pickard took over the family business he dreamed of manufacturing fine china in Illinois. His dream began to be realized in 1930 when Pickard started to experiment with porcelain. It took seven years before the Pickard formula was fully developed. Further experiments produced a glaze that was both hard and brilliant and still is considered by many experts to be the finest in the industry. Production moved to Antioch in 1937. Soon Pickard became known for creating beautiful white china as well as decorations. Today **Pickard, Incorporated** manufactures a wide array of collector's plates, and beginning in 1989 was responsible for "The Presidential Bowl," which commemorates the bicentennial of the United States Presidency. The first order was placed personally by President George Bush.

Though Pickard has been in the ceramic business for one hundred years, it did not always manufacture porcelain. The Pickard China Studios was established in Edgerton, Wisconsin in 1893 by Wilder Austin Pickard and moved to Chicago in 1897. For the next four decades Pickard China Studio was a decorating company specializing in hand painted art pieces, dessert and tea sets. Many of the artists at the time were from the Art Institute of Chicago. The staff was increased by renowned ceramic artists from Europe. Since most of the fine china was manufactured abroad at the time, the Pickard studios imported blank ware, mostly from Germany and France, to be decorated.

Wedron was the nation's largest producer of silica flour in 1925.

Illinois
manufacturers
fine porcelain.

Some of Pickard's painted porcelain products from the 1930s.

In 1977 Pickard was selected by the United States Department of State to manufacture the official china used by American Embassies and other diplomatic missions abroad. The special decoration has an embossed gold border of stars and stripes and an embossed reproduction of the Great Seal of the United States. Since then, the contract to produce the Embassy service has been renewed twice, following competition open to all American manufacturers. Further, Pickard has been selected to produce exclusive fine china services for heads of state and many hotels, restaurants and corporations. Recently Pickard was commissioned to produce a new custom china for Air Force One, Blair House and Camp David.

CONVENIENCE RUNS ON ELECTRICITY

The 1920s and 1930s saw a flood of new appliances brought to market as the desire for a more comfortable life through material consumption became a possibility for many. At the same time electricity became more convenient as it began to reach the most distant corners of habitation. Utility companies sprang up everywhere, resulting in competition which lowered the price of electricity, which in turn spurred on the development to satisfy the desire for electric appliances and other things that used electricity. The utility companies also got in the act by offering appliances as premiums for services bought. Among the new appliances was the pop-up toaster, developed in 1919 by the Waters-Genter Company of Minneapolis who, in 1924, also gave it the now world famous Toastmaster trademark. Two years later the company was bought by Chicago's **McGraw Electric Company**. Other appliances had been around for a few years but were given a new look in the 1920s. Among these was the dishwasher invented by George Walker, a Chicagoan, in 1909. The same year the electric stove was invented by George Hughes in a basement just south of the Loop. Hughes would later found Hotpoint.

The 1920s and 1930s were also a time when high schools were becoming more accessible through the automobile. High schools, in turn, started to develop after school programs such as athletic activities that required keeping accurate time and scores easily. The **Nevco Scoreboard Company** of Greenville was founded in 1939 by Ralph A. Nevinger at a time when electric scoreboards were not well known. Nevco was among the first companies to replace the "flip-card" score keepers with electric scoring and timing scoreboards. Allowing the fans to see the time, instead of having only the game's time keepers controlling it with their watches, helped add excitement to the game and accuracy in timing. The first scoreboard was manufactured by Nevinger and two employees as a wooden cabinet of oak, with a few dozen wires and some bulbs behind painted glass discs for the scores. The first scoreboard was sold to Williamsville High School, in Williamsville. At first the scoreboards were mostly for basketball and manufactured one at a time and then taken out and sold, but as they gained in popularity orders began to come in and scoreboards went into production. Today Nevco scoreboards are used for many sports and operate on only two wires that feed sophisticated solid state electrical equipment.

Keeping score made games more popular.

An early Nevco scoreboard.

MAKING DENTISTS SMILE

The mass production of candy also came into prominence during the years between the world wars. **Heath Brothers Confectionery**, founded in Robinson, today stands at the core of the international candy conglomerate, Leaf. Leaf was formed in December of 1983, when Huhtamaki Oy, a Finnish conglomerate, purchased **Leaf Confectionery**, the confectionery division of Beatrice Foods and the Donruss Division of General Mills. The acquisition included many products, among them: Whoppers, Milk Duds, Jolly Ranchers, Switzer, Good & Plenty, Good n' Fruity, Super Bubble, RainBlo and Pal Bubble Gum. There are also baseball card packets such as Donruss, Studio Set, Leaf Set and Triple Play. Heath Brothers Confectionery was established in 1914 in Robinson. As their items grew in popularity, the brothers became more interested in the candy making aspects of the business. They took a basic recipe of butter, sugar and almonds cooked together and developed it further. After many months of trial and error, the brothers declared their formula for "English Toffee" to be "America's Finest," and dubbed it Heath English Toffee in 1928.

At the height of the Depression, in 1932, a Heath bar was introduced weighing only one ounce. At the time most other candy bars weighed four ounces and many in the industry were doubtful that the Heath bar would succeed. It proved to be the right size for the times.

In 1964 Heath entered the fundraising business by selling candies directly to schools and other organizations for the purpose of re-selling to raise funds for special events. In early 1970 Heath acquired the Fenn Brothers of Sioux Falls, South Dakota and added their Butter Brickle brand to the Heath line. At the same time Heath introduced Bit O'Brickle, small bits of toffee for baking. In 1980 Heath developed an industrial division to supply other manufacturers with the Heath products. Among the users were Ben & Jerry, Nabisco and Dairy Queen. In 1987 Heath introduced Mint Meltaways. In January 1989 at the start of Heath's 75th year, it was acquired by **Leaf, Inc.**

Another member of the Leaf line-up is Hollywood Brands. By purchasing the Pratt and Langhoft Candy Company of Minneapolis, Minnesota in 1922, Frank A. Martoccio, who was a macaroni producer, got in the candy business. Six years later he acquired the Pendergast Candy Company, also of Minneapolis. In 1936 Frank and his son Clayton sold the macaroni factory to focus on candy. Searching for an appropriate manufacturing site, **Hollywood Brands** found it in a former envelope factory in Centralia. At the time of the move, Hollywood Brands was producing Butternut, since 1916; Polar, since 1924; PayDay, since 1932; and Milkshake and Zero, since 1933. Over the years the Hollywood line expanded and contracted with such candies as: Red Sails, Smooth Sailin, Hail, Big Time, Three Little Pigs, Three Bears, 747, Dazzle, Picnic, Chills, Pecan Picnic, Big Pay, Top Star, All Star, Magic, Nut Sundae, Spot Pecan, Taffy Nut, Aero, Snow King and Hollywood.

In the 1960s Hollywood Brands was the number two producer in total volume of candy nationally, with plants in Centralia (employing up to 700 people), Ashley and one in Montgomery, Alabama. In 1967 the Matoccio family sold Hollywood to **Consolidated Foods, Inc.** of Chicago (later to become **Sara Lee Corporation**). A disastrous fire in 1980 almost put an end to Hollywood, but within three years the plant was rebuilt and Centralia was the home to a state-of-the-arts candy making facility, capable of producing nearly three million candy bars per day. In 1988 Hollywood Brands was acquired from the Sara Lee Corporation by Leaf.

Milk Duds, the brain child of Milton J. Hoolway in 1926, six years after he acquired **F. Hoffman & Company** of Chicago, combined two of the most popular candy ingredients, chocolate and caramel. The name came about because the original idea was to have a perfectly round piece. Since this was impossible, the word "dud" came to mind and the main ingredient, milk, made up the other half of the name. In 1960 Holloway sold his company to Beatrice Foods from whom it was acquired by Leaf. From 1926 to 1992 Milk Duds were produced in Chicago, then production moved to Leaf's Robinson facility.

Only a Chicago-area based company since 1966, **Tootsie Roll Industries** has long been viewed as a local firm, for reasons known best to its marketers. The round piece of chewy, chocolate candy that delights Americans today is said to still look and taste amazingly like the first Tootsie Roll Leo Hirschfield, an Austrian immigrant, hand-rolled in 1896 in New York from recipe he had brought from Europe. The roll was the first penny candy to be individually wrapped in paper. Another famous Tootsie Roll product was the soft-center lollipop, first produced in the 1930s. Today the company turns out about 12 million pops daily. In 1966 it was necessary to open a Midwest facility in the Ford City Industrial Park on Chicago's south side. By 1968 this facility had become the company's main plant.

Arguably among the most profound innovations in food products came about in 1930 when James Dewar of Schiller Park, while he was manager of **Continental Baking Co.**'s Hostess Bakery, invented the Hostess Twinkie. At the time Continental Baking (now headquartered in St. Louis, but with a number of baking facilities in Illinois) was producing a line called little Short Cake Fingers, which were baked in aluminum pans, but only during strawberry season. Dewar thought that if he could inject cream into the fingers they could be sold year-round. Originally Twinkies were filled by hand, a laborious process that has since been automated to an air injection cream filling. Twinkies got their name from a billboard advertising "Twinkle Toe Shoes" which must have looked like two little yellow ballet shoes, and originally sold two for a nickel, the same price as a pound of sugar in 1930. For over sixty years Twinkies have been popular. Today more than a half million hens lay the 160 million eggs it takes to produce the 500 million Twinkies eaten annually by Americans.

It's not perfectly round, it must be a dud.

ILLINOIS OIL MADE THE 20TH CENTURY MOVE

Just as coal was found under Illinois soil to power the communal needs of the 19th century, so oil from beneath the corn, soybeans and pastures of the state has made our 20th century the one for individual mobility. Illinois ranked third among crude oil producing states in 1907; by 1990 Illinois ranked 10th by bringing in about 23 million barrels of oil (from an estimated six billion barrel reserve), most of it through stripper wells that yield two to five barrels a day. This may seem piddling stuff compared to the pumpers of West Texas or the Middle East, where some wells produce 10,000 barrels a day, but it is ours, it is another product of the resource rich Illinois Basin that begins in Champaign County and sprawls in a wide oval south into Indiana and Kentucky.

Litchfield was the scene of Illinois' first oil production.

In 1882 Litchfield was the scene of the first commercial oil production in Illinois. The small pocket then tapped has long ago gone dry. Bridgeport, which gave its name to the first oil producing sand in Illinois, was the center of another early oil boom. Other towns quickly followed. Crude oil production climbed steadily for a time: 1889-1890, two barrels; 1890-1900, four barrels; and 1900-1910, 12,713 barrels.

A town such as Lawrenceville, in the heart of the Lawrence County oil fields, brought in its first oil well in 1906 and produced the first paraffin-free oil in 1924. Martinsville was platted in 1833, but didn't really develop until 1904, when it became an oil and gas boom town. By 1916 the oil was drained out of Martinsville.

In 1940 the Illinois Pipeline Tank Farm stored oil pumped to Martinsville from Texas, Oklahoma and points in the Illinois basin. A major Standard Oil Refinery was established at Wood River, near East Alton, in 1907 because of superb river and rail access. In 1927 a Shell Refinery was established in Roxana, next to Wood River. For a decade Illinois oil boomed, but by the start of World War I, when the nation began to really need oil, Illinois' wells produced only a trickle. But the search continued. In 1928 oil was discovered in Dupo. A boomlette followed.

Then, in the late 1930s, came a second boom. A few miles southeast of Clay City, the first oil well in Clay County was brought in on February 26, 1937. In the same year, Patoka was the center of an oil boom. In 1939 Salem, seat of Marion County, was home to the second largest oil field in the United States. That year, too, Linco Tank Farm in Martinsville contained 43 oil storage tanks and St. Elmo, founded 1830 by a group of Kentucky Catholics, was an important brick manufacturing center before it became an oil boom town in 1939.

And again in the 1960s oil gushed forth. This time oil was found by Lloyd Harris, a geologist and oil man from Matoon who was nearly broke from investing in failed wells, while examining core samples taken by a power company looking for underground storage for natural gas. The geologist went to an area near Wapella in DeWitt County and took more samples. Collecting a few very skeptical investors, among them Alf Thompson, the near legendary oilman of central Illinois, a test well was sunk. The field has produced oil ever since, over four million barrels. Other companies followed, but none have hit oil in the area.

Most of the oil pumped in the Illinois Basin ultimately went to Chicago, the area around which has had the second or third largest concentration of petroleum refineries in the United States for much of this century and which, at Petoca, is still the major pipeline crossroads of America. This crossroads was the primary target of Soviet ICBMs during the "Cold War." If it could be knocked out, it was thought by some, the United States would quickly come to a standstill and its defeat would be assured.

Petoca was a hot spot in the "Cold War."

During the 1940s and 1950s these underground pipelines supplied the refineries in the Chicago area, the largest of which was Standard Oil Company of Indiana at Whiting and East Chicago, Indiana. Other refineries included Sinclair, Petco, Cities Service, Socony-Vacuum, Pure Oil and Texas Companies, plus many independents, all located in the Lake Calumet area.

In 1952 Illinois consumed 1.5 billion gallons of gasoline at an average price of 28.3 cents a gallon. It was dispensed through 13,600 service stations. By the mid-1970s there were just over 10,000 service stations in the state and in 1990 there were about 5,800 service stations pumping out 5.3 billion gallons of fuel per year. The decline in the number of service stations was due to the increasing costs of the business. In 1990 a station had to sell about 600,000 gallons a month just to stay in business, while in the 1950s, 50,000 to 60,000 gallons would have sufficed.

Illinois was the 4th largest refining state in the nation in 1990, after Texas, California and Louisiana, and the 10th largest producer of crude oil, with some 60,000 employees in oil and oil related industries.

In the early 1980s there were 10 refineries in the state; by the early 1990s there were seven. These seven refineries are located in three general areas: Blue Island, Romeoville and Joliet; Roxana by St. Louis; and in Robinson and Lawrenceville. Of these, the Shell refinery at Roxana is the largest in the state and the Mobile refinery in Joliet is the last refinery site allocated by the United States Government to date; that was in 1970.

The interstate transmission of natural gas began in a big way in 1930 when the Continental Construction Company, now the **Natural Gas Pipeline Company of America (NGPL)** was organized to build a 900-mile gas pipeline from the Texas Panhandle to the Chicago area. In its day the company was a leader in developing underground storage techniques. Today NGPL operates some 12,500 miles of pipeline along two routes extending from the southwestern United States and from onshore and offshore Gulf Coast production areas to the Upper Midwest. NGPL is also a coordinating partner of the Trailblazer Pipeline System, which brings gas from the Rockies. By the 1980s NGPL supplied gas to 49 utility companies serving some 12 million persons, delivered 65 percent of the gas used in Illinois and 75 percent of the total gas consumed in Chicago.

The use of manufactured gas in Illinois goes back to the late 1840s. In 1855, when the town of Ottawa passed an ordinance providing for manufactured gas to be used in lighting, the **Ottawa Gas Light & Coke Company** sent gas through hollowed logs to illuminate homes and make street lighting possible. In August of 1858 Ottawa's Gas Light & Coke Co. illuminated the first Lincoln-Douglas debate, which was attended by an estimated 10,000 people at a time when Ottawa had a population of only 5,000.

In Ottawa gas was sent through hollowed logs to illuminate homes and streets in 1855.

When the **Chicago Gas Light & Coke Company** provided the first gas service to Chicago on September 4, 1850, there were 36 gas lamps in City Hall, 125 in "private establishments" and 99 in streets. The *Chicago Tribune* reported, "At about 2 o'clock p.m., the gas pipes were filled and brilliant torches flamed on both sides of the street as far as the eye could see. ... In the evening the lamps were again lighted, and for the first time in the history of Chicago, several of the streets were lighted in regular city style."

This was the start of what is today the **Peoples Energy Corporation**, parent company of the **Peoples Gas Light and Coke Company**, the gas utility serving the city of Chicago, and the **North Shore Gas Company**, serving northeastern Illinois. Peoples was chartered on February 12, 1855, but several obstacles hampered the start, and manufacture and distribution of gas did not begin until June 1, 1862. The plant was at 22nd Street and Racine Avenue and was unharmed by the Chicago Fire. The Fire destroyed the gas plant erected by Chicago Gas Light at Monroe and Market Streets. The fire touched off unbridled competition and several more gas companies began to lay mains in streets. At first, efforts to consolidate some of these competing firms were rebuffed on antitrust grounds. A bill passed in the 1897 session of the Illinois General Assembly made it legal for one gas company to sell property and franchises to another, and that paved the way for the absorption by Peoples Gas of seven other gas companies, including Chicago Gas. In 1907 the firm leased the properties of the **Ogden Gas Company** and **Universal Gas Company**. Peoples alone has provided the city with gas service since that year, although Ogden and Universal were not dissolved until 1950.

GAS GETS HOT

Gas as a source of light began to decline within two decades after the introduction of the electric light bulb, but gave rise to a whole new line of products, gas appliances. In 1898 Peoples sold 20,343 gas ranges for home cooking. Gas also caught on as an industrial fuel. By the end of the 1920s the success of gas as a fuel created supply problems and Peoples decided to become partner, in 1930, with **Continental Construction Company** to construct a high pressure gas pipeline from the Texas Panhandle to northern Illinois. The first deliveries through this new line reached Chicago on October 16, 1931 and for the next thirty years users in the city received a mixture of natural and manufactured gas, a product of higher heating value than previously had been available solely with manufactured gas. The line also provided a transmission system that made it possible for single companies to serve large geographic areas. Completing this project marked the beginning of the Natural Gas Pipeline Company of America, which became a wholly owned subsidiary of Peoples Gas in 1948.

Another pipeline became necessary during World War II. It went into service in 1949 and parallels the first. The remarkable increase in home-building after the war necessitated the laying of a third pipeline. It was completed in 1951. In 1962 Peoples acquired North Shore Gas Company, based in Waukegan. Six years later, in 1968, Peoples Gas Light, North Shore and Natural Gas Pipeline became subsidiaries of a new parent firm named **Peoples Gas Company**. Quickly, the new parent began to diversify within the energy field, acquiring an oil company, a coal mining and marketing firm, a drilling unit, and venturing into oil and gas exploration and development. This activity set the scene for another name change, and in January 1980 the parent firm became known as **Peoples Energy Corporation**.

At first gas was produced from coal, from distilled bituminous coal and left as coke and other residue. Coke was usually considered a useless by-product. Technology did not exist then to distribute manufactured gas long distances and municipal gas companies were small, serving only immediate needs. Then, in 1902, a breakthrough occurred when the **Aurora Gas Light Company** laid an eight mile steel pipeline to take manufactured gas from the plant in Aurora to Batavia. Engineers came from all over the world to study the new technology.

As in all technical fields, innovation led to change. By 1910 Ira C. Copley, the son of the founder of the Aurora company, had put together ventures to form the **Western United Gas and Electric Company**. The following year, 1911, Samuel Insull and his associates incorporated the original Ottawa firm and others to form the **Public Service Company** of Northern Illinois. Many well known people were associated with this firm, among them United States Vice-President Charles G. Dawes and Charles Wacker. A third merger occurred in 1912 when six northwestern Illinois gas firms formed the **Illinois Northern Utilities Company**. While the companies merged, technology improved. In 1916 Western United Gas & Electric Company was one of the first gas utilities to adopt welded joints on steel pipes, instead of using the threaded joint method then preferred.

In 1954, after years of mergers and acquisitions, the Western United, Illinois Northern and Public Service gas companies became **Northern Illinois Gas**. In its first year of service, NI-Gas ranked 13th among gas distributors in the United States. Company operations were franchised in 236 communities. By this time manufactured gas had been almost completely replaced with natural gas brought in from Texas and Oklahoma in high-pressure transmission pipelines. This fuel was plentiful and inexpensive. Demand was stimulated.

Serving a territory within one of the fastest growing areas in the country and having a waiting period list for connections, opportunities abounded for NI-Gas. Recognizing the limitations of above ground gas holders currently in use, company engineers searched for

At first gas was produced from coal.

an underground formation where gas could be stored for withdrawal when needed in winter. By 1958 a dome-shaped water-bearing aquifier was discovered near Troy Grove, about 70 miles southwest of Chicago. Soon other locations were found near Pecatonica, Ancona, Pontiac, Lake Bloomington, Hudson and Lexington.

Dome-shaped water-bearing aquifiers made perfect gas stores.

While storage problems were being solved, NI-Gas developed other innovations such as an improved method of creating taps on large-diameter pipe without shutting down customers, and a moling technique for inserting pipe beneath roads, eliminating blocked streets and broken pavements. In the early 1960s a "lawn-saver plow" minimized much of the yard restoration required by previous methods. The use of prefabricated meters reduced installation time of new services, while temperature compensated meters permitted out-of-doors installation and improved access to meters for reading.

The growth of the 1950s and 1960s brought about improvements in communication. A centralized computer-based inquiry system became operational in 1974, altering 20 years of customer service practices. That same year the utility completed a supplemental natural gas production facility, the first of its kind in Illinois. It converted liquid hydrocarbons to pipeline-quality gas. In 1976 NI-Gas became a major subsidiary of **NICOR Inc.,** an exempt holding company. By 1982 NI-Gas served 544 communities in a 17,000 square mile service territory in the northern third of Illinois, generally outside Chicago.

MEDICAL TECHNOLOGY FOR ALL

In the 1930s some aspects of chemistry and medicine became important and still have a profound effect on us. **Baxter International, Inc.,** founded as the **Don Baxter Intravenous Products Corporation** by two physicians, Dr. Donald Baxter of Los Angeles and Dr. Ralph Falk, a surgeon from Boise, Idaho, and Dr. Falk's brother, Harry Falk. Their intention was simple: to simplify and mass produce modern medical technology so that all doctors could use it. Intravenous (IV) restoration was their starting point.

The technique showed great promise as a method for building up the strength of weakened patients, but the technology of intravenous therapy remained primitive because its development had never been organized. At the time only a few large teaching hospitals were applying IV therapy and each of them was experimenting with its own chemical formulas, containers and tubing. As a result of these fragmented efforts, IV solutions were easily contaminated and many patients experienced side effects.

In 1933, in the company's first manufacturing facility, a renovated automobile showroom in Glenview, Dr. Baxter, the Falk brothers and their six employees followed scientific and engineering principles to effect their conclusions. The result was IV fluids, containers and administration equipment in large uniform quantities produced under constant monitoring for quality. Contaminants were eliminated and adverse patient reactions minimized. The line was marketed under the name travenol, a name extracted from TRAVENous sOLution. In 1976 the term became part of the company's name.

In 1935 Dr. Falk purchased Dr. Baxter's interest in the firm and made research a permanent feature. Among the first products developed was the TRANSFUSO-VAC container. With it a new chapter in blood-preservation technology was written. Where blood formerly could be stored only a few hours, the glass of the new container allowed practical storage for up to 21 days. Blood banking was now possible. Demand for the containers knew no bounds with the onset of World War II. New facilities were opened to supply the demand. During the war years Baxter developed a way to separate plasma from red blood cells. Unlike whole blood, plasma could be stored indefinitely. With the end of the war the demand slowed and shifted to the civilian market. By 1947 business had improved enough to warrant the move to larger quarters in Morton Grove. The company's international renown was yet to come. In the early 1950s a Dutch physician, Willem Kolff, sought assistance from the then chief executive, William B. Graham, in perfecting an invention whose theoretical success he had already demonstrated —the artificial kidney. Two United States medical supply houses had already rejected Kolff's device, but Graham agreed to develop a working model, and by 1956 the U200A was a reality. Acceptance came slowly. As the machine's technical difficulties were overcome and its performance improved, the machine gained recognition and has saved countless lives since then.

Blood banking draws interest.

The company's pioneering efforts led, in the 1960s, to the development of the first heart-lung system. This development made open-heart surgery a commonplace procedure. The current company was formed by the merger of Baxter Travenol Laboratories, Inc. and **American Hospital Supply Corporation** in November, 1985. To reflect the merger, a new name was chosen in May of 1988: **Baxter International, Inc.**

Baxter's TRANSFUSO-VAC made blood storage possible

"And here we have a fine Aldrich product ..."

ILLINOIS, KEY TO WAR EFFORT

The first half of the 1940s was a time of war, and manufacturers adjusted their production to meet the nation's needs. The result was a boom in production that continued through 1948, as wartime needs were translated into peacetime wants.

The war effort provided the best impetus for economic growth. The estimated number of unemployed in March, 1940 was 600,000 out of a labor force of 3.355 million, or 17.9 percent. In March, 1945 there were 24,000 unemployed out of a labor force of 3.293 million, or 0.7 percent. In September, 1939 there were 1,226,686 public aid recipients. In August, 1945 there were 214,712. By the end of 1943, 267 new plants had been built and over 1,000 factories expanded to further the war effort. In 1943, at the height of the war related production, industrial employment stood at 931,000 persons and total employment at two million in the Chicago industrial district alone. Chicago outstripped New York, Detroit, Philadelphia and Los Angeles as an ordnance manufacturing center and had long been a source for aviation production components, such as precision machine parts, steel castings and forgings and electrical wiring and equipment. But it suddenly acquired several primary parts makers, three aircraft engine plants and large producers of aircraft engines, aircraft carburetors, Norden-bombsights and airplane propellers.

The already vast steel industry required little conversion when war production began, and little reconversion was necessary when it was over. Chicago's steel mills — 40 blast furnaces — poured forth steel day and night, operating near 100 percent capacity and setting one production record after another. Nearly 18 million tons of steel issued forth per year from the plants. That amount would taper to about 15 million by the end of the decade.

Pressed Steel Car Company and **Pullman-Standard Car Manufacturing Company** made M-3 tanks (at 28 tons each). Pullman also made howitzer carriages, trench mortars and shells. International Harvester produced military crawler tractors, 37 and 75 mm shells and huge refrigeration units, which after the war were for a brief time modified into home refrigerator units. **Diamond T Motor Truck Company** turned out heavy duty, six-wheel drive trucks at a rate of 100 per week. **Elgin National Watch Company** made time fuses for antiaircraft shells. **Link Belt Company** made antiaircraft guns, **Western Electric** created a wide range of military communications equipment, **General American Transportation Company**, a large manufacturer of tank cars, concentrated on 90 mm antiaircraft shells and Sta-Rite of Shelbyville, a hairpin manufacturer, made millions of arming wires and cotter pins.

At the start of the war Chicago's six largest industries in order of gross income were iron and steel, food, printing and publishing, textiles and apparel, non-electrical machinery and electrical machinery. By the end of the war the six largest industries were iron and

Chicago was America's leading ordinance production center.

191
▲

steel, electrical machinery, transportation equipment, food, non-electrical machinery and ordnance. Most of these plants were easily converted to non-war needs. An aircraft engine plant, for example, turned to making telephones, another turned to diesel engines and a third to auto parts. A state survey found that there were 11,983 manufacturing establishments in Illinois when the war began, and in 1947 the number was 15,988. In Chicago, the number of firms grew from 9,058 to 12,284 in the same period.

New technologies created a burst of industrial growth.

The war's end had manufacturers employing 50 percent more workers, from 625,000 to 925,000. While consumers flocked to stores in record numbers, retail sales hit a peak of $4.2 billion in Chicago in 1948 and wages were at an all time high. Chicago's financial community was happy, too, when consumer credit reached $8 billion in 1948, from $2 billion in 1942, and from the pre-war high of $6 billion.

Although labor had agreed at the outset of the war to restrict strikes and stoppages, that agreement did not hold after the war. Strikes occurred in 1946 in several industries, such as coal, steel, meatpacking and metalworking.

By 1948 overstocking began to be noticed in many stores and warehouses. The heady momentum began to slow. New technologies softened the effect of this trend and in many instances created bursts of industrial growth.

Aside from these events that have been well documented elsewhere, Illinois invented, produced and manufactured many items during and after the war which were, and in many instances still are, of national significance, but which have never stood in a spotlight. The following stories will tell of some of the people who have made and continue to make Illinois a primary manufacturing state.

In the 1930s Paul B. Roberts opened a retail store in Roseland, specializing in American Colonial Furniture. Sometime in the early 1940s a customer asked him how she could display a ceremonial plate on her wall. Roberts began working with a used tin can and developed a hook for holding the plate. As the non-war use of tin was restricted, he had to get special permission from the government to develop his plate hanger. Eventually his firm sold more than 70 million of the hangers — just one of the more than 1,000 products that his company handles that are used in showrooms and conventions throughout the United States and the world.

Alvin W. Bohne founded the **Tapecoat Company** of Evanston in 1941 to manufacture the first hot applied coal tar tape designed to protect buried steel pipe from corrosion. This has been especially useful to gas and oil companies everywhere. Over the past 50 years the company has developed a variety of products, many of which were patented. Eventually Tapecoat formed into a division of **T C Manufacturing**, a holding company, which also included **Unit Dose Laboratories** of Rockford. Today UDL is the largest packager of generic unit dose pharmacutical products in Illinois.

Raymond Houston Neisewander, Sr. founded the **Capitol Wood Works** of Springfield in 1929 and the **Raynor Garage Doors** of Dixon in 1944. At the time the Dixon to Sterling corridor along the Rock River was known as the hardware capital of North America. Neisewander grew up on a farm in Gibson City and dropped out of school in the ninth grade, the year his mother died in the Great Flu epidemic. It was 1920. She left him an inheritance of $500, which he could not touch until he was 21. In 1929, when he was 23, funded by his inheritance, Neisewander started Capitol Wood Works in the rented rear room of a small grocery store in Springfield. Here he made cabinets and did general millwork. Over the years the firm manufactured Sock-o paddles, bar tops and bar fixtures, munitions boxes and wood garage door sections.

Since 1962 Capitol has devoted itself to making movable wall partitions, based on an invention patented by Neisewander. The Raynor Garage Door Company is an outgrowth of Capitol's garage door section production. Raynor began in Quincy in 1944, but moved to Dixon in 1946. Starting with 37 employees and 28,000 square feet of space, Raynor has developed into the largest employer in Dixon, with over 600 people and 700,000 square feet of manufacturing space.

Camcar Screw & Manufacturing Co. of Rockford, a division of Textron since 1975, was founded in 1943 by Robert Campbell (Cam), Ray Carlson (Car) and Eugene Aspling to solve a problem facing military-aircraft: failure of a screw machine part and the lack of screw machine capacity. The part Camcar made was a control cable fitting. This device controlled the aircraft engine and flight patterns and was used on bomber aircraft in World War II and the Korean War.

In 1963 the Camcar team developed a new process to extrude head parts, a patented process named Raycarl in honor of its inventor, Ray Carlson. The machine, called a header, was designed to manufacture screw parts using one continuous roll of wire. The process is called cold heading or forming. A header can produce from 50 to 450 parts per minute, depending on the kind of part and machine.

The patented process is both elegant and simple, and makes up a unique screw heading process which combines extrusion with heading to allow production of more complicated fastener shapes. The result is a large diameter head which is cold formed on a much smaller body screw or component. This improved cold forming machine and process is now utilized all over the world and has been recognized as a revolutionary concept in the field of cold heading. It has been called the most significant breakthrough in the cold forming industry in 50 years.

In 1969 Camcar's Aerospace Division supplied over 600 different parts for the Rocketdyne engines on Apollo 7. And Camcar's titanium parts were used to construct Grumman's Lunar Module which served as the launch platform for the ascent stage from the moon — where they were left behind and remain on the moon as relics of human activity.

Over the years Camcar's management has encouraged its employees to develop creative solutions to customers' fastener problems. For example, in 1965 the TORX Drive System was invented. This patented system provides equal contact on all six lobes of the screw

A header can produce 50 to 450 parts per minute.

head, making it easier to turn, and is now utilized as a superior fastener drive system throughout the world. Currently 49 domestic and 44 foreign firms are producing TORX fasteners, and the system is quickly becoming a world standard. Today the firm has over 2,000 employees at ten divisions and four distribution centers.

Anderson Physical Laboratories (APL), and since February, 1989 **APL Engineered Materials**, was set up in the summer of 1944 in Champaign-Urbana by Dr. Scott Anderson as a private, independent physics laboratory. Shortly after the founding, the A.M. Todd Co. of Kalamazoo, Michigan asked Anderson to develop an objective analysis for peppermint oils. He arranged to buy Perkin-Elmer's 16th infrared spectrometer and developed a five-point spectroscopic analysis for four components of the oil.

The five-point spectroscopic analysis was developed to analyze peppermint oil.

With the acquisition of the Perkin-Elmer instrument, APL became the only independent infrared laboratory in the United States. Toward the end of its first year, and for the next nine years, APL became the virtual "Physics Department" for the Pittsburgh Plate Glass Co. During this time APL built a staff of 15 people who authored numerous papers in technical journals. In 1959 APL obtained a contract with the United States Atomic Energy Commission to purify salts, with the expectation that the new zone refining technique could be used. This was done, but the technique was quickly found not to be practical. APL developed a more commercially viable approach and soon supplied most of the laboratories working on fused salt batteries with salt purified by chemical treatment only. The yield with these salts changed from grams to kilograms. The main client was **Argonne Laboratories**.

In 1962 GTE Sylvania's lamp business bought some of APL's distilled iodides, applied them, and found lamp performance was far superior to anything they had seen previously. APL was now in the lamp business and on its way to a brighter business future in a real niche market. Later APL developed and patented a process for manufacturing high purity, ultra dry halides in precise size spheroids. This led to the development of high speed dosing systems for metal halide lamps, a concept soon expanded to include sodium-mercury amalgams for high pressure sodium lamps. APL's current list of customers for these materials includes every major lamp manufacturer in the world.

Over the past several years APL has developed several new materials and components which are used in the lighting industry including getters, thermionic cathode emission materials, fluorescent lamp amalgams, pellet dispensers and precision rare earth metal chips, to name but a few.

OIL BURNERS

The post-war economy allowed for much more leisure, a concept that had been slowly developing in the American mind since the 1920s. And as leisure became more common, fishing developed from a lazy summer activity to a serious sport, involving millions of Americans. Fishing required worms and, with the great demand, it was not practical to always go dig them up in the garden as needed. Availability of worms became a problem and their storage was a concern. **Buss Manufacturing Company** of Lanark has, since 1946, produced Buss Bed-ding, a product that is a complete concentrated worm food and habitat that keeps nightcrawlers, redworms and their ilk alive for longer periods of time: this is a great aid to fishermen. Don Buss coined the term "Bedding" in association with worms, and was the inventor and originator of this product.

It was also the post war years that brought us the concept of suburbs on a large scale and along with it the mass production of the private home. Each of these homes had to have its own, self contained heating unit, most of which operated on oil, a cheap resource at the time. To burn the oil efficiently, specially designed burners were required. Lloyd Aldrich was a pioneer in the manufacture of the oil burner, facilitating the conversion from coal to oil fired heating equipment, such as boilers, furnaces, water heaters and other power generators. Beginning with crude designs in the 1920s, Aldrich made his first burner in his basement in the town of Wyoming and sold it on May 1, 1935; over the next seven months he manufactured 250 Aldrich Heat Pak burners.

> To burn oil efficiently, specially designed burners were required.

With the assistance of the small town of Wyoming, the Aldrich factory was built and by 1941 burner production reached 26,000 units annually. Soon the **Aldrich Company** considered itself the "World's largest oil burner manufacturer." As the use of coal for home heating waned, so did the need for converters and Aldrich started producing boilers and water heaters fired by the company's burner. These developments made the oil burner much more reliable and most important, serviceable in place. Aldrich's other inventions

The motor-transformer department of Aldrich Company in 1948

include the elimination of high tension transmission of high voltage between the transformer and electrodes by using contact springs; the use of slip friction of the running contact providing the safe operation of switches; development of the double universal joint between the motor and bump. These developments had a profound effect on the industry and are still in use.

Sunbeam
introduced the
Mixmaster
in 1930.

For many years the Aldrich Company has been the largest employer in Stark County, providing the county with an important tax base and stability. Today the Aldrich Company is still locally owned and manufactures a wide variety of hydronic heating equipment. Most notable are their indirect fired water heaters and primary/secondary modular boiler systems. The indirect heaters are known world wide for their longevity and ease of maintenance. Their newest introduction of primary/secondary modular boiler systems is fast becoming the model for efficient hydronic space heating. This is accomplished by an innovative multiple vessel concept run by a computerized control technique.

With World War II, Stewart-Warner of Chicago became one of the nation's top defense contractors, with some plants completely devoted to military production. In an arsenal at Dixon Stewart-Warner built bombs, grenades and artillery shells. Other plants converted to the production of radar devices, aircraft engine components, hydrostatic fuses for explosives and other military hardware. But the company had its roots some 40 years earlier.

Stewart-Warner Corporation began in 1897. That year, John K. Stewart and Thomas Jefferson Clark incorporated their **Chicago Flexible Shaft Company** which was then dedicated to making commercial animal clippers and shearing equipment. As a sideline they brought out the first electric iron in 1910. By 1930, and known as the **Sunbeam Corporation**, the company introduced its now well-known Mixmaster electric mixer.

Meanwhile, in 1910, in Meriden, Connecticut, a young businessman named Edgar W. Bassick joined an 18-year old furniture-hardware manufacturer, the Meridian Screw Company. Bassick moved fast. By 1911 he was president of Meriden Screw and six years later had acquired a whole series of furniture-hardware manufacturers and merged them into a new corporation, the **Bassick Company**. Attracted by the fast growing car building industry, Bassick adapted some of his firm's hardware to automotive applications and began producing hood latches and grease cups for low-pressure lubrication. Rapid growth followed. Bassick moved from Bridgeport, Connecticut to Chicago, where he acquired the Gullborg family's patents on the Alemite Lubrication System in 1919, and the even more advanced Zerk system in 1924. A new venture, Bassick-Alemite, was formed to manufacture and market high-pressure auto lubrication equipment. The product became the standard for auto lubrication throughout the Western Hemisphere.

While Bassick wowed the auto industry with lubrication technology, Stewart and Clark rode the automotive boom to success with their Flexible Shaft Company speedometers. In 1905 they formed **Stewart & Clark Manufacturing Company** for the express purpose of building these devices. A small plant was erected on West Diversey Parkway near Damen

Avenue in Chicago. Today the giant shell of the Stewart-Warner headquarters and plant still dominates the neighborhood. In 1912 they acquired their major competitor, Warner Instruments Company of South Beloit, and named the new company **Stewart-Warner Corporation**, and consolidated all operations at the Chicago plant.

As America's love for the automobile became an obsession, Stewart-Warner grew. In 1924 it made a decisive move by acquiring Bassick-Alemite with its high-pressure lubrication system. The new product-mix found application in much of America's original equipment manufacturing industry, both automotive and non-automotive.

Today,
Revell-Monogram
is the world's leading
manufacturer
of plastic model kits.

PLASTIC BECOMES POPULAR AFTER WORLD WAR II

After the war increased emphasis was placed upon new product development, the reapplication of military technology and the acquisition of promising businesses. The new lines now included automotive service equipment, instrument products, industrial lubricating equipment, fluid materials handling equipment, casters and chair control devices, heat transfer products, lighting equipment and electromechanical devices, combustion-heating products, military electronics, commercial-industrial electronics, hand-held power tools and furniture and cabinet hardware.

Plastic became a popular material after World War II and many toy companies used it. Two companies are typical of this trend. The **Processed Plastic Company** of Montgomery was founded by Ross Bergman in 1948. They made many inexpensive, injection-molded toys sold by such mass market stores as Woolworth.

Another company, **Revell-Monogram Models** of Morton Grove, founded in 1945, in the 1960s became one of the world's largest manufacturers of plastic kits. Today Revell-Monogram is the world's leading manufacturer and marketer of plastic model kits, and still manufactures its world famous models in Morton Grove.

The predicted post-war depression did not materialize. Non-agricultural employment rose to more than 3.1 million from 2.3 million in 1940 and remained above three million during the next decade, including the relatively mild 1949 recession. Until the mid-1970s the economy continued to grow, although at a decreased rate, and the average annual unemployment remained below five percent except for cyclical troughs in 1954, 1958 and 1961.

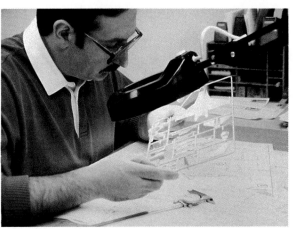

Preparing a model at Revell-Monogram

One small step ...

THE GOLDEN AGE OF MATERIALISM

The end of World War I had brought about major changes in the economic and political make up of Europe, which affected manufacturing in the United States greatly. It made the United States much more independent and self sufficient. World War II, viewed in hindsight by many as the inevitable second chapter that had to give closure to the first World War, set America up as the industrial and political power of the world, countered only by Soviet aspirations, which presented themselves as chapter three, the Korean War. The Korean War gave the United States a clear enemy, one it would strive against for more than three decades. To Illinois manufacturing, the various wars and military actions America was party to were good for production. New products could be developed, tested and produced at military expense. Just as sure as spring follows winter, peace follows war, and peace for most manufacturers means one thing: adapt wartime production to a commercial market demanding products they have had to do without. Thus it was in the 1950s. During the Korean War a company like **Hotpoint,** which had a plant that made refrigerators, converted to jet engines as soon as the war started. With the end of the war Hotpoint reverted back to refrigerators, making 400,000 per year — one every 40 seconds — for the next few years.

The decade from 1954 to 1964 was one of history's great shopping sprees, as many Americans went on a baroque spender bender and adorned their mass-produced houses, furniture and machines with accoutrements of the space age and of the American frontier. "Live your dreams and meet your budget," one advertisement promised, and unprecedented numbers of Americans were able to do it. It was, materially, a kind of golden age. There was so much wealth brought on by new found prosperity that it did not need to be diluted. Each householder was able to have his own little Versailles along a cul-de-sac.

Despite growth in almost all sectors of the economy, spurred on in no small part by an increase in births, the 1950s brought changes to Illinois that past experiences could not foresee or have the where-with-all to meet. During these years the population of the six-county metropolitan area of Chicago increased by more than one million people, while the city of Chicago itself lost population. The composition of the population of Chicago was changing in significant ways, too. At the turn of the century the non-white population amounted to about 2 percent of the metropolitan total. By 1950 it stood at 11 percent.

Access to the market has always been of primary importance to the manufacturer and the 1950s saw a revolutionary change in transportation: the popular use of the airplane. The airplane had proven itself indispensable in World War II and it carried over into peacetime. It should also be noted here that the airplane had a long history in Illinois, all the way back to 1840, with the first documented flying machine built in Illinois. This machine

New products were developed at military expense.

was an ornithopter created by Hugh Newell — known as Crazy Hugh — a farmer living in Newton, six miles west of Danville. The crank powered machine plunged to the ground from a hay stack. No one was hurt.

By the mid-1950s airplanes, as well as the miles of the expanding interstate highway system, were contributing significantly to the decline of the railroads. In 1944 the East-West Expressway was started, the first of a series of superhighways to speed the flow of automobiles and trucks in and out of Chicago.

Midway Airport handled 2,000 flights per day in 1955.

Chicago, as America's transportation hub, accepted the airplane in a big way. Midway Airport, which was handling up to 2,000 flights a day, was choked with passengers, who in 1955 numbered eight million and made it the world's busiest airport. The Near South-west side of Chicago was booming. Air transport of manufactured goods became feasible and many manufacturers and warehousers moved close to the fields for easy access. In 1956 it became clear that jet air travel would be the way of the future and that Midway could not expand accordingly, being hemmed in by residential areas and industrial zones. Something had to be done. The answer came in O'Hare International Airport, which began accepting its first commercial flights in October, 1955.

Only 10 miles north of Midway, O'Hare was originally an aircraft rest field for the Douglas Aircraft Company. It was first known as Orchard Place, hence O'Hare's baggage labels "ORD." In 1946 the city of Chicago obtained the property, 10 square miles and enough room to park 10,000 cars. When it opened, O'Hare was the largest airport in the world; it soon would be the busiest, too.

Envisioned as an airport to relieve some of the pressure on Midway and with passenger traffic expected to be about eight million at O'Hare by 1960, it actually took on many more passengers than predicted and caused the marked decline of the South Side field. O'Hare's expansion plans were speeded up when it became clear that the airport would be the better choice for jet planes, with its new and longer runways. In 1957 Midway had 28 gates; O'Hare was expanding to 54 from 16. Quickly, the area around O'Hare began to sprout new buildings and businesses eager to be near the airport, among them **United Airlines**, which moved its headquarters from Midway to Elk Grove Village in order to be near the airport it saw as its destiny.

The jet age officially began in Chicago in March, 1959, when the first Boeing 707, bound to New York from San Francisco, touched down. O'Hare went international the same year, when a TWA flight from Paris disembarked at the newly completed international terminal.

The jet plane quickly evolved into a symbol not just of physical speed but also of the social change that was believed to be happening faster than ever before. The very short time that had elapsed between Kitty Hawk and the step into space proved to be very difficult for many people to comprehend. The difficulties of dealing with such rapid change was nicely suggested by Tex Avery's 1953 MGM animated cartoon, *Little Johnny Jet*. This film, an Oscar nominee, which tells the story of a family of airplanes, combines the sonic boom with the baby boom and dramatizes the often disconcerting combination of wonder, envy, fear and resentment that parents might have felt when confronted with their confident, fortunate children.

TUNING IN

In 1948 there were 18 TV stations on the air.

As people moved to the suburbs they became physically separated, out on their own in a new, muddy and unfinished landscape, but they were also linked as never before through advertising, television and magazines. Industry saw them as something new, "a mass market," an overwhelmingly powerful generator of profits and economic growth. Among the new products demanded by the post-war population was telelvision, which literally grew up overnight, and Chicago companies like **Zenith**, **Motorola** and **Admiral** soon accounted for 40 percent of America's television set production. Sears marketed its first receiver in 1949, a black-and-white model that sold for $149.95. Today it is difficult to imagine the impact television had in those years, when consumers went from no TV to one. By 1948 about 30,000 Chicagoans were employed in manufacturing televisions; the next year 40,000 people were employed to turn out 90,000 TV sets a month in Chicago. At the time 28 companies were listed as television set manufacturers; in 1950 there were 80 nationwide; in 1968 there were 18. Competition had thinned the ranks. In 1948 there were 18 stations on the air and some 200,000 sets received their signals in the United States The next year 45 stations were broadcasting, 77 more applications were granted and 311 applications were being reviewed by the FCC. Television was everywhere. In 1951 there were about 10.5 million TV sets in the United States; the year before that, there had been 3.5 million. Now Chicago was not only the nation's crossroads of transportation, but also the hub for communications. Chicago was the cradle of TV broadcasting, the place live shows originated and advertising became correspondingly significant. The following year, 1952, TV advertising outspent radio commercials for the first time, and Arthur C. Nielsen was prepared to rate audience preferences from his Chicago base.

As with so many products, Illinois had a leader in television, too — **Motorola, Inc.** of Schaumburg. In 1952 television sets accounted for the largest segment of Motorola's sales. The following year, Motorola opened a 280,000 square foot television assembly plant in Franklin Park.

The company's 1957 annual report noted that: "It is clear that a strong demand for color is still somewhere in the future." Not that Motorola had not tried to stimulate that demand. In 1954 the company had introduced its first color television, which was withdrawn from the market in 1956 because it fell short of success. It was beset with technical problems, a high price tag and most importantly, the failure of the broadcasters to offer an adequate amount of color programming. The same year, 1956, Motorola introduced a remote control tuning device for its Golden Satellite TV. Four years later Motorola introduced the Astronaut television, the first transistorized, AC- or battery-operated receiver. The set contained 23 transistors, 11 diodes and only one vacuum tube. That year the company was ranked as the world's leading supplier of combined audio systems, specializing in affordable, well-engineered sound equipment for the home.

In a joint venture with **National Video**, Motorola developed, in 1963, the first rectangular picture tube for color television. It was smaller in volume, yet had a larger viewing screen than the older round color television tubes. The tube quickly became the standard for the industry. Four years later, in 1967, Motorola introduced the Quasar line of color receivers, America's first all-transistor color television set. These sets were designed to be easily repaired, the feature stressed in their Works in a Drawer trademark.

In 1974 Motorola sold its home television business, including the Quasar trademark and the manufacturing facilities in Franklin Park and Quincy to **Matsushita Electric Industrial Company Ltd.** Motorola's new focus was to be on the development and manufacture of advanced semiconductor and radio telecommunications products and technologies.

But before television technology made Motorola a household name, the company was already important. Motorola was founded when Paul V. Galvin and his brother Joseph E. Galvin purchased the battery eliminator business of the bankrupt **Stewart Storage Battery Company** in Chicago in 1928. The first product, a battery eliminator, was a separate component that enabled a home radio to operate on ordinary household current. As battery-operated radios became obsolete, so did the battery eliminator. With the October stock market crash, business ground to a halt. The following year the **Galvin Manufacturing Corporation** produced the first practical and affordable auto radio. At the time auto radios were not available from automobile manufacturers, so the Galvin auto radios were sold and installed as an accessory by independent automotive distributors and dealers. The original model 5T71 auto radio sold for $110 to $130 installed, about half the cost of custom models. The radios sold well and Galvin decided on the brand name Motorola, to suggest motor (i.e. car) and sound, ola as a suffix as in victrola. In 1947 the Galvin corporation was christened Motorola, Inc.

By 1936 the company's share of the car radio market was well established and the company was a leader in the United States market. The following year Motorola's auto radios were the first to feature push-button tuning, a vibrator power supply, fine-tuning and tone controls. From 1942 on, Motorola devoted most of its manufacturing to the war effort. Its expertise was radio communication.

EVERYBODY'S TALKING

With the announcement of its first mobile police receiver in 1936, police radios began to supplant the telephone call-box communication system. Three years later Motorola introduced its first two-way radio, the T69-20, a mobile transmitter and the companion to the Police Cruiser mobile receiver. The device was an AM set designed to use FCC-assigned police channels in the 30.5 to 39.0 mhz band and was priced under $300, making it the

Motorola equals motor (i.e. car) plus ola (i.e. sound) from victrola.

least expensive mobile two-way radio equipment available. In 1940 Motorola developed the world's first hand-held, two-way, radio on its own initiative. The result was the five-pound Handie-Talkie radio, an AM unit with a range of one to three miles. Convinced that FM radio communications technology was the way of the future, Paul Galvin hired Daniel E. Noble, a pioneer in FM radio communications and semiconductor technology, as director of research. A communications department was established.

Unique in its small size and weight, the Handie-Talkie was the only hand-held portable radio in production when Pearl Harbor was attacked. Within three weeks production exceeded 50 units per day and by 1945, over 130,000 had been built. It became the best known item of all the Signal Corps equipment used by the military.

In 1941 Motorola was the first to commercially manufacture FM two-way radio systems and equipment: the FMR 13 mobile receiver, the first with an FM squelch circuit, and the FMT 30 mobile transmitter. Both items were designed by Dan Noble.

Motorola manufactured the first commercial FM two-way radio system.

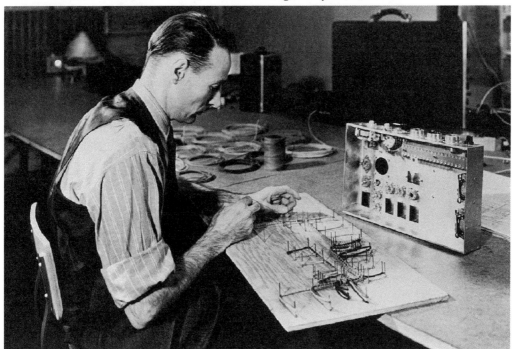

The final assembly in the 1940s

In 1942 four manufacturers attempted to design a radio that met the Signal Corps specifications for a high-frequency portable radio: Hazeltine, Wilcox-Gay, Philco and Galvin. Dan Noble's design won the contract for Galvin. The new design, called the SCR-300, replaced the older Signal Corps radio and got the descriptive name "walkie-talkie." The SCR-300 weighed 35 pounds and had a maximum range of 40 miles, with an average range of 10 to 20 miles. It featured a dial which enabled the unit to be tuned to various frequencies between 40 to 48 mhz. The first units were used in battle in 1943 and quickly received universal praise from foot soldiers on all fronts. The same year the first radio teletype hook-up used by the army (in Italy) relied on Motorola police radios. The previous year the first radio relay system for behind-the-lines communications was set up in North Africa. Motorola was authorized by the U.S. War Department to supply civilian

FM two-way radio equipment to civil defense units and local and state police operations. More than 80 percent of all the FM radio communication systems installed during the war in the United States were made by Motorola.

Between 1942 and 1945 supplies of quartz radio crystals ran short and Motorola was asked to organize more than 30 other radio crystal manufacturers. Motorola supplied them with production equipment and taught them the proper manufacturing processes. By the end of the war more than 35 million radio crystals had been delivered by Motorola, half the total amount of quartz radio crystals used. Motorola also began to experiment with microwave radio. In 1951 two 1,000-mile microwave radio systems, the two largest industrial systems in operation, were among the more than 20 supplied by Motorola.

In 1956, Motorola was the sole supplier of radar equipment for air traffic control.

As a result of supplying such enormous quantities of radio technology during the war years, Motorola was one of the few companies that did not have to re-tool these manufacturing lines for civilian use. This same technology and much of the product line was readily adaptable to commercial uses.

At the dawn of the commercial jet age, in 1956, Motorola was the only company to offer radar equipment specifically designed for air traffic control. Two years later a closed circuit television system was developed and Motorola provided radio equipment for the Explorer 1, a 31-pound Earth-orbiting satellite. In 1960 the company's first push-button mobile radiotelephones were installed and a fully transistorized Handie-Talkie VHF radio paging system, the first capable of signaling any one of 7,000 pagers on a single radio channel, was installed in hotels, hospitals and industrial facilities.

Motorola's auto radio assembly in the 1940s

In 1962 the industry's first fully-transistorized portable two-way radio, the 33-ounce Handie-Talkie HT-200, was introduced. The unit was nicknamed the "brick" because of its shape and durable construction. Other radio equipment was also developed. Among them was the radio link to Mariner II on its flight to Venus, and images of Mars were relayed back to Earth from aboard Mariner IV in 1964. Motorola also supplied transponders for the Gemini manned-space program. In 1965 the transistorized Pageboy pager, supplied by the Bell system as the Bellboy pager, was used on capitol hill as part of a system of 15 transmitters covering all of Washington, D.C. In 1971 the Pageboy II radio pager was introduced. It was the smallest, most sophisticated pager available, at 4.8 cubic inches and 3.9 ounces. It had 80 components, compared to the 210 for the Pageboy I.

In 1977 Motorola began to test the "cellular" phone.

In 1977 an experimental radiotelephone system, the Dyna-T.A.C. (called a cellular system because of its short-range radio coverage areas called cells) began to be field tested in the Washington, D.C./Baltimore area, after the first such experimental license was granted by the FCC to Motorola. Three years later Motorola supplied AT&T with cellular radiotelephones for a Chicago-area test. In 1983 the outcome of a 15-year development program was the first non-wireline cellular system to be granted a commercial license by the FCC.

In 1978 a congressional task force on Japanese trade was initiated. It marked the first organized action regarding efforts to enter the Japanese market. Nippon Telegraph and Telephone was urged to enter discussions with Motorola regarding the purchase of Motorola pagers. By 1984, 200,000 Motorola pagers were in use in Japan. Seven years later Motorola shipped its millionth pager to Japan.

THE TRANSISTOR LAUNCHES MODERN ELECTRONICS

When, in 1948, the opportunity arose to supply radios to automobile manufacturers, Motorola arranged a deal with Ford by which it acquired Detrola, and one Friday evening proceeded to move all that company's machines, tools and other materials from Detroit to Chicago. Production started the following Monday morning. At the same time Motorola also began supplying auto radios to Chrysler. Soon Motorola was producing all the radios used by General Motors as well. To meet the demand, Motorola established its first manufacturing facility outside of Chicago, in Quincy. By 1954 Motorola was producing one-half of the original equipment auto radios for Ford and Chrysler, and all the auto radios for American Motors and International Harvester, too, and also continued to produce radios to be sold and installed after the car has been purchased. That year a new technical development was Motorola's first auto radio to use plated circuitry. Two years later, in 1956, Motorola became the first commercial radio maker to incorporate transistors in an auto radio. This radio was smaller and more durable than previous models and required less power to operate.

The invention of the transistor in 1948 launched modern electronics. A transistor utilizes a semiconductor for controlling the flow of current between two terminals and a third. Its function is similar to those of a vacuum tube without the current to heat a cathode.

Transistors are smaller, generate less heat, require less power and are much more reliable than a vacuum tube. In 1953 Motorola applied for its first semiconductor related patent and, two years later, Motorola was the first company to put a high-powered transistor into commercial production. Soon the company produced enough transistors and semi-conductors to supply other manufacturers.

In 1965 8-track tape players enter the automotive market.

By now Motorola was producing new audio products with astounding regularity. In 1959 the company's semiconductor line of products included the mesa transitor, the smallest mass-produced transistor manufactured to date. It had an electrically active area smaller in size than the width of a human hair. The same year Motorola introduced the FM-900, the first FM auto radio to be mass produced in the United States. It was an immediate success. Also in that year an all-transistor auto radio was introduced. It was considered the most reliable in the industry. By then almost one-third of all auto radios were made by Motorola. Another important auto innovation occurred in 1961 when Motorola, working with Chrysler, introduced the first practical, low cost, press-fit, siliconrectifiers that made

Motorola puts it all together in the 1940s

all-electronic automotive alternators possible. This device allowed an auto battery to recharge while the engine was idling. The following year Motorola's Semiconductor Products Division was making 95 percent of all auto rectifiers used in American cars. In 1963 more than three million units a month were delivered.

As the cost of semiconductors declined in the 1960s, their applications in industrial and consumer electronic products increased to create a major market. Motorola helped accelerate this trend by introducing a low-cost, plastic-encapsulated transistor, called a TO-92. It also developed a mass production technique, called lead-frame packaging, whereby strips of 100 transistors were assembled at once. Within one year Motorola was producing two million plastic-packaged devices per week. This design was eventually adopted by the entire industry.

Working in joint venture with Ford and RCA, in 1965, Motorola designed and manufactured the first eight-track tape player for the automotive market. Next to auto radios, the eight-track tape player was the Automotive Products Division's best seller. Motorola entered the space age in 1971 when one of their FM radio receivers was used by the Lunar Roving Vehicles to provide a voice link over the 240,000 miles between it and the Earth. The receiver, dubbed "the first car radio on the moon," was 100 times more sensitive than a standard car radio, yet weighed only one and a half pounds. By 1977 Motorola's automotive customers also included British Leyland, Citroen, Renault and Volkswagen.

An important ecological breakthrough was achieved in 1980 when Motorola supplied the first electronic engine control modules to Ford. In 1991 Motorola shipped its ten millionth power train controller to Ford. These modules, developed in 1977 for the 1980 line, were designed to control fuel efficiency and emissions. They became the first major market for Motorola's microprocessors. Similar products were developed for General Motors and Chrysler. Motorola had introduced its first microprocessor in 1974, the eight-bit 6800. Containing 4,000 transistors, it was the first to only require a single 5-volt power supply. In the following year, 1975, General Motors approached Motorola for a custom-chip derivative of the 6800. Its first application was for a trip-mileage computer in 1978. The following year, Motorola introduced its first 16-bit microprocessor, the 68000. Capable of completing two million calculations per second, it could be used both to run and to write programs for scientific, data processing and business applications. It was eventually adopted by Apple Computers for its Macintosh line.

In 1984 Motorola introduced the world's first true 32-bit microprocessor, the MC68020. Its three-eighths inch square chip holds 200,000 transistors that can access up to four billion bytes of memory. That year the MC68HC11, the first advanced microcomputer adjustable to specific applications, was also introduced. By 1989 Motorola had sold more than 30 million microprocessors. And the next year the company produced the world's densest, most complex semiconductor yet, for a United States Department of Defense program. This device is an experimental half-micron microprocessor containing four million transistors that can perform 200 million floating point operations per second.

In 1991 10 of the world's largest automakers, representing approximately three quarters of current market sales, agreed to use Motorola's microcontrollers in their next-generation powertrain control systems.

THE PINBALL WIZARD, THERE'S GOT TO BE A TWIST

Among new industries of the 1950s were ones that focused on a single product, a product that had little or no prewar history, and that did not require the manufacture or invention of new parts. The finished product was born through an assemblage of already existing parts. Such were an assortment of coin-operated machines whose manufacture, starting in the 1930s to well into the 1970s, was based in Chicago. For over four decades the city was the center for the design and manufacture of such coin-operated devices as pinball

Chicago was the center of pinball machine production.

machines, slot machines and jukeboxes. In the Depression year of 1932 a Bally customer received 10 balls for a penny in Ballyhoo, a pinball machine introduced to Chicago and named after a contemporary satirical magazine. Ray Moloney, a principal of **Lion Manufacturing Corporation**, helped create the pinball industry with Ballyhoo. The machine sold 50,000 units within seven months and fostered a separate division of Lion, **Bally Manufacturing Company**. The company quickly developed a line of new games which required skill and coordination of hand and eye. Moloney's machines were the most attractive and the most challenging. He introduced electricity to the mechanical game board and lighted its vertical back glass with optical themes that would be very influential on Chicago fine arts.

The 45 rpm

becomes

the new standard

for pop singles.

During the 1940s and 1950s most of the pinball games in the world were made by three Chicago companies: Bally Manufacturing Corporation, which claimed to be the world's biggest, **Williams Electronics**, and **D. Gottlieb and Company**. As profits soared, controversy got so thick around pinball machines that they were banned for a time in the mid-1950s in Chicago and elsewhere. In the 1960s Bally was directed by William T. O'Donnell, who introduced an entirely new, electric slot machine that captured the Nevada gaming market, and made obsolete the totally mechanical machines. Within a few years Bally had become the leading manufacturer of slot machines in the world, having invented the "progressive" machine and the one-dollar machine for greater player appeal. In 1968 Lion Manufacturing formally merged with Bally, forming Bally Manufacturing Corporation.

Recognizing the broader dimension of the industry, Bally acquired **Midway Mfg. Co.** in 1969 to provide a myriad of arcade machines and games. Acquired in 1974, Bally's Aladdin Castle family centers quickly increased from 30 regional sites to some 400 locations in 45 states.

Then, in the late 1970s, new technology based on video, microchip and computer related circuitry was introduced and the electric-mechanical gave way, resulting in Chicago losing its predominance in the market. Bally recaptured market leadership by introducing two games that immediately achieved an unprecedented popularity: Space Invaders, in 1978, and Pac-Man, in 1980. Each game quickly sold more than 70,000 units in an industry where 20,000 sales are significant. The game industry has not been the same since, especially in the last decade with the introduction of foreign manufactured games.

The jukebox experienced a similar story. In 1954, 61,000 coin-operated phonographs were produced nationwide; of these, 80 percent were made in Chicago. The top local manufacturers, all nationally recognized names at the time, were **Rudolph Wurlitzer Company, J. P. Seeburg Corporation, H.C. Evans Company**, and **Rockola Manufacturing Corporation**. It was an odd business; earning, so claimed Billboard magazine, an average of $10.25 per week at a nickel a play; yet nationwide 7,500 distributors paid $800 to $1,200 per jukebox to play the hits to come out of the 200 or so new pop releases per week.

When Raymond Loewy, the noted American designer of industrial products, called the 1955 cars "jukeboxes on wheels," he meant to condemn automobiles for becoming loud, colorful and vulgar, like the entertainment machines he believed to embody the worst of American culture. As it turned out, the influence of the late-1950s cars would end up transforming the jukebox. As the 1950s progressed, the familiar, flashing, curvy, arch-topped jukeboxes disappeared from bars, diners and soda fountains, to be replaced by newer models that played 45 rpm records, the new standard for pop singles. These new jukeboxes had a lot more glass, wrapping all the way around the record storage and playing mechanism. But this new transparency did not appear to serve those who were dropping their coins into the slot and pressing the buttons. Rather, it seemed more as if the jukebox itself had turned into a vehicle of sorts, one that incorporated the kind of transparency that would be found in a jet plane or a new car. The whole machine had angular lines and tended to lean forward, poised and looking eager. The jukebox wasn't going anywhere, physically at least, but symbolically it was a harbinger of the new. It was delivering the latest music at a moment when the music was itself shaped by new stirrings of sensuality and dynamism. The heavy-looking, old jukebox still had memories of Glenn Miller bouncing around inside. The new-style jukebox, which was both larger and airier-looking than the old one, matched the new Chevy V-8 as a symbol of teenage liberation and was the appropriate vessel for "Rock Around the Clock," "Peggy Sue" and "Hound Dog." By the mid-1960s the craze was past and, though jukeboxes still exist, they draw little attention today.

The suburbs needed lawn mowers and covered barbecue grills.

THE 1950s GRILL AND CHILL

Along with the need to flip and twist, the desire to burn one's beef as domestic entertainment expressed itself in the joy and pain of home barbecuing, which came into style in the 1950s, just as the suburbs developed and man began to mow lawns and play chef. Sadly, the available grills were either too hot or open to rain and wind — whatever, they didn't do well. Even George Stephen had problems, but he decided in 1951 to do something about it: create a barbecue with a cover.

At the time George Stephen was employed by the **Weber Brothers Metal Works** (since 1960 known as the **Weber-Stephen Products Co.**), where he had worked in fabrication and sales since the early 1940s. For his first barbecue he selected two spun metal shapes being produced by the com-

A Weber Grill maker

pany for a product totally unrelated to the grill. These shapes, when put together, formed a kettle-covered charcoal grill. The grill proved so popular among his friends and neighbors that in July, 1952 Stephen began selling "George's Barbecue Kettle," the ancestor of today's Weber kettle. Odd in shape, the performance of the kettle was nothing to laugh at, and it sold briskly.

Ardco pioneered glass door refrigerators.

By the 1980s Weber had grown to be the number-one manufacturer of charcoal barbecue grills and accessories in the world, employing 500 people.

Another need that developed on a broad scale during the war and then came into its own in the course of the 1950s was refrigeration, and it has stayed with us, in fact expanding rapidly over the past four decades. While much investigation and research has gone into why manufacturers of the past, traditional American companies, have not been able to cope with world markets, other manufacturers seem to be doing very well. These appear to share a common thread in that they all seem to be market driven, with a major commitment to advanced technology. Through ongoing product development programs in all divisions and aspects of their product line, these manufacturers inhabit niches that are very specific and which they know very well. Within these market niches they prosper and develop. An example of this type of niche company is **Ardco**.

Ardco, located in Chicago, was founded in 1957 by Henry M. Buchbinder. Originally called **Aluminum Refrigerator Door Co.** and located in a 7,000 square foot loft in Chicago, the company manufactures glass refrigerator doors, the frost-free type that protects

Ardco cleared the fog from frozen food selection in the 1950s

frozen foods in every larger food store and many other places. Ardco is the world's leading producer of glass refrigerator doors. Ardco pioneered energy saving, low temperatureglass display doors for the frozen food and supermarket industry. This came about through the development of electrically conductive, insulated glass that keeps glass display doors clear and free of condensation.

During this same period, Ardco introduced vertical, full length, automatically closing, self-service cooler doors to the growing convenience food industry. The company's complete door line and merchandising accessories continue to meet the changing needs of the dynamic food industry. In 1968 Ardco introduced TemperBent curved glass products to the United States market.

Today curved glass display cases are widely used in retail food outlets to dramatically merchandise bakery, deli, meat, fish and other perishable food products. In addition to these applications, TemperBent is used for glass solariums, curved shower doors, non-food fixtures and office partitions. Ardco employs a technically advanced, automated and computerized bending system capable of producing fully tempered shapes up to 78 inches in length.

The Buchbinder Division produces and markets floral coolers and accessories to the retail floral industry and supermarket industry throughout the United States. Ardco's Heat Transfer Products Group is the second largest producer of commercial refrigeration products in North America. Within this Group, the extensive Russell product line is used in all commercial refrigeration applications, ranging from reach-in refrigerators to large refrigerated warehouses. Russell is the West Coast's largest refrigeration equipment manufacturer.

There is a growing market for compressorized engineered systems that are energy efficient, factory built and warranted. These systems are specifically designed for hospitals, hotels, restaurants, airport kitchens and other food service facilities. ColdZone + Filco builds packaged compressorized refrigeration systems for the food service industry and is the country's largest manufacturer of food service packaged refrigeration systems, while the Witt line pioneered a quick delivery system for replacement coils used in heating, cooling and refrigeration.

A greater awareness of history and the realization of the frailty of structures to the ravages of man and bird, brought about the introduction of such protective devices as Nixalite (**Nixalite of America**, East Moline) which was introduced in 1950. Nixalite is a splayed row of stainless steel prongs that is a simple, easy to install and humane way to keep birds from landing and to discourage other animals from climbing of trees, fences and other man-made obstacles.

Today
curved glass
display cases
are widely used.

KINGS OF THE ROAD CARRY THE LOAD

Although begun in 1944, the greatest reminders of the 1950s are the expressways which serve us everyday. The building of Chicago's expressway system consumed about $1.1 billion and preserved the city's reputation as the center of national commerce. Though trucking companies complained about the traffic, they could brag that Chicago was the largest handler of motor freight in the United States. From 1945 to 1955 trucker business quadrupled. The new use of diesel engines increased a truck's capacity and efficiency. About 100,000 trucks employing some 30,000 people made up the fleet of 2,000 local and 500 long haul firms active on Chicago streets. To handle the increased truck traffic, the city organized trucking terminals and built new warehouses and loading docks. Private firms did the same. Later studies would show that once the highways were built, the development of the trucking firms followed quickly, resulting in more congestion.

In the 1950s road construction was among the greatest of the state's public expenses and the federal government helped by funding the construction of the interstate system. This system, in turn, helped develop and expand the trucking industry which, as the railroads had before it, sought out Illinois, and most specifically Chicago, as the hub of its industry.

In the second half of the twentieth century, roadways have helped small towns such as McHenry which, in the mid-1960s, had a population of 3,600, and was predominantly a rural community with only a few manufacturers. The major employers were construction related. In 1992 McHenry supported a population of over 17,000 and was a rural diversified community with over 30 manufacturers.

Road construction reached a new level of automation in the mid-1960s, when the Miller Brothers founded the **Miller Formless Company** of McHenry, after they had developed and patented the first "automated guidance control" slip form curb and gutter machine. By early 1970 the evolution of the first Barrier Wall slip formed by "automated guidance control" was developed. These two developments were crucial to the construction of roads in the United States and elsewhere. Currently four manufacturers supply 90 percent of the United States market. The vocational and technical nature of companies such as Miller Formless encourage a close working relationship between industry, community and educational institutions, inspiring training and skill development for all levels of employment needs.

From 1945 to 1955 truck business quadrupled.

JUST PUSH THE BUTTON

Electronics was another growth industry that truly came to fruition in the 1950s. Clearly, by the late 1950s, America had progressed beyond the age of the "ordinary automatic." Merely saving labor was no longer a very remarkable thing. Products began to offer something more, something magical, something that could only be achieved at the press of a button. The "push-button age" seems the most comprehensive and evocative phrase used by people of that age to describe their remarkable, product driven culture. There was a tremendous proliferation of push buttons on products during the late 1950s and well into the 1960s. Electric stoves turned into keyboard ranges, with push buttons for each gradation of temperature. Washing machines sprouted buttons that specified particular types of wash. In some automobile models, the automatic transmission selector ceased to mimic an old gearshift lever and was replaced by a series of push buttons. In the Edsel, these push buttons were in the center of the steering wheel, where the horn used to be. In each of these instances there was no real technological advance. The significance of the push button was entirely symbolic. It had merely replaced another kind of control device that had been doing the job satisfactorily for many years. In most cases push buttons replaced rheostat dials, which were not merely as good as push buttons for most applications, but quite a lot better, since they allowed even more subtle and exact adjustment than could hundreds of push buttons.

But the push button had a meaning beyond practicality or convenience. It embodied promise. It told us the machine was complex and that it could function without our intervention. Pushing the button was a smaller, less intimate gesture than twisting a dial. And what we could not see was that the button we pushed was connected to a switch that really made everything happen. These switches could turn electronics on and off, even at the speed of light. The Cherry Corporation was founded in 1953 as the **Cherry Electrical Products Corporation,** by Walter L. Cherry in Highland Park, to manufacture a single

Switches are the work horses of electronics.

An early snap switch

product, the snap switch. Over the next two decades Cherry expanded, built and moved several times, finally settling in Waukegan and there expanding into a three building complex on a 30 acre site, with offices and production facilities in eight national and international locations.

Though Cherry has grown markedly in the past 40 years and holds hundreds of patents, both in the United States and abroad, and many more patent applications are on

A snap action switch of the 1990s

file, its original orientation as a component manufacturer selling to original equipment markets has not changed. Among the more significant developments since 1953 is the general purpose appliance switch (1957), the workhorse for the first 15 years and a standard in thousands of products from home appliances, automobiles, office machines, to computers. automotive electrical switches (1965) provide vehicle manufacturers with hundreds of customer specific configurations of in-dash, armrest, console, under the hood and weather exposed electrical and electronic devices. Printed circuit boards (1967), low energy gold crosspoint switches (1967), electronic keyboards (1969), electronic calculators (1971), exposure control crcuits (1977), motor speed controls (1984), waterproof switches (1985) and full travel membrane keyboards (1987) are all part of a fast growing industry in a world that is highly dependent on switches.

A small switch on Apollo 8 made Plainfield part of the space age.

The optoelectronic switches (1988) are the newest in contactless design. Depending on the intended application and service life specified by equipment and machinery designers and engineers, the optoelectronic switch is rated at 50 million cycles. This makes it ideal for office machines, vending machines, computers and telecommunications; applications in which dust and vibration threaten the life of traditional snap action switches. Today's product lines are divided into three main segments: Electronic Assemblies and Displays, Semiconductor Devices and Electromechanical Devices.

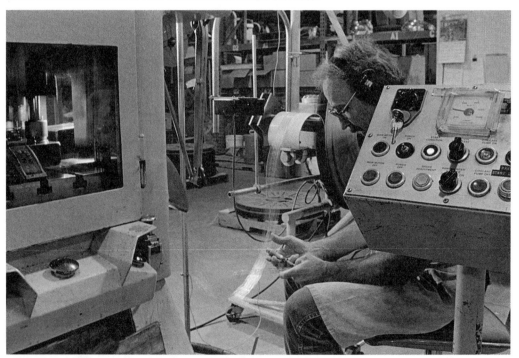

Plainfield Stamping with precision

Two tiny pieces in a swich no larger in diameter than a dime and one-half inch long were **Plainfield Tool and Engineering Company**'s (today known as **Plainfield Stamping - Illinois**) contribution to the Apollo 8 flight and Plainfield's entry into America's space program. The company had been founded in April of 1959 by Clifford W. Berglund, Clarence F. Schmitz and Allan R. Behl, with the goal to produce tooling and stamping for the electronic industry. Education and training of tool, die and mold makers has been of the utmost importance to the founders of PT&E. To this end they implemented a five year apprenticeship program approved by the United States Bureau of Apprenticeship Training. Classes were taught by the company principals at Plainfield Tool and Joliet Junior College. Today, Plainfield Stamping - Illinois, a part of **Plainfield Companies**, is known throughout the country and internationally for precision and innovation in producing complex parts in plastic and metal for the space aircraft and electronics industries.

Another pioneer in precision switch design is **Otto Engineering, Inc.** of Carpentersville, founded in 1961 by Jack Roeser, who started off building and marketing switches for other firms. Otto is the largest maker of cockpit controls for aircraft, and 800 Otto switches are in the space shuttle, yet its manufacturing and product development facilities are housed in a remodeled historic building dating from 1865.

Otto Engineering is housed in a remodeled historic building dating to 1865.

Otto's first sale was not a switch, but the A-5 Epoxy Applicator that Roeser had developed to apply epoxy to switch terminals. When Cook Electric saw it in action, they purchased one. This sale led to the creation of a separate equipment division, which sold mixing, dispensing and computer controlled application equipment. In 1988 the Equipment Division was sold to 3M.

Otto's first switch was a rotary one for Cook Electric, followed closely by the P1 Push-button line, which became the core of Otto's business for many years. In 1971 a second switch followed, the P2 Push-button for the McDonnell Douglas F-4 fighter; and a third, the B3 basic for Jay El Products, a maker of lighted cockpit controls; and a fourth, the T1 Toggle for the F-4.

The next year the product line expanded dramatically with the T2 and T4 Toggles and the P6 environment-free Push-button for the McDonnell Douglas F-15 Fighter. A slide switch for the Electro-Motive Division of General Motors soon followed. The rapid technology developments of the 1970s was fed on switches and the P1, EMD, B2 and B3 Basic Switches followed in quick succession. Switches originally designed for military needs found broad commercial application, including the Boeing 727 and the DC-8. By 1981 Otto employed almost 100 people. Today Otto employs over 150 people.

The 1980s saw many new Otto products, such as the U2 Trigger for the Sikorsky UH60 helicopter, the T6 Toggle for the General Dynamics F-16 fighter and the T5 for the McDonnell Douglas F-18, the P6-3 Sealed Basic, the B5 Basic, the B5-7 Basic, the B1 Basic and V1 Engineering Assembly, the P8 Mini Push-button and the T3 Toggle. Today Otto products are in the F-117A stealth fighter, the B1 and B2 bombers and find ever increasing commercial applications, such as the V1, which was developed for Motorola communication devices. Switches are now an integral part of farm tractors, lift trucks, boats, medical equipment and computers.

Another important innovator in electronics was the **Square D Company**, which in 1960 moved from Detroit to Park Ridge, then into a new building in Palatine in 1979. The Square D Company is a leading manufacturer of electrical distribution and control equipment, and a major supplier of electronic materials, components, products and systems.

Square D was founded in Detroit in 1903 as the McBride Manufacturing Co., and made cartridge-fuses. Five years later the firm acquired patent rights to make a revolutionary new safety switch housed in a cast-iron enclosure and designed to prevent direct exposure to electrical shock. In 1915 the operation, then known as Detroit Fuse and Manufacturing Co., began housing the switches in sheet-metal enclosures embossed with a new trademark, the letter "D" in a decorative square. Customers began referring to the product as "that square D switch" and in 1917 the name was changed to Square D Company. Since then, through development of new products and a series of successful mergers and acquisitions, Square D has earned a leadership position in the electrical equipment industry.

Hydrocarbons not fluorocarbons propelled aerosol.

The founder of **Hurley Chicago Company**, Jason Hurley, invented the company's first product, the Hurley Town & Country water filter in 1969, and started production in 1972. This product pioneered the use of hot water backwash to maintain home drinking water filters. At the time of its introduction, there were about seven companies with similar products. Now there are 200.

LET US SPRAY

DuPont has recognized Edward Seymour, founder of **Seymour** of Sycamore, as the inventor of pigmented spray coating — in the vernacular, spray paint. The year was 1949, and the color was aluminum. Not that aerosol was not known; it had been used for insect repellent sprays called spray bombs and for a clear paint spray called Crylon. In the early days the propellants were fluorocarbons, but they were expensive to produce and difficult to control. At the time their long term effect on the earth's atmosphere was unknown. By the mid-1960s enough evidence had been gathered against fluorocarbons to ban them. At the same time the aerosol industry was already shifting to hydrocarbons as the propellant of choice, because they were cheaper to produce, easier to control and kinder to the environment.

Seymour knew that pigments suspended in a medium, such as oil, had the urge to settle on the bottom of the can, and that it was necessary to stir paints. But the paint in a sealed aerosol can could not be stirred by conventional means, a stick. What to do? To stir the paint something had to be inside the sealed can, so Seymour invented, then patented the device that mixes the color inside the container. We hear it as the rattle. It's actually a bead, usually polygonal in shape for greater efficiency and made of metal. Seymour patented all possible shapes for the bead except the sphere, which was not possible. Today there are about 20 companies in the aerosol paint industry, producing about 350 million units annually, of which Seymour produces about 20 million.

BABY BOOMERS ARE THE FUTURE, NOW

During the 1960s Americans finally did see their countrymen land on the moon, and a great many of them sent their children off to college and a wholly different kind of life. For the most part the promises of the 1950s had been, more or less, fulfilled. Still, by 1964 it was becoming clear that the look — and the meaning of things — was starting to change. Ultimately, the age was limited by the same demographic phenomena that had brought it into being. As early as 1953 Fortune had predicted major changes for the market in about 1965, as the first wave of the baby-boomers started to consume things. Actually, the change came a little earlier than that, because the clothing, record, fast-food and cosmetic industries succeeded in tapping into the baby-boom market early, and sixteen-year olds were acquiring cars by 1962 and 1963 at a pace nobody would have dared predict a decade earlier. And while their parents had been conditioned to look toward the future, anticipate it and plan for it, the baby-boomers took a very different signal from all they had been exposed to while growing up. They were not waiting for the future. They *were* the future. The Mickey Mouse Club had told them daily that they were "the leaders of the twenty-first century," but who wanted to wait until 50?

MacLean-Fogg's taping machine was first offered to the market in the 1960s

AN AGE OF RAPID CHANGE

In 1970 seven of the United States' top 22 industrial plants employing more than 4,000 workers were in Chicago. Throughout the 1970s Illinois remained a strong manufacturing state.

Cleaning up is hard to do.

Where there were once single great manufacturers in each aspect of manufacturing, the 1970s and 1980s saw specialization and downsizing become bywords for industry. Manufacturers saw themselves competing on an international level as they never had before. For some manufacturers, international competion proved disasterous, especially for those who had not kept pace with technology that throughout the 1970s was changing at an unprecedented pace. Others adapted and have contributed significantly to Illinois. A case in point is **Walterscheid, Inc.** of Burr Ridge, which successfully introduced the wide angle constant velocity universal joints for farm implements, first in Europe, and then to the agricultural industry of North America in 1978. By the late 1980s Walterscheid was the world leader in the manufacture and sales of these joints. The application of this invention to agricultural machinery made it possible to transmit power smoothly through corners and thus increase the efficiency and productivity of farm operations. The market importance of the joints to the American farmer can be seen by the entry of three other manufacturers with similar designs. To date Walterscheid remains the clear market leader.

The cult of health and physical fitness that began to emerge in America in the 1970s brought with it the beginning of an awareness by some that major changes had occurred in the state's, nation's and world's environment over the past few decades. This awareness led to efforts to find the culprits. Soon the fingers began to point at industry, especially American industry. Public and political agitation soon led to restriction on automobile exhaust emissions, factory smoke stack emmissions, factory noise level and many others. Often the restrictions added great cost to doing business, and the traditional attitude of passing the cost on to the consumer wasn't always found to be the best solution. As a result, industry suffered and critics flourished. While nuclear fuel production (thought by many in the 1950s to be the fuel of the immediate future) was singled out and severely curtailed through governmental action in its traditional methods of production and disposal, others, such as steel production, were found not only to be dirty, but non-competitive when it came to meeting cheaper foreign steel production head on. The need to clean up not just the immediate debris from these industries, but to comply with retroactive demands, put a great burden on some Illinois industry, while it spurred others on. Starting in the 1970s the growing awareness of all kinds of refuse has led to the growth of the waste management industry. Containing and sealing corrosive fluids has become a serious consideration.

Row, Inc. of Addison, founded in 1976 for the development of "resilient teflon" O-Rings, has faced the challenge as the only company in the world to manufacture teflon encapsulated silicone and viton gaskets. Their O-Rings have the capability of acting as an elastomer, but with the added feature of being resistant to practically all known chemicals and temperatures ranging from minus 177°C to plus 260°C. Handy, when we consider that we have to dispose of some very toxic stuff that as a side-effect may have cured our ailments, powered our air conditioners and allowed us to drive cars. Row is one of the very few manufacturers that has settled into this niche.

Acme recycles barrels

Over the last hundred years the **Acme Barrel Company** of Chicago has maintained a level of leadership and innovation which is the model of that industry. Today Acme Barrel is the largest steel drum reconditioning facility in the United States — almost 2,000,000 steel drums a year. On a typical day Acme reconditions over 3,500 30-55 gallon capacity tight head drums and over 4,000 30-55 gallon capacity open head drums. As soon as the drums enter the Open Head Plant, they are sent through the oxidation process and then are steel shot blasted to remove all identification. Unlike most reconditioners who store "raw" drums with residues present and original labels left on, Acme's inventories consist of clean, processed containers. This gives Acme a larger ready-to-paint inventory with shorter lead times while virtually eliminating customer's environmental exposure. With tight head drums the goal is the same: an unidentifiable, ready-to-paint steel drum. The tight head drums are first sent through a chemical flush, then processed through a unique Acme system that removes all labels. After this the exteriors are shot blasted to remove all paint and identification. Then the drums are inventoried to customer specifications. Because they are tougher, safer, cheaper and can be almost infinitely recycled, steel drums have proven to be environmentally safer than most alternative products.

The manufacture of stock and custom knives for the plastic, paper, agricultural and recycling industries is a niche that **Zenith Cutter Co.** of Rockford has grown into. Founded in 1923, Zenith made cutters for the furniture and woodworking industry, became involved with the corrugated box industry. As the industry grew, so did Zenith's share of the business, to the point of now supplying blades for virtually every domestic and foreign machine used in box manufacturing plants.

Another company that has found its niche is **MacLean-Fogg**. The primary product of MacLean-Fogg of Mundelein, from its beginning in 1925 through about 1975, was a lock nut that prevented the loosening of bolted joints when exposed to vibration fatigue and shock loads. At first the lock nuts were used almost exclusively by the railroads, but as automobile usage increased, that industry also required them.

For the first few years the company was very small; then, in 1929, John MacLean became aware of the Water-Tight Bolt, which had been turned down by a number of bigger companies. MacLean saw the impact the invention could have: water tight bolts could eliminate seepage of water into box cars, which was then a severe problem. He bought the invention. In 1954 the Industrial Locking Fastener Division was formed.

One of its most important tasks was to educate manufacturers of the superior performance of fasteners. In the 1930s before lock nuts were used on automobiles, every joint of a new car had to be tightened after the factory assembly and before the new owner took her first spin. Periodic tightenings were then required as part of regular maintenance. The lock nut eliminated the need for periodic tightenings by having the nuts locked at the time of assembly in the factory, once and for all.

From this one product serving a narrow market, MacLean-Fogg grew into three major business groups, serving communities such as Savanna with employment opportunities, and a broad spectrum of markets with engineered fasteners and assemblies; high voltage

Lock nuts eliminated the need for periodic tightenings.

MacLean-Fogg's nylon insert locking nuts

connectors; silicone rubber insulators and support devices; precision suspension and power train components. A current trend among many larger companies is to have outside engineering design a product for the company. MacLean-Fogg has been especially capable of responding to these needs with its own engineering and support staff.

Specialization, service and niche marketing have become important.

Among MacLean-Fogg's many products is the Compositz Suspension Insulator. This insulator weighs 10 percent as much as one made of porcelain, providing significant cost savings in shipping and installation. Since the cost of an insulator includes such factors as transportation, storage, handling, breakage, cleaning, installation, maintenance and line losses, in addition to the insulator itself, a new material can amount to a considerable savings in time and money.

Fastener making at MacLean-Fogg in 1925

Each new product is thoroughly tested; starting with the inspection of incoming raw materials. The finished product is distributed through 30 selected companies, with 100 stocking locations nationwide. In case of an emergency or disaster, MacLean-Fogg maintains a separate storm stocking facility at O'Hare Field.

Other operative words of the 1970s were specialization and service, with the corporate management targeting niche markets which rewarded specialized skills with a loyal customer base. Among the manufacturers who developed this outlook was **Goodman Equipment Corporation**, one of the world's premier suppliers of mining locomotives and parts. Goodman Equipment was not a new company in the early 1970s when it began to adapt niche thinking, but it did have a new management team and ideas to sell a product for which the company had been respected for over one hundred years. Herbert Goodman had begun manufacturing underground mining locomotives in Chicago in 1889, making

Mimeograph offered new heights in duplicating

his first delivery in 1891. The original locomotive was designed by ElmerAmbrose Sperry, the inventor of the Sperry gyroscope. By 1904 Goodman locomotives were moving freight through Chicago's underground maze of tunnels. Two years later the company's first export went to New Zealand. Since then Goodman has been exporting worldwide. In 1965

Goodman locomotives moved freight through Chicago's underground tunnels.

An Elmer Ambrose Sperry designed locomotive

Goodman was sold to Westinghouse Air Brake Company, which in turn was acquired by American Standard in 1968, only to be bought shortly thereafter by a group of investors headed by Calvin A. Campbell, Jr., who returned the company to its roots under the name Goodman Equipment. Goodman entered the plastics processing market in 1979 with the purchase of the **Improved/IMCO Plastics** machinery lines. This diversification allowed the company to form two plastics divisions: Improved Parts & Service and **Improved Blow Molding Equipment Company**. Today Goodman Equipment Corporation is head-quartered in Bedford Park and, besides plastics molding machinery, still manufactures locomotives from 1.5 to 50 tons to transport people, materials and supplies. In mines they haul gold, silver, tin and uranium. Above ground they move tourists around Disneyland and through Chicago's Museum of Science and Industry's coal mine exhibit.

Goodman's 3 ton Titan BN storage battery locomotive

When it
rains it pours.

On September 24, 1982 **Morton Norwich** was merged with **Thiokol Corporation**. The result was named **Morton Thiokol, Inc.**, a Chicago-based company with four areas of specialization: specialty chemicals, high-technology propulsion systems, salt and household products. The Morton of Morton Thiokol refers to **Morton Salt Company**, founded in Chicago in 1848, which is today the largest domestic salt producer and the only national distributor in the United States. The company has many evaporated and rock salt mine production facilities. Its trademark image, the Morton Salt Umbrella Girl on Morton Blue Package table salt, is world famous.

The Texize division of Morton Thiokol began in 1945 as a manufacturer and marketer of cleaning and household laundry products. Over the years Texize products such as Spray 'n Wash soil and stain remover, Fantastik spray cleaner, Glass Plus glass, appliance and cabinet cleaner, Pine Power pine oil disinfectant and Yes detergent have become market leaders in their categories.

The by-word of the 1980s was recycle and a number of Illinois companies entered into this field with innovations that are not much yet heralded. One of these, **Equipco** of Monmouth, organized in 1980, introduced the idea of re-manufacturing commercial soda fountain dispensing machines to Coca Cola USA, saving the company money and the nation raw materials, over replacing an old dispenser with a new one. Coca Cola now places more re-manufactured units than new units.

The computer came of age in the early 1980s and by the end of the decade its application has become almost universal. The first and only computer designed corneal contact lenses for low vision applications, using only a math model of the patient's cornea, was developed by **IVM Corp.** of Decatur. The company may be the only manufacturer of "night vision contact lenses" for retinitis pigmentosa and 100 percent protective UV-vision enhancing contact lenses for ocular albinism, sports, police and military use.

Since 1990 **International Superabrasives Ltd.** of Elk Grove Village has been in a joint venture with a company in the Ukraine to process industrial diamond crystals that meet United States manufacturing needs and standards.

Brewing was a mainstay of Illinois economy for much of the last century. Then, in the last three decades, large firms bought up the small ones and local beer production tempered to local tastes, became a thing of the past. But the return to nature of the 1960s came to a head in the 1980s with the founding of numerous small breweries. One of these is Elmhurst-based **Pavichevich Brewing Co.**, founded in 1989 by former Chicago policeman Ken Pavichevich.

MIXED RESULTS

Other specialized companies of the 1980s include **Fluid Management** of Wheeling, the world's leading manufacturer of mixing and tinting equipment for the paint industry. The company's equipment has helped create an industry, not just for consumers but also for original equipment manufacturers by providing equipment and engineering systems to other industries — food, ink, coatings, chemical and cosmetics.

Fluid Management started in 1987 by acquiring the Addison based firm of **Miller Paint Equipment, Inc.** This firm began as a hardware store in 1927. Ten years later the family patriarch invented the first vertical armed paint mixer. This machine was the first in a long line of other innovations for paint industry equipment which opened up a vast new business for paint retailers, hardware stores and other manufacturers. The simple to use machines dispense and mix fluids, among them colorant that satisfied the demand for a wide variety of affordable, custom-tinted paint. This machinery was the forerunner to Just-In-Time concepts and flexible manufacturing, since it enabled paint manufacturers and original equipment manufacturers to produce just the quantities of custom colors needed. Nabisco uses the machines to add flavorings and other ingredients that once were mixed by hand. The result is a more consistent product and lower labor costs.

Harbil Manufacturing Company of Wheeling was acquired by Fluid Management in November, 1988. Harbil began business in 1946 as a sales organization for **Chicago Commutator, Inc.**, a 1942 founded manufacturer that produced Harbil's exclusive twin-cradle oscillating paint mixer. The principals of the firm, Harry Rossett and Bill Weismann, combined their names, "Har" and "Bil," to name the firm.

Only a handful of companies produce ink vehicles in the United States; one of them was **Lovite**, which since 1989 has been known as **Akso Resins and Vehicles** of Matteson. The material is sold to ink manufacturers. Ink has traditionally been petroleum based and difficult to dispose of properly. Until quite recently, as with so many other potentially damaging liquids, much ink just went down the drain. It's a bit differnt now. To meet environmental concerns, Akso and others in the ink vehicle industry have been moving away from a petroleum-based chemistry to a soy-based one. The soy-based inks have been shown to be environmentally more responsible than petroleum based ones, for now.

COPY MACHINES

An environment that has gone through major changes in the past few decades is the one found in the office. Over 200 manufacturers of office equipment have called Chicago home in the past century. Office equipment has been an important aspect of Chicago manufacturing. In the 1950s the modern office could not function without an Addressograph, Comptometer or the Ditto. **Victor Adding Machine Company**, organized in 1918, made the Comptometer.

Among the most important of the office equipment manufacturers is the **A. B. Dick Company**, founded by Albert Blake Dick III who originated the Ditto trademark in 1918 and coined the word "mimeograph," which was invented in 1884. The mission of the company, to quote A.B. Dick, was to "put marks on paper." And it did. The fluid that made the Ditto possible was supplied by T.A. Heyer, who had established a business in 1903 that produced and sold his Chicago Hektograph. The **Heyer Company** is still a producer of stencil and spirit duplicating machines. Ditto also made addressing machines and out of this business a revolutionary technology developed — the Videojet — the world's fastest printer.

Much of manufacturing is about new products and new products are about research and invention as well as risk. So it was with the Videojet. During the research and development of this project Jim Stone, head of a team charged with the responsibility of developing new technologies for A.B. Dick, noticed very interesting technology being developed at Stanford University. At Stanford the possibility was becoming a reality that the electron beam in a CRT, or "picture" tube in lay terms, could be used to place an electrostatic charge on paper. The latent image formed by these charges could then be developed and fused to create a permanent image. In theory this would occur at the speed of light, because the images were placed by beams of electrons.

At the time integrated circuit, solid-state or RAM memories had not been developed; in fact, very little technology was available to make the theory work. But inventing and testing ideas quickly led to a CRT with a faceplate with vacuum-tight imbedded wires which could conduct the electron beam to paper sensitive to electrostatic images. The practical breakthrough came when the research team determined how to form characters on the faceplate using an electron beam. Electric light writing was on view. At the same time mechanisms needed to move a web of paper, develop latent images, and cut and spool the printed paper, all at very high speed, were also being devised.

The work paid off with the invention of the world's fastest printer, fastest, at least the 1960s. Soon related products were developed, including the full page Fax machine and high speed graphic printers for the United States Government. One unit was used to print a continuous picture of freight trains as they passed by.

Once this first step towards electric character generation had been taken, others followed quickly. Soon marks were made on TV screens. These occurred after a fast core memory and a new circuit designed to work at TV speed, which was programmed by data entered using an electronic keyboard, had been created.

A very early public application of this technology occurred when the ballot totals for the 1968 elections were broadcast. Forever handwriting would be obsolete and TV screens could scroll information to the viewer horizontally or vertically. The most dramatic use of this technology may very well have been when Neil Armstrong stepped on the moon and millions of TV viewers read the text "One small step for a man, one giant step for mankind" scrolling horizontally across the bottom of their screens.

> Handwriting almost became obsolete.

During the development of the display control unit, the DCU, Richard Sweet, a scientist at Stanford University, wrote to the Vice President of Engineering at A.B. Dick describing a primitive oscillograph that had no moving parts and produced an image of electrical signals using drops of ink. The idea that "we can generate characters electronically and this can print an image of electrical signals" was born.

Bar code printers save materials.

"But can it print in ink without moving parts?" was the next question. So non-contact printing began. And within a few years **Videograph Operations**, as the Industrial Development Division of A.B. Dick was known, introduced the first commercial ink jet printer, a high speed, noiseless line printer. It was called the Videojet, and it was ahead of its time. It could print so fast that it had to slow down to let the then fastest computers feed it data. It was also very fussy, demanding much care and maintenance. It was not yet office trained. The breakthrough came when a large can manufacturer inquired regarding the feasibility of printing date code identifiers onto beverage cans. The beverage industry had spent a great deal of money over the years trying to code their cans, all without success. The challenge was to code cans moving at 2,000 feet per minute, or 22.7 miles per hour. A prototype was installed in Milwaukee. Cans of beer were coded so efficiently that the brewer would not stop it until after a permanent installation was in operation. What began as an experiment is today a worldwide standard, coding over two billion beverage cans per year. For many years **Videojet Systems International, Inc.** has been world dominant in the marking and coding industry, printing over 14 billion codes and product identifiers on everything from milk cartons to computer chips every year.

THE BAR CODE TENDER KNOWS ALL

Ink jet technology was introduced in the United States in 1980. The basic technology is driven by a microprocessor which is operated by special software. The software drives each print head which is connected to the controller by a data line. A canister of pressurized ink is connected to the print head serving as an ink reservoir. Inside the print head is a series of electro-magnetic solenoids that activates a plunger to control the ink which is propelled from the orifices. The orifices are arranged vertically so that one cycle of each solenoid creates one vertical column of dots. Characters and symbols are formed by the solenoids opening and closing selectively based on the program. The first LP (Large Character Print) ink jet printed bar code was created in 1981. These bar codes were printed with a print head containing seven valves, each firing one droplet of ink at a time. Each drop of ink measured approximately 80 thousands of an inch in diameter.

Among the early applications of this technology, called the 80 mil bar coding system, was by a manufacturer of salad dressing and cooking oils. The products were produced and packed in one building and then they were sent along conveyors to another building to be warehoused. The 80 mil bar system proved a cost advantage over printed labels and a great aid in efficiency. Today the 80 mil bar system does not meet any industry specifications and is thus primarily used for internal, company specific controls, such as counting, sorting, quality and inventory control. In the past decade the bar code has expanded its functions greatly to include such information as dates, time codes, batch codes and sequential numbers, and is used on a wide range of handling systems. The Uniform Code Council (UCC) has responded to the demands of industry and developed a bar code symbol specification for shipping containers which is called the "UCC shipping container code." The purpose of this specification is to provide a series of guidelines for manufacturers to bar code their shipping containers.

Real time production information has become important.

DISTRIBUTED BY:
JEWEL FOOD STORES, INC.
MELROSE PARK, IL 60160
©Jewel Food Stores, Inc. 1991

0 41280 03223 7

Reg. Penna. Dept. Agr. RPB　　　　　　**Made in U.S.A.**
SATISFACTION GUARANTEED OR YOUR MONEY BACK

Once the UCC specifications became accepted, ink jet manufacturers were requested to develop a bar-code printer that would comply with the new regulations. The 80 mil didn't. Soon a bar code print head was developed to meet all industry specifications. The latest generation of ink jet printers is called the Symbol Jet and is capable of printing a 40 mil bar code.

Saving on materials is another advantage of the bar code printer. By printing on a wide range of materials, including generic cartons — ones that are not product specific, the user does not need to maintain his own inventory of cartons, but can use cartons purchased in quantity as needed. These cartons are fresh, strong and uniform and take up less space than stored cartons which have gathered moisture and fatigued. Another important factor is that an ink jet printer operates in real time. This means that every label can have a unique identity. And because of advances in printer technology, the desired information can be printed in human readable format or in bar coding. Real time production information has become important in the food and drug industry. Since the very first relatively primitive seven-dot versions to today's high quality printers, ink jet printer manufacturers have provided the food and pharmaceutical manufacturing industry and others with a low cost method of coding and control through direct to carton non-contact printing.

SURVIVAL IS CHANGE

The survival of a manufacturer over many years usually shows a great ability to adapt to changes in the industrial environment. Many Illinois manufacturers have adapted well; among them is **Navistar International Corporation** which was born out of International Harvester in 1986. That year the International Harvester name and the IH symbol were sold to **Tenneco Inc.** as part of the sale of the IH's agricultural equipment assets.

A leader in
farm equipment
switches
to trucks.

International Harvester lands

The eventual metamorphosis of Navistar out of International Harvester began in 1902. The two leading manufacturers of harvesting machinery at the turn of the century were McCormick's organization and the **Deering Harvester Company**, both located in Chicago. Deering had been founded in 1869 by William Deering. In 1902 the two companies combined with three smaller concerns — the Milwaukee Harvester Company; Warder, Bushnell and Glessner Company; and the Plano Manufacturing Company — to form the **International Harvester Company**. The prime reasons behind the organization of the new Company were to develop new products, to bring about a more diversified line and to give more attention to the foreign market.

During the latter part of the nineteenth century, the farm equipment industry, influenced by the rapid expansion of agriculture for which it was so largely responsible, grew into one of the most highly competitive businesses in America. This period of severe competition had a restricting effect: so many companies entered this market that no single enterprise could muster enough capital to engage in normal development or expansion. At one time it was estimated that more than 2,000 concerns were manufacturing one or more lines of equipment. Most were barely able to keep abreast of the times — much less anticipate the farmer's needs.

With the exception of the Warder, Bushnell and Glessner plant at Springfield, Ohio, that of the Milwaukee Harvester Company and a Deering factory at Hamilton, Ontario, all manufacturing properties acquired by the consolidation were located in or around Chicago. The plant of the Plano Manufacturing Company on Chicago's south side became the company's **West Pullman Works**. The company also established its General Offices in Chicago, where they have remained. In addition, Deering, which had reached the forefront in its field largely through its manufacturing sagacity, contributed to the corporation coal, iron and timber lands and a steel mill in South Chicago, better known as the **Wisconsin Steel Works**, giving the company a source of raw materials sufficient to provide for expansion and product diversification.

The first step in the development of a complete line was the acquisition of the D.M. Osborne Company, at Auburn, New York, which manufactured a line of harvesting and tillage implements designed to meet the eastern trade. Because of its location near the eastern seaboard, the addition of that plant was also in line with the company's desire to expand its foreign trade. In 1904 the purchase of the **Keystone Company** of Rock Falls added an historic line of tillage and haying tools. This factory, subsequently sold, became known as **Rock Falls Works**. About this time the **Weber Wagon Works** of Chicago became an IH property. The company's line of farm implements became complete with the acquisition in 1918 of steel and chilled plows through the purchase of companies which operated the Canton Plant in Canton, a plant in Chattanooga, Tennessee and the addition of a line of seeding machines manufactured in Richmond, Virginia.

Pneumatic tired tractors were introduced in 1933.

Throughout this period there was a general tendency to simplify the various lines of traditional harvesting machinery. The pioneer light harvester-thresher was introduced in 1914; the stationary thresher four years later. Every new machine developed was in response to definite needs of agriculture.

In the last century many attempts were made to apply the steam tractor to plowing, the farmer's most difficult job. Because of its cost, size and general unwieldiness, it could be employed profitably only on the immense acreages of the West. Farmers of quarters and half sections never seriously considered the steam tractor. Its real importance lay in the fact that it was a step in the right direction. As the internal combustion tractor emerged from its experimental stages, the steam tractor was doomed. During those first years designers were convinced that there could be neither power nor traction without great weight. It quickly became obvious that lessening the weight per horsepower would improve the machine's performance. Deering had already experimented with gas engines as early as 1889. As might be expected, IH was one of the first companies to explore the possibilities of this new kind of power in 1905. Production of various models began in 1908.

The incentive provided by the huge wartime demand for tractors led many automobile manufacturers into the farm power field. The influence of the automotive design led to many changes in the farm tractor and began a trend toward a smaller machine, more suitable for the ordinary small farm of the Middle West.

The Farmall model by IH was the first successful attempt at building a genuine all-purpose tractor. Its introduction in 1922 revolutionized the tractor industry. A landmark in tractor production was reached in October, 1926 when production of Farmall tractors was begun at the newly equipped Farmall Works in Rock Island.

Pneumatic tired tractors were introduced in 1933. Although they increased the original cost of the tractor, rubber tires had many advantages, the most important of which was the lessened rolling resistance and consequent reduction in fuel costs. Rubber tires for the first time admitted the tractor to the paved highway.

When roads improved, wheel diameters were reduced.

The International Harvester company's entry into the field of motor transportation was inspired by a recognized need of the farmer. Farmers who were not near a railroad were finding the horse and wagon an utterly inadequate, time-consuming means of hauling their product to the market. Trips to town were necessarily infrequent when they involved an expenditure of long hours or days of indispensable horse and manpower.

As early as 1898, E.A. Johnston of the Engineering Department had installed a gas engine in a wagon-type chassis and driven it successfully between his home and the McCormick Works for many months. In 1905 Mr. Johnston designed and developed an Auto Buggy at the Rock Falls Works. Its purpose was to haul moderate amounts of produce to and from the market and take the farm family to church on Sundays. Production was abandoned in 1911. Development efforts now concentrated on the engineering and manufacture of trucks. The volume of truck production had reached a point in 1937 that justified the erection of a plant to be devoted exclusively to the production of truck engines. Indianapolis was chosen as the site. International Harvester trucks have long been famed for their ability to stand up under tough conditions. The high-wheeled construction of the original Auto Buggies and Auto Wagons was designed to allow these vehicles to traverse the muddy, rutted country roads the average farmer was forced to cope with. Only after improvement had been made in the nations's highways was the diameter of the wheel reduced.

Some International Harvester trucks from the past

Tractors became really practical for construction and industrial use when the regular McCormick-Deering 10-20 was modified by the addition of a tracklaying device to make the first International crawler tractor. Later IH crawler tractors were built with more and more horsepower to meet the needs of heavy construction and logging work, and also to satisfy the demand from farmers who needed the extra power and traction of the crawler-type tractor to pull heavy combines and gang plows over the immense hilly acreages of the West. By 1933 the first diesel engine was installed in an IH crawler tractor, the TD-40. This was the first American made diesel engine that started on gasoline and after a minute or less shifted to full diesel operation.

Cooperation can create jobs.

In 1938 IH produced the TD-18, its first tractor designed for exclusive industrial application. No longer were industrial tractors simply modifications of farm tractors; an entirely new field had been opened with its own distinctive characteristics.

Early in the 1940s the company's management recognized the need for a major reorganization of a corporate structure that had remained virtually unchanged since the time of the merger in 1902. To make sure that the proper attention would be given to the design, manufacture and sale of each of the product lines, it was decided that separate divisions, each responsible for a single group of products, should be established. The company's product lines were represented by the Agricultural Equipment Division, the Truck Division, the Pay Line Division, covering Industrial and Construction Equipment, the Solar Division, responsible for gas turbine engines, the Overseas Division and the Wisconsin Steel Division.

In 1964 the Wisconsin Steel Division became the first Chicago area steel producer to convert to the highly efficient basic oxygen furnaces. Two years later a continuous casting facility was completed which eliminated three steps from the former methods of making steel. This was the first time the basic oxygen and continuous casting operations had been used together on a commercial basis in the United States. A third improvement, put in operation in 1968, was vacuum degassing, a process that improves the quality of steel by removing nitrogen, hydrogen and oxygen from the molten liquid.

Throughout the 1970s and 1980s IH weathered out of the most difficult series of crises any American corporation had ever faced. It came out of the storm in 1985-86 with a new corporate identity and a new corporate name, Navistar International Corporation. The name, Navistar, is derived from "navigate" and "star" and is meant to express direction, progress and destination. The "star" in the name indicates not just the goal seeking objectives, but "outstanding performance."

Navistar manufactures and markets International brand medium and heavy trucks, school bus chassis and mid-range diesel engines in North America and selected export markets. Since its founding, Navistar has led the North American combined medium and heavy truck market and is the world's largest supplier of diesel engines in the 130-270 horsepower range. The company's products, parts and services are sold through a dealer network spanning approximately 950 outlets in the United States and Canada.

COOPERATING INTO THE FUTURE

Cooperation between an American company and a foreign one can be positive and help keep domestic jobs and revenues in Illinois. Beginning production in September of 1988 with the Mitsubishi Eclipse and Plymouth Laser, **Diamond-Star Motors** in Normal has been a joint venture between Chrysler and Mitsubishi since 1985. The venture continued a long tradition of automobile manufacturing in Illinois. Six years later the Diamond-Star Motors became a wholly-owned subsidiary of Mitsubishi. The facility has an annual capacity of 240,000 cars.

UNO-VEN achieves high fuel yields.

Since its appearence in December, 1989, **The UNO-VEN Company**, of Arlington Heights and Romeoville, a partnership between affiliates of Unocal Corporation's Union Oil Company of California and Petroleos de Venezuela, S.A. (PDVSA), has proven its ability to extract high yields of valuable light products from each barrel of crude oil it receives. These products, manufactured at the company's 153,000 barrel-per-day refinery, are predominately the high volume fuels used by midwestern motorists, airlines, railroads, trucking fleets and industrial and agricultural consumers.

The UNO-VEN Company's refinery provides a reliable supply of petroleum products to the Midwest

UNO-VEN's single refinery in Romeoville, currently one of the most modern in the United States, also manufactures solvents used by the chemical industry to produce plastics, paints and coatings, carpeting, detergents, dyes, pharmaceuticals, synthetic fibers, adhesives and even food preservatives. Amazingly, only about 2 percent of a barrel of crude is used to make these solvents, yet they are key ingredients in the production of many of the products which improve our standard of living.

The company employs approximately 1,200 people, 750 of these at the refinery. While stressing the manufacture of valuable light petroleum products, the importance of maximizing the uses for lower value residual products is not neglected.

The production of "needle coke" serves as an example. **Lemont Carbon, Inc.,** a Unocal subsidiary, and UNO-VEN each hold a 50 percent interest in **The Needle Coker Company**, which owns and operates a plant adjacent to the UNO-VEN refinery in Romeoville. Utilizing Unocal's proprietary technology in its production of needle coke, a highly specialized product is produced that is used internationally to make electrodes for the steel industry. By further processing oil that would otherwise be sold at residual fuel oil prices, the production of needle coke results in a considerable upgrade over the stock from which it is manufactured.

A related refinery product is petroleum coke. This coke remains after the maximum yield of valuable light products has been extracted from crude oil. Used as an industrial carbon feedstock or fuel, it is shipped from the refinery by barge to the Great Lakes region and the United States Gulf Coast.

Finding relatively higher value uses for traditionally lower valued products is a very important application of technology that will help feed Illinois' manufacturing in the future.

For well over a century, Illinois has been home to the nation's leading manufacturers. Some of these have entered their golden years, while others are just developing their positions in a rapidly changing world of demands. Demands not even dreamed of five decades ago are now the motivating force of many manufacturers.

As materials changed from metal or wood to synthetics, whole new supply systems developed. These new systems often demanded an interdependence and cooperation on an international level, which has occasioned some discomfort to many, yet is absolutely necessary for manufacturing to survive. It is with all this in mind, and the weight of more than a century of manufacturing strength, that the IMA has advised its members and guided government to act in ways that will be more than immediately gratifying and effect them personally for the next century to come.

Applying technology to find higher value uses for lower valued products is essential.

*IMA President James Donnelly and U.S. Secretary of State
John Foster Dulles, Annual Meeting, 1955*

A HISTORY OF THE IMA

From its start, the purpose of the Illinois Manufacturers' Association (IMA) has been to inform and educate its membership and the general public; promote government policies beneficial to manufacturers and advocate a free enterprise system. For one hundred years, the IMA has looked out for the interests of the people of Illinois.

The relative freedom from laws against industry was one of the key reasons for Illinois developing an important manufacturing base. The IMA was founded in 1893 in response to a perceived threat to individual freedom. On August 24, 1893 an organizational meeting was held at the Medinah Temple by "a number of manufacturers of the city of Chicago for the purpose of cooperating to test the constitutionality of a recent act of the legislature of this state limiting the hours of female labor." The group maintained that the law deprived women of the liberty of making a contract for their labor, and also of the wages that could be earned during longer work days.

The charter members of the IMA were all in one way or another involved in piecemeal manufacturing, such as was common in garment and shoe production. This type of manufacturing was among the earliest threatened with foreign competition, tariffs and unionization. Pushed along by the influx of immigrants from Europe, the unionization of American industry began in earnest in the 1880s. The Knights of Labor enjoyed phenomenal growth between 1880 and 1887, at which time they counted a membership of over 700,000. By 1893 manufacturers, especially those in Illinois, felt themselves pressed enough to form a protective organization of their own. After a series of open confrontations the IMA was formed. What was essential was that the members be firmly united in their determination to defend their interests against the pretensions of organized labor at the workplace and in the legislatures.

The bylaws, as well as the certificate for organization of the corporation, "to be known as the Illinois Manufacturers' Association," were filed with the Secretary of State, W. H. Hinrichsen, on November 23, 1893. Further, it was stated that "the object for which this Association is formed is to protect and further the business and interests of the manufacturers in Illinois, to develop the relations existing between them, and to facilitate the interchange of ideas relating to any kind of manufacturing industry in said State." The IMA has pursued these objectives vigorously for the past century.

The first challenge faced by the newly-founded IMA was the suit challenging the women's work law brought by J. E. Tilt, a member of the IMA's Executive Committee. Its outcome would affect many manufacturers. The legislation had passed in the last session of the General Assembly and many manufacturers considered it a violation of their rights and those of working people alike. The law was seen as a piece of dangerous radicalism. The manufacturers believed that the women's work law was unconstitutional in that it was an arbitrary infringement of the right of free contract. The suit was carried all the way to the

Illinois Supreme Court, which declared the law unconstitutional in 1894. The manufacturers of Illinois had scored their first victory, which set the direction the IMA would take for the next few decades.

In Illinois, as elsewhere, organized labor was extremely aggressive in its fight for power, and aroused great resentment among employers. What was most feared was that labor had definite economic and social objectives toward which it was striving. The Chicago Typographical Union, in 1879, began a campaign for the eight-hour day. This campaign was largely managed by the Socialist Labor Party. In their demand for the eight hour day, the socialists had the support of over 20 labor unions. The movement eventually became so threatening that in 1887 the Chicago Typothetae Association was organized among Chicago printing houses to offer specific resistance.

From the way the IMA was organized, it had all the indications of being a one time, "face one law" kind of organization. In the founding year, 144 or so manufacturers supported the efforts of the IMA and joined the membership. The next year saw a growth in new membership, while many of the first year members did not renew. The years 1894 to 1898 must have been trying times for the organization; members joined and fell away with each legislative season. In its first decade, the IMA did not seem strong. It could only focus on one issue at a time, muster its militia and then disband again until the next threat.

But the IMA survived and did so mostly through the efforts of a few individual manufacturers who saw a clear and long term mission for the organization. They believed the IMA could be useful on a permanent basis, not just as an occasional muster for defense against political and social confrontations. The IMA's first few boards were rather uniform in their almost expected diversity, with one board member per industry. Levy Mayer, of Moran, Kraus & Mayer, was appointed the first General Counsel in 1893. The General Counsel, starting with Mayer in 1893, has attended meetings of the Board of Directors, has presented the viewpoint of industry to legislative committees at Springfield and at Washington, advised the staff and committee members on legal problems and has issued legal opinions to member firms on legal issues which were of general interest to industry.

The first printed legal opinion sent by the Association was issued by Mayer on August 13, 1898, and was entitled "Opinion of Mr. Levy Mayer, General Counsel for the Association, Upon the Right of Railroad Companies Under the War Revenue Law to Require the Shipper to Pay the Cost of the Stamp on Duplicate Bills of Lading." The first standing committee created by the Board of Directors was the Committee on Legislation.

The IMA was the one voice of industry that had been in training for most of the decade, and by 1899 many manufacturers heard the voice and listened. Membership began to climb and renewals were a matter of course for many. In 1897, 50 firms were members; by 1898, 200 were; by 1904, 750; by 1928, 3,000; by 1953, 6,600; and by 1965, 9,780.

The records of the IMA show that the Board met regularly and frequently; the directors took active interest in the affairs of the Association; Board meeting attendance increased;

and the Board adopted a militant, constructive attitude on issues affecting the welfare of the state of Illinois and its industry.

From time to time, the directorate enlarged as the industrial development of the state, the extension of the activities and the growth of the Association warranted. For many years the Board met regularly on the second Friday of each month. As a rule, the members of the Board were (and remain today) the principal officers in their respective firms. They came from all parts of the state, represented industries of all sizes and engaged in practically all lines of production. They represented a true cross-section of Illinois and, by extension, American industry.

The records of the IMA were initially kept by the secretary, a part-time honorary office. The first of these was Harry Jacobson, who served from August 24, 1893 until February 21, 1894. The second, J.E. Tilt, served through 1894, and the third, Joseph Biefeld, served until February, 1898, when the first staff officer to be employed on a full-time basis, John M. Glenn, was hired as secretary of the Association. Glenn was dynamic and inventive in his leadership of the IMA. Under his tutelage, from 1898 to 1928, many of the policies and positions now taken as a matter of course were initiated.

For many years, the Committee on Legislation was an important factor in the affairs of the Association. Although the IMA has from the start engaged in a wide variety of activities, it has never lost sight of its primary responsibility: the protection of the welfare of the industries of Illinois in local, state and federal legislative matters. That the Association has effectively represented the interests of its members over the years is evident in the legislation that has been passed. As a result of the IMA's efforts, Illinois has been regarded as one of the best states in which to manufacture.

Even in the first year of the IMA the volume of state legislative proposals was formidable. In the 1893 session of the Illinois General Assembly there were 782 separate bills introduced in the House and 425 in the Senate, of which 22 bills under the title of "Labor" were introduced in the House and 10 in the Senate. As the state developed industrially, and it boomed for the next six decades, legislative proposals directed at industry grew proportionally. By 1943, in the regular session of the Illinois General Assembly, 1,713 bills and resolutions were considered. Of these, 717 measures were on the docket of the Association as affecting the interests and the welfare of Illinois industry. Twenty years later, in 1963, 3,251 Bills were introduced, of which about one-third either directly or indirectly had a bearing on Illinois industry. Thirty years later, in 1993, the IMA followed 1,224 of the 5,000 bills introduced in the Illinois General Assembly.

The volume of unsound, unwarranted legislative proposals with which the IMA has had to contend throughout the years has necessarily caused the Association frequently to adopt an attitude of opposition in its legislative work. However, and this is important to recognize, the IMA has always been prepared to initiate and support legislative measures which were, in fact, calculated to benefit the worker and not unreasonably burden the employer.

This policy was already acted out in the first years of the IMA, when on March 21, 1895, at a special meeting of the membership, the following resolution was unanimously adopted:

> Resolved, that it is the sense of this meeting that the law passed by the Legislature of this State, approved June 17, 1893, entitled "An Act to Regulate the Manufacture of Clothing, etc." in this state, with the exception of that portion which has recently been declared unconstitutional by our Supreme Court, meets with the hearty support of this Association. That we are in full accord with legislation regulating the sanitary condition of factories, shops, etc., the preservation of the health of employees and the prohibition of child labor, and that the officers of the state, under this act be upheld and assisted by us in their labors toward these ends.

Over the years the IMA has led the way toward reason and understanding in many conflicts that set popular opinion against the facts. More often than not, the IMA has been persuasive in its reasoning. When Upton Sinclair published *The Jungle*, in 1906, it immediately became a best seller. Politicians reacted quickly. President Theodore Roosevelt was an early reader of the novel and directed his Secretary of Agriculture, James Wilson, to investigate the escalating charges against the packing industry. At the same time, the IMA established its own committee to investigate the world-wide charges that the products of the Illinois packing houses were unfit for human consumption. After extensive investigations, the committee reported that the products of the Chicago meat industry were wholesome, but recommended some changes in the practice of preparation. The same year, the IMA organized a telephone company which prepared and introduced an ordinance in the Chicago City Council in protest against rates proposed by the existing telephone company operating in the city. The IMA's resistance prevented the existing telephone company from securing authority from the City Council to charge higher rates, thus saving money for the users of the new service.

In 1911 Charles Piez, president of the Link Belt Company, member of the IMA Board and a subsequent IMA chairman, served as the chairman of the committee of industrialists who, in cooperation with a group representing labor, worked out the provisions of the first Illinois Workmen's Compensation Act. The recommendations of this joint group were approved by the Illinois General Assembly in 1911. This Act was one of the first adopted in the United States and served as a model for legislation of this character throughout the country. Since then, all major changes made by the Illinois General Assembly to the Act have been in conjunction with the recommendations of management and of labor, arrived at in conferences between representatives of these groups.

In 1913 the IMA organized the Illinois Manufacturers' Casualty Association, because liability insurance rates had increased 300 to 500 percent since the passage of the Workmen's Compensation Act. Had the IMA, in effect, not become an insurer, many of its smaller members could have drowned under the new financial burden, or the prices of their products would have increased to such an extent that they would not have been competitive in a free and open market.

Two years later, in 1915, the IMA published for the first time, and made available to members, the "Pink Sheet"— a printed digest of daily legislative proceedings. Never before had this kind of service been offered by an association of businessmen. The next year, 1916, the IMA organized the Illinois Manufacturers' Costs Association. At the time, Edward N. Hurley, former IMA president, was vice-chairman of the Federal Trade Commission. Many manufacturers wrote Hurley that their competitors were fixing sales prices without reference to the cost of production, with the result that there was a lack of profits at the end of the business year. Hurley looked into the matter and then publicly advocated the necessity for an accurate cost-finding system. Following this suggestion, the IMA called a meeting of representative cost accountants and heads of bookkeeping departments in Illinois and formed a temporary organization called "The Illinois Manufacturers' Costs Association." It soon became a permanent organization with its own bylaws. It was the first organization of its kind and became a model for other trade associations across the country.

For a number of years, the Costs Association devoted itself to furthering the development of cost accounting systems and practices. The Cost Association aided in the development of this particular accounting practice and helped manufacturers understand and institute its principles. When cost accounting became common among manufacturers, the Costs Association greatly expanded its efforts into related fields by keeping an eye on laws and regulations that were being adopted by various governmental bureaus. Articles on a broad range of subjects affecting accounting were printed in the *Monthly Costs Bulletin*. Among the subjects of concern were state sales and use taxes, Social Security deductions, withholding taxes, various types of federal corporation and excise taxes, wage and salary stabilization practices and many others that are all part of the burden carried by accounting departments, and which impact a company's bottom line.

As World War I broke out, the nation was in need of the best products for the war effort. But how to get at them? To team up Illinois manufacturers with the war effort, the War Industries Board was organized by the IMA. The Board gave small members direct representation in Washington through an office that helped them obtain federal government contracts. In short order, more than $100 million in contracts were obtained for Illinois companies. This kind of cooperation and involvement by the IMA with its members' needs extended beyond the armistice to the founding, in 1920, of the Illinois Industrial Council, whose purpose it was to knit together "in common interest all the Industrial Organizations of the State in the consideration of questions involving legislation, labor, taxation and general business policies."

In 1922 the city of Chicago imposed a license fee on factories and workshops. The IMA counsel was of the opinion that the fee was unconstitutional and the IMA urged its membership not to pay, or if they did, only under protest. The following year the IMA obtained an injunction restraining the city of Chicago from collecting the fees. The City then took the matter to the Illinois State Supreme Court. For its part, the IMA organized a committee of influential businessmen who appeared before the Governor and argued against a bill pending in the legislature for license fees to be imposed on factories and workshops by communities that passed the legislation. Two days later, the governor vetoed the bill.

President Ronald Reagan awards John J. Jecmen, president of Harris Preble Company, the President's "E" award as Gov. James Thompson looks on.

On the other hand, in 1925, the IMA secured the passage of a bill permitting the organization of credit unions among employees. Two years later the IMA opened a legislative office in Springfield. The volume of legislative work had grown to such an extent that a separate department became necessary, with its own director, Allan T. Gordon. When the legislature was not in session, he traveled over the state contacting candidates and noting their views regarding problems facing Illinois.

Upon the death of John M. Glenn in 1928, James L. Donnelly was elected executive vice president and secretary. Donnelly held this position for the next 36 years, until 1964, and then served as director of the IMA's Executive Committee for one year. Donnelly came from a manufacturing background and had served the IMA in a number of capacities, first as vice president of the Association and chairman of the southern division, before he accepted the post of secretary. He was followed by E. Edgerton Hart, executive vice president from 1965-71; Orville V. Bergren, executive vice president from 1972-74 and president from 1974-83; Arthur R. Gottschalk, president from 1984-91; and Gregory W. Baise, president since 1991.

In 1929 the IMA secured one of its most important public achievements when it took the governor, a state senator and other state political leaders on an inspection trip of the proposed Deep Water Route. On the trip, a Congressional Committee was appointed to secure the necessary appropriations. A short time later, President Herbert H. Hoover agreed to ask Congress to appropriate the funds. As a result, Illinois recovered the business to the western coast states and South America which was lost to eastern competition favored with low rate transportation through the Panama Canal.

In 1931 the IMA participated in the organization of, and affiliated itself with, the Midwest Manufacturers' Association, Inc. This Association incorporated the state industrial associations in Indiana, Iowa, Kansas, Michigan, Minnesota, Missouri, Nebraska, Ohio, Oklahoma, Wisconsin and Illinois. Its function was to act as a clearing house for the viewpoint of Midwest industry and to coordinate the views and influence of Midwest industry on federal legislative problems and other issues of mutual interest.

In 1933 a committee of industrialists under the chairmanship of O.E. Mount, vice president, secretary and treasurer of the American Steel Foundries, and at the time chairman of the IMA's Committee on Workmen's Compensation, Health and Safety, worked out the provision of the Illinois Health and Safety Act in cooperation with representatives of labor, after deliberations over a period of many months. The recommendations of this joint management-labor group were unanimously approved by the legislature. The Illinois Health and Safety Act was enacted at a special session of the legislature in 1936.

When the federal government adopted the federal Social Security Act in 1935, requiring the states to enact unemployment compensation insurance laws, Illinois industry, through a representative committee of industrialists working in conjunction with their counterparts from labor, worked out the provisions of the original Illinois Unemployment Compensation Act, which passed in 1937. The Industry Committee was responsible for the inclusion in the Act of the Merit Rating Provisions. Much of the next year, 1938, was spent explaining the provisions of the new law to IMA members. Eight interpretive bulletins were issued by the general counsel in that year.

With America's entry into World War II, the IMA was again in a position to help secure the finest materials and provisions for the war effort from Illinois manufacturers. But the effect of priorities, shortages, ceilings and concentration of war contracts in the hands of large industry gravely concerned small businesses. The IMA argued for a broad distribution of sub-contracts and civilian production among small businesses, and cooperated with the War Production Board to this end.

After World War II, local and state governments raised taxes on assessments, and many new license bills were introduced to make up for revenues lost during the war years. A curb on this "wild" taxation was introduced in Springfield, with strong IMA participation in its drafting. Through the Association's tireless advocacy, the legislation passed resulting in downstate counties and towns being limited to maximal extended taxes of between 15 and 20 percent instead of the 100 percent they had been subject to in earlier legislation.

The nature of city councils is to meet frequently and often quite informally, with the result that industry is in a constant state of uncertainty as to its local responsibilities, especially regarding its tax burden. Under these conditions many industries, especially the smaller ones, could be seriously injured in many parts of the state if the power to tax were delegated to city councils. Among the most controversial measures to be successfully opposed by the IMA was one that would have given unlimited power to the City Council of Chicago to license and tax all industry and business within the city. This measure was similar to proposals which the Association had opposed at many previous sessions of the City Council, on the grounds that the "power to tax is the power to destroy" and that this great power should be left with the State Legislature. This measure, if adopted by Chicago, would have undoubtedly been extended to all municipalities throughout the state quickly.

In the post-war years, the IMA became even more actively involved in the nomination and election process of public officials. By reviewing the merits of the candidates, the

Association provided manufacturers with a better understanding of the positions of the candidates regarding industry, which, in turn, allowed for a more educated vote to be cast in elections.

In 1950 the IMA held a series of conferences with leaders of the Casualty Insurance Industry, resulting in substantial rate reductions on premiums to buyers of workmen's compensation and occupational disease insurance. By doing its own research on workmen's compensation insurance rates and then effectively presenting the findings to insurance officials, the IMA entered a new phase of involvement on behalf of its membership. From now on, the Association would research and check the facts on whole industries and thus, in effect, become the conscience of those eager to change laws or institute legislation beneficial only to a few or without having a full understanding of the consequences.

For more than 90 years, the IMA has provided its members and legislators with the facts through its own publications: the *Annual Report*, since 1903; the *Legislative Bulletin*, first published in 1903 (pink in color since 1915); the *IMA Labor Review*, 1922-1954; the *IMA Law Digest*, since 1955; the *Executive Memo*, since 1960; *Springfield Highlights*, since 1955; the *IMA Public Affairs Report*, first published in 1973; and *The Illinois Manufacturer*, since 1990. The work of the IMA's standing committees, such as Federal Taxation, Foreign Trade, Industrial Health, International Relations, Patents and Trademarks, State and Local Taxation and Workers' Compensation, Unemployment Insurance, Environmental Quality and Technology have for almost a century been the source of information for most of the Association's publications, legislative activities and public education on the issues facing industry in Illinois.

The 1950s and 1960s brought the IMA a whole new set of problems, some of them old, but many of them new. As the demand for material goods increased, the impact of manufacturing on the environment began to be noticed by some, and noises began to be made to save the world from industry. These sounds were not unfamiliar. They had been heard for decades. Every generation has had its affair with business and painted its emotions in different colors. The result has been fairly uniform. Society generally feels threatened by manufacturing, while demanding all the benefits that it has to offer. At the same time, society is unwilling to pay for the consequences of these wants. Again, the IMA set out to educate and help its members cope with the new issues. In 1963 the IMA was actively concerned with water pollution. Measures were introduced in Congress to place water pollution control under the federal government. The IMA presented testimony stating that water pollution control should be primarily the responsibility of local government. Chicago was cited as an example. Air pollution was also a newer issue, which the IMA again emphasized should be handled at state and local levels, rather than through the federal government.

Each year since its founding, the IMA has held a special dinner for its members. The 70th Anniversary dinner was marked by a telegram from former President Hoover. His message read: "Although I cannot be present at your Anniversary Dinner-Meeting, I want to congratulate your organization on its 70 years of public service to the state of Illinois and the nation. I send my good wishes for your continued contribution to the American way of life." Three years later, the 73rd annual dinner meeting of the IMA featured Richard M. Nixon as speaker. The dinner set a new IMA attendance record: 2,500 people.

Throughout the 1970s the issues of the day were not new ones, and many are still with us today. The hand of government was falling increasingly heavily on the shoulders of industry; pollution control, occupational safety and health, equal employment opportunity and the various aspects of consumer protection were all worthy issues and important to society, but some unrealistic laws and regulations governing them could spell trouble for the economy. The IMA noted that organized labor had more power and legis-

IMA's Annual Dinner speaker, 1966

lative clout than ever before, and that the image of industry was not very bright in the public's eye. And probably the most important observation of the day was that international trade was causing America to experience an increasing trade deficit, as more American products became non-competitive. Inflation, a result of the huge federal deficit, was seen as the number one problem facing manufacturers.

The IMA showed its member firms a way out of the political and legislative maze by providing a strong basis for collective, effective action through committees. The standing committees at the time were: Consumer Relations, Environmental Quality, Foreign Trade, Industrial Relations, Industrial Safety and Health, Legislative, Patents and Trademarks, Public Affairs, Small Industry, Taxation, Unemployment Compensation and Welfare and Workers' Compensation. Each committee kept a vigilant eye on regulations, ordinances and laws of local governments, the state of Illinois and the federal government that concerned manufacturers.

The Illinois voters elected Gov. Dan Walker (1972-1976), a populist governor who was allied with Democratic majorities in both the House and Senate. Beginning in 1975 the General Assembly was pro-labor, and remained so for the next 18 years. This was the first time that labor controlled the General Assembly since the Depression. As a result, the workers' and unemployment compensation laws were ripped open in 1975, the unemployment compensation system went $16 billion into debt that year and by the late 1970s, Illinois' workers' compensation had become the most expensive in the nation.

The Walker Administration forced the IMA to increase its lobbying activities to protect its members. William E. Dart, a highly-skilled lobbyist, joined the IMA in 1976 and his first mission was to attack the unemployment compensation laws. Under Dart's leadership, the IMA's lobbying efforts moved unemployment compensation out of bankruptcy and into a model system with agreements in 1982, 1987 and 1992. Other states were quick to follow the IMA lead.

As a result of the IMA's making over 100 successful amendments to the Workers' Compensation Act, an inherently bad system became a fairly competent one, especially when compared to the systems in other states of the nation. In the arena of employer-employee relations the IMA was instrumental in defeating repeated attempts at the state level to ban lie detectors (ultimately passed by Congress). In the area of elementary and secondary education the IMA developed and passed into law, over the initial powerful opposition of the entire organized school community, the first ever accountability system for Illinois elementary and secondary schools, effective in 1994. The IMA also supported an income tax increase to help fund schools.

The IMA was also active in tort reform when it introduced and lobbied successfully for passage of the Illinois Statute of Repose. The IMA organized 130 statewide and regional associations into the largest coalition ever to speak on any issue before the Illinois General Assembly, the Illinois Coalition of the Insurance Crisis, which subsequently became the Tort Reform Alliance of Illinois. The Coalition is an IMA affiliate and has led an all out effort to enact radical changes in the Illinois tort law. To date the efforts have been rewarded with only minor changes passed by the Illinois General Assembly.

In the recent past, protecting our air and water from pollutants and individual people from themselves by placing restrictions on industry, and charging industry retroactively for any oversight or infraction of the current rules, was seen as a one-step solution for all our ills. For the IMA, environmental issues have been of vital concern, too, and the Association has spent much effort to keep Illinois manufacturers competitive with those in surrounding states. The IMA was successful in defeating an attempt to place environmental clean up taxes solely on Illinois chemical manufacturers. Furthermore, the IMA helped in the passage of comprehensive solid and hazardous waste legislation that had minimal negative impact on the state's manufacturers. Lobbying efforts of the IMA defeated attempts by radical activist groups to get business and industry to underwrite large percentages of residential power costs. The IMA also led a successful effort to rewrite the Illinois Utility Act and defeat repeated attempts to tax direct purchase of natural gas.

Throughout the 1980s, the IMA struggled with state and local governments hungry for more taxation, as consumer wants and personal debt pushed the national debt until it spiraled up and out of consciousness. It led the effort to keep the personal property replacement tax at a minimum and successfully supported passage of legislation repealing the Illinois inheritance tax. The IMA created and passed a bill for full exemption from sales tax for manufacturing machinery and equipment used in production. Then the IMA supplemented this and succeeded in expanding the scope of this exemption to now include repair and replacement parts, research and design equipment and other manufacturing equipment not necessarily related to production. The IMA authored and promoted the Illinois investment tax credit allowing an income tax credit for investments in manufacturing equipment. It successfully lobbied to pass an income tax credit for all expenditures in research and design. Among its greatest successes was the defeat of legislation that proposed a 40 percent tax increase, while supporting a temporary 20 percent one year income tax increase. The IMA was successful in resisting the efforts of those wanting to make this tax permanent. It was also successful in defeating repeated attempts to enact a service tax, and in defeating efforts to pass local income tax.

Created in 1976 in response to the growing number of Illinois political action committees, the IMA membership was urged to support its own Manufacturers Political Action Committee (MPAC). It was organized to help pro-business and pro-manufacturing candidates throughout the state. In its first year, MPAC specifically targeted and defeated the Illinois state senator who authored the 1975 anti-business workers' and unemployment compensation legislation. This defeat of the Senate Chairman of the Labor and Commerce Committee which resulted in a renewed call by labor for the creation of a new "Agreed Bill Committee" to negotiate workers' and unemployment compensation changes. This was accompanied by pleas to remove these issues from the electoral debating agenda.

Over the years MPAC has maintained a constant alliance with Senate Republicans and in 1992 helped them achieve a majority in the state senate for the first time in 18 years. Today, MPAC is recognized as the largest and most effective pro-business PAC in Illinois and continues to seek qualified individuals to run for public office. In addition, the IMA is recognized as the leading lobbying force for business in Illinois. Today the IMA has a lobbying staff of four located in Springfield.

In the early 1970s the IMA began to experience a decline in membership which reflected the decline in the number of manufacturers in Illinois. The decline accelerated in the mid-1970s after the United States went off the gold standard and American manufacturers had to compete seriously in world-wide markets for the first time. The decline in membership leveled off after the 1982 recession, which also culled the ranks of manufacturers of the ones unable to compete in the new markets. The manufacturers who succeeded had fine tuned their operations to produce more quality goods with automated machinery and lower overhead costs resulting in reduced production costs. Today, Illinois manufacturers are producing more goods than they have at any time in the past 100 years: the IMA owns a building in Springfield and is leading the effort to train and retrain manufacturers to compete in the global marketplace. The IMA has held true to its mission statement written 100 years ago:

> The object for which the Illinois Manufacturers's Association is formed is to strengthen the economic, social, environmental and governmental conditions for manufacturing and allied enterprises in the state of Illinois, resulting in an enlarged business base and increased employment.

THE IMA CENTENNIAL BOARD

CHAIRMAN

James A. Peterson, president, Bimet Corporation, Morris; manufacturer of bimetal thermostats for the small appliance industry.

VICE CHAIRMAN

Calvin A. Campbell Jr., president, Goodman Equipment Corp., Bedford Park; manufacturer of underground mining and tunneling machinery and plastic blow molding machinery.

TREASURER

John R. Moore, president and CEO, Midas International Corporation, Chicago; manufacturer of exhaust replacement parts, specifically pipe, straight tubing and mufflers for the automotive repair franchising industry.

CENTENNIAL BOARD

Charles S. Allen, president and CEO, Sloan Valve Company, Franklin Park; manufacturer of freight car electrical equipment, electronic faucets, flush valves, vacuum breakers, shower heads, soap dispensers and hand dryers.

Davis G. Anderson, president, Chicago Extruded Metals Co., Cicero; manufacturer of brass shapes, rods and wire.

John R. Anderson, president, Anderson Industries, Inc., Rockford; holding company of various manufacturing firms serving the automotive, packaging and plastic molding industries.

David C. Arch, chairman and CEO, Blistex, Inc., Oak Brook; manufacturer of medicated health-care products for all consumer retail outlets.

Norman A. Berg, president, American Steel Foundries, Chicago; manufacturer of steel components for freight cars and locomotives.

Clifford W. Berglund, chairman and CEO, Plainfield Stamping-Illinois Co., Plainfield; manufacturer of metal stampings and fabrication.

Cedric W. Blazer, president, Zenith Cutter Co., Rockford; manufacturer of replacement machine knives serving the plastics, corrugated, recycling, agricultural, ice rink and wire industries.

Linda S. Breuer, president, Breuer/Tornado Corporation, Chicago; manufacturer of floor maintenance equipment and industrial vacuums for industries including janitorial and healthcare, in addition to schools, hotels and factories.

Barry J. Carroll, chairman of the board, Carroll International Corp., Des Plaines; manufacturer of confections, equipment for concentrating mineral ores and cleaning coal to reduce sulfur emissions, commercial kitchen ventilator hoods, utility distribution systems and commercial kitchen stainless steel fabrications.

M. Blouke Carus, chairman and CEO, Carus Corporation, Peru; manufacturer of manganese compounds used to purify drinking water and remove a variety of impurities from waste water. The corporation also publishes elementary school textbooks and children's magazines.

Gregory P. Cozzi, vice president, Cozzi Iron & Metal Inc., Chicago; processor of scrap iron, steel and non-ferrous metals.

William C. Croft, chairman, Clements National Co., Broadview; manufacturer of electric products for construction and industrial maintenance industries.

Paul J. Darling II, president and CEO, Corey Steel Company, Cicero; manufacturer of precision cold finished steel bars, and is also a primary metal service center engaged in the slitting of carbon sheet coil for subsequent sale. In addition, Corey is a wholesaler of aluminum, copper bearing metals, pure iron, stainless steel and silver brazing alloys for industries that include appliance, automotive, farm equipment and screw machine products.

Carl K. Doty, president, R.R. Donnelly & Sons, Chicago; printing and related information services; value-added products for retailers, catalogers, owners and users of information.

Craig J. Duchossois, president, Duchossois Industries, Inc., Elmhurst; manufacturer of garage door openers for consumers; railway freight cars for the transportation industry and small arms for the national defense.

Harold V. Engh Jr., chairman, North American Plastics Corp., Aurora; manufacturer of plastic trash and lawn bags.

Alexandra H. Estes, chairman and president, Haeger Industries, Inc., Dundee; manufacturer of ceramic decorative accessories for the florist and retail industries.

James N. Farley, chairman, SpeedFam Corporation, Des Plaines; manufacturer of equipment for high technology and other industries; also manufactures lapping polishing and grinding machines for industries that include semi conductors and computers.

Salvatore Ferrara II, president, Ferrara Pan Candy Co., Forest Park; manufacturer of confectionery products for all food-related outlets.

Clark W. Fetridge, president, The Dartnell Corp., Chicago; printers of books, newsletters and advertising brochures for all industries.

Federick P. Foltz, vice president and general manager, Admiral Refrigeration Div. of Maytag Corp., Galesburg; manufacturer of major brand-named refrigerators for both domestic and international markets.

Frank E. Furst, president and CEO, Furst-McNess Company, Freeport; manufacturer of livestock feed premixes for livestock producers in hog, dairy and beef industries.

Jerry Hayden, president, Peacock Engineering Co., Itasca; contract assembly and packaging business for consumer, industrial and government industries.

Glen A. Johnson, president, Oakley Millwork, Inc., Frankfort; manufacturer of windows, doors and trim for residential construction serving new home contractors in northern Illinois, northwest Indiana and southern Wisconsin.

Philip P. Kaiser, chairman, P-K Tool & Manufacturing Co., Chicago; manufacturer of precision metal stamping for industries that include automotive, electric appliance, electronics, specialty hardware and computers.

Dennis J. Keller, chairman and CEO, DeVry Inc., Oakbrook Terrace; DeVry owns and operates DeVry Institutes, Keller Graduate School of Management and Corporate Educational Services. The schools offer bachelor and associate degrees and diploma programs in electronics technology, computer information systems, telecommunications management, business operations and accounting, as well as master degree programs in business administration, project management and human resource management.

H. W. Knapheide III, president, The Knapheide Mfg. Co., Quincy; manufacturer of truck bodies for the agriculture, public utilities, service industries, railroads and construction industries.

John K. Lawson, senior vice president, Deere & Company, Moline; equipment manufacturer for all agricultural and industrial markets.

Barry L. MacLean, president and CEO, MacLean-Fogg Company, Mundelein; manufacturer of engineered plastic and metal components serving automotive, truck, power and telephone utility, medical and general consumer hard goods markets.

Thomas M. McKenna, president and CEO, Moorman Manufacturing Company, Quincy; manufacturer of livestock feed products, livestock equipment, soybean meal, soybean oil and vegetable oils, for the cattle, swine, dairy, poultry, food and industrial industries.

Albert R. Miller, president, Phoenix Closures Inc., Naperville; manufacturer of plastic bottle caps for agricultural, chemical, food and pharmaceutical industries.

Mark S. Nussle, president, Viking Metal Cabinet Company, Inc., Chicago; a designer and manufacturer of a wide variety of custom fabricated metal parts and casework involving steel, stainless steel, and enamel systems. Industries served include electronics, food service, architectural and construction.

Massie E. Odiotti, sr. vice president, Sun Chemical, Northlake; manufacturer of printing ink for publication and packaging printers.

Henry B. Pearsall, chairman, Sanford Corp., Freeport; manufacturer of housewares, hardware, drug and office supplies.

David A. Peterson, president, Nashua Precision Technologies, a division of Nashau Corp., Champaign; manufacturer of ultra-precision machined products serving the personal computer and laser printer industries.

John R. Power, publisher and general manager, *Jacksonville Journal Courier*, Jacksonville; newspaper printing and typesetting.

David P. Ransburg, chairman, L.R. Nelson Corporation, Peoria; manufacturer of lawn and garden sprinkling equipment serving lawn and garden industries.

Alan J. Rassi, vice president, Caterpillar, Inc., Peoria; design, manufacturer and marketer of earthmoving, construction and materials handling machinery for industries including transportation, energy, housing, forest products, mining, commercial and industrial construction.

Kenneth J. Rollins, president, Quincy Compressor Div., Coltec Industries, Inc., Quincy; manufacturer of reciprocating and rotary screw air compressors and vacuum pumps for general industrial air, hospital air and vacuum, climate control air, instrument air and printing plant air and vacuum.

Nancy Rus, vice president and corporate director, organizational development, Motorola, Schaumburg; manufacturer of FM two-way radio and data communications systems.

F. Eugene Schmitt, CEO, Berlin Industries, Inc., Carol Stream; commercial printer specializing in long run Web offset, four-, five-and six-color printing serving direct mail marketers and publishers.

Lewis L. Smith, CEO, Premier Plastics Corp., Elk Grove Village; manufacturer of custom injection molding of thermoplastics for appliance, electronic, medical, electrical, automotive aftermarket, consumer products, lawn and garden industries.

Stephen S. Stack, president, SeamCraft, Inc., Chicago; manufacturer of quality sewn products serving companies that include, Ford, General Motors, G.E. Toro and E.R. Squibb.

George A. Vincent III, chairman, president and CEO, The C.P. Hall Company, Chicago; manufacturer of specialty plasticizers and rubber chemical ingredients serving an assorted number of industries including rubber, plastics, food and pharmaceuticals.

Frederick G. Wacker III, president, Liquid Controls Corporation, Lake Bluff; manufacturer of liquid measurement tools.

John F. Wahl, president and CEO, Wahl Clipper Corporation, Sterling; manufacturer of small electrical appliances, mostly personal care appliances, for the retail industry.

Marvin R. Wortell, chairman, Triton Industries, Inc., Chicago; a manufacturer of formed metal products. Production capabilities include stamping presses and fabricating equipment such as turret presses, laser cutting and press brakes for industries that include computer/electronic enclosures, vending mechanisms and enclosures, flow control (mechanical assemblies) and food processing.

John A. Zenko, CEO, Telemedia, Inc., Buffalo Grove; manufacturer and distributor of high-quality training materials for improving productivity. Telemedia also provides multi-media technical skills and computer systems training worldwide.

Richard W. Ziehm, president, Precision Extrusions; manufacturer of custom aluminum extrusions, fabrication, finishing, CNC machining and anodizing serving industries including electronics, telecommunications, lighting, computer and machinery manufacturers.

ELECTED IMA LEADERS 1893-1993

1893-1899   W. B. Conkey, W. B. Conkey Company, Chicago

1900   Charles A. Plamondon, A. Plamondon Mfg. Co. Chicago

1901   Martin B. Madden, Western Stone Co., Monmouth

1902   Charles H. Deere, Deere & Company, Moline

1903   B. A. Eckhart, B. A. Eckhart Milling Company, Chicago

1904   John H. Pierce, Western Tube Co. Kewanee

1905   John E. Wilder, Wilder & Company, Chicago

1906   U. G. Orendorff, Parlin and Orendorff Co., Canton

1907   C. H. Smith, Western Wheeled Scraper Co., Aurora

1908   F. W. Upham, Upham and Agler, Chicago

1909-1910   Laverne W. Noyes, Aermoter Company, Chicago

1911   P. A. Peterson, Union Furniture Company, Rockford

1912-1913   Charles Piez, Link-Belt Company, Chicago

1914   H. G. Herget, Pekin Wagon Company, Pekin

1915   Edward N. Hurley, Hurley Machine Company, Chicago

1916-1917   Samuel M. Hastings, Computing Scale Co. of America, Chicago

1918   William Butterworth, Deere & Company, Moline

1919   Dorr E. Felt, Felt & Tarrant Mfg. Co., Chicago

1920   William Nelson Pelouze, Pelouze Mfg. Co., Chicago

1921   George R. Meyercord, The Meyercord Company, Chicago

1922   Herman H. Hettler, Herman H. Hettler Lumber Co., Chicago

1923-1924   E. C. Heidrich, Jr., Peoria Cordage Company, Peoria

1925-1926   Charles Piez, Link-Belt Company, Chicago

1927   Paul F. Beich, Paul F. Beich Company, Bloomington

1928-1929   James D. Cunningham, Republic Flow Meters Co., Chicago

1930-1931   Theodore R. Gerlach, Gerlach-Barklow Co., Joliet

1932   Samuel M. Hastings, Computing Scale Co. of America, Chicago

1933   Thomas S. Hammond, Whiting Corporation, Harvey

1934-1935   R. E. Wantz, Rockford Fiber Container Co., Rockford

1936   Thomas S. Hammond, Whiting Corporation, Harvey

1937-1938   B. C. Heacock, Caterpillar Tractor Company, Peoria

1939-1940   W. Homer Hartz, Morden Frog & Crossing Works, Chicago Heights

1941   Robert M. Gaylord, The Ingersoll Milling Machine Co., Rockford

1942-1943   Sterling Morton, Morton Salt Company, Chicago

1944-1945   J. C. MacKeever, The Gerlach-Barklow Co., Joliet

1946   T. Albert Potter, Elgin National Watch Co., Chicago

1947   R.J. Koch, Felt & Tarrant Mfg. Co., Chicago

1948   Arnold J. Wilson, General Time Instruments Corporation, LaSalle

1949   Edmund F. Mansure, E. L. Mansure Company, Chicago

1950   Henry Pope, Jr., Bear Brand Hosiery Co., Chicago

1951   John Slezak, The Turner Brass Works, Sycamore

1952   L. K. Ayers, C. K. Williams & Co., East St. Louis

1953   George H. Williamson, Williamson Candy Company, Chicago

1954   Charles C. Haffner, Jr., R. R. Donnelley & Sons Co., Chicago

1955   Arthur J. Schmitt, American Phenolic Corporation, Cicero

1956   Gordon S. Culver, Richards-Wilcox Mfg. Co., Aurora

1957   Charles S. Craigmile, Belden Manufacturing Co., Chicago

1958   William S. North, Union Special Machine Co., Chicago

1959   Merle R. Yontz, LeTourneau-Westinghouse Co., Peoria

1960   Harold Byron Smith, Illinois Tool Works Inc., Chicago

1961   H. C. Mueller, The Powers Regulator Company, Skokie

1962   Leonard C. Ferguson, Western Newell Mfg. Co., Freeport

1963   Bennett Archambault, Stewart-Warner Corporation, Chicago

1964   Alan C. Mattison, Mattison Machine Works, Rockford

1965   Kenneth Kroehler, Kroehler Mfg. Co., Naperville

1966   William B. Graham, Baxter Laboratories, Inc., Morton Grove

1967   William C. Croft, The Pyle-National Company, Chicago

1968   R. A. MacNeille, St. Charles Manufacturing Co., St. Charles

1969   Stanley M. Sorenson, Hammond Corporation, Deerfield

1970   Gregson L. Barker, Uarco Inc., Barrington

1971   Ellwood F. Curtis, Deere & Company, Moline

1972   John D. Gray, Hart Schaffner & Marx, Chicago

1973   John A. Wagner, Jr., Wagner Castings Company, Decatur

1974   Raymond Hollis, Graymills Corporation, Chicago

1975   Frederick G. Wacker, Jr., Ammco Tools, Inc., North Chicago

1976   Edmund B. Thornton, Ottawa Silica Co., Ottawa

1977   John W. Kendrick, Met-L-Wood Corporation, Bedford Park

1978   Dean A. Olson, Rockford Acromatic Products Co., Rockford

1979   Mitchell P. Kartalia, Square D Company, Palatine

1980   John A. Lawrence, Lawrence Brothers, Inc., Sterling

1981   Robert W. Hawkinson, Belden Corporation, Geneva

1982   Arthur E. MacQuilkin, Industrial Filter & Pump Mfg. Co., Inc., Cicero

1983   William D. Leighton, Oak State Products, Inc., Wenona

1984-1985   Maurice J. O'Brien, Marblehead Lime Company, Chicago

1986-1987   Clifford W. Berglund, Plainfield Tool & Engineering, Inc., Plainfield

1988-1989   Erwin E. Schulze, Ceco Corp., Oak Brook

1990-1991   Barry L. MacLean, MacLean-Fogg, Co., Mundelein

1992-1993   James A. Peterson, Bimet Corp., Morris

SELECTED BIBLIOGRAPHY

Andreas, Alfred T. *History of Cook County*. Chicago, A.T. Andreas, 1884.

Bach, Ira J. "Pullman: A Town Reborn," *Chicago History*, (Spring 1975): 44-53

Buisseret, David. *Historic Illinois from the Air*. Chicago: The University of Chicago Press, 1990.

Casey, Robert J. and Douglas, W.A.S. *Pioneer Railroad: The Story of the Chicago and North Western System*. New York: McGraw-Hill, 1948.

Casson, Herbert N. *The Romance of the Reaper*. New York: Doubleday, Page, 1908.

Clayton, John. *The Illinois Fact Book and Historical Almanac, 1673-1968*. Southern Illinois University Press, Carbondale, 1970.

Cronon, William. "To Be the Central City," *Chicago History*, 10 (1981): 130-40. Cronon, William. *Nature's Metropolis. Chicago and the Great West*. New York: W.W.Norton, 1991

Cutler, Irving. Chicago: *Metropolis of the Mid-Continent*. Dubuque: Kendall-Hunt, 1973.

Davenport, Eugene. "A Century of Agricultural Progress," *Illinois Blue Book*, 1917-19.

Darling, Sharon S. *Chicago Ceramics and Glass. An Illustrated History from 1871 to 1933*. Chicago: Chicago Historical Society, 1979.

Darling, Sharon S. *Chicago Furniture Art, Craft and Industry, 1833-1983*. Chicago Historical Society. 1984.

Derber, Milton. *Labor in Illinois. The Affluent Years, 1945-80*. Urbana, University of Illinois Press, 1989.

Federal Writers Project. *Illinois: A Descriptive and Historical Guide*. Chicago: A.C. McClurg & Co., 1939. reprint, New York: Pantheon Books, 1983.

Forrestal, Dan J. *The Kernel and the Bean. The 75-Year Story of the Staley Company*. New York: Simon and Schuster, 1982.

Gayle, Margot "A Heritage Forgotten: Chicago's First Cast Iron Front Buildings," *Chicago History*, 8,2 (Summer 1978): 98-108.

Gladding, Alfred E. *Mechanical Belt Fastening, A Brief History*. For the 75th anniversary of Flexible Steel Lacing Co. Privately printed, 1982.

Glauber, Robert H. "The Necessary Toy: The Telephone comes to Chicago," *Chicago History*, 8,2 (Summer 1978): 70-86.

Hartmarx Centennial Celebration 1887-1987. Chicago: privately printed 1987.

Heise, Kenan and Michael Edgerton. *Chicago, Center for Enterprise*. Windsor Publications, 1982.

Hogan, John. *A Spirit Capable, The Story of Commonwealth Edison*. Chicago: Mobium Press, 1986

Hotchkiss, George W. *Industrial Chicago*, vol. III: Ch.1 The lumber trade of Chicago.

Hughes, Thomas P. *Networks of Power: Electrification in Western Society, 1880-1930*. Baltimore: Johns Hopkins University Press, 1983.

Illinois Guide and Gazetteer, 1969. Chicago, Rand McNally & Co. Prepared for the Illinois Sesquicentennial Commission.

Jensen, Richard. Illinois; *A History*. New York: W.W. Norton & Co., 1978.

Kelly, Alfred H. *A History of the Illinois Manufacturers' Association*. The University of Chicago, Dissertation, March 1938.

Leech, Harper, and Carroll, John. *Armour and his Times*. New York: D. Appleton-Century Co., 1938.

McCollough,Albert. *The Complete Book of Buddy "L" Toys*, Greenberg Publishing, 1982.

McDonald, John F. *Employment Location and Industrial Land Use in Metro.Chicago*. Champaign: Stipes Pub. Co., 1984.

McLaughlin, Patricia. "Zip!!!," *The Chicago Tribune* February 3, 1991, Women section.

Mansfield, John Brabdt. *History of the Great Lakes*, 2 vols. Chicago: Beers & Co., 1899.

Mayer, Harold M., and Wade, Richard C. *Chicago: Growth of a Metropolis*. Chicago: University of Chicago Press, 1969.

Mayer, Harold M., *The Port of Chicago and the St. Lawrence Seaway*. Chicago: The University of Chicago Press, 1957.

McCormick, Cyrus. *The Century of the Reaper*. Boston: Houghton Mifflin, 1931.

Pierce, Bessie Louise. *A History of Chicago*. New York: Alfred A. Knopf, 1957.

Poole, Ernest. Giants Gone: *Men Who Made Chicago*. New York: McGraw-Hill Book Company, Inc., 1943.

Putnam, James William. *The Illinois and Michigan Canal: A Study in Economic History*. Chicago: The University of Chicago Press, 1918.

75 years of Distribution, *Industrial Distribution* magazine, 1980.

Smith, Wes. "Well oiled," *Chicago Tribune*, October 4, 1990. Tempo, section 5.

Sommers, Steven. "A Century of Chicago Toys, 1880 - 1980," *Chicago History*, 11,3 (1982).

Sterling, Robert E. *A Pictorial History of Will County*, vol. II. Joliet: Will County Historical Publications Company, 1976.

Stover, John F. *History of the Illinois Central Railroad*. New York, Macmillan, 1975.

Strickland, Arvarth E. "The New Deal Comes to Illinois," *Illinois State Historical Society*, (vol. LXIII), 1963:55.)

Sutton, Robert P. *The Prairie State. A Documentary History of Illinois. From the Civil War to the Present*. Grand Rapids, Wm. B. Eerdmans Publ. Co., 1976.

Swift, Louis F., with Arthur Van Vlissingen, Jr. The Yankee of the Yards: *The Biography of Gustavus Franklin Swift*. Chicago: A.W. Shaw, 1927.

Wade, Louise Carrol. Chicago's Pride: *The Stockyards, Packingtown, and Environs in the Nineteenth Century*. Urbana: University of Illinois Press, 1987.

Weiler, N. Sue. "Walkout: The Chicago Men's Garment Workers" Strike, 1910-1911," *Chicago History*, (Winter 1979-1980): 238 - 249.

Weinrott, Lester A. "Sweet, Sweet Scent of Soap," *Chicago History*, (Spring 1977): 44-52.

Wieland, James and Edward Force, *Tootsietoys: The World's First Diecast Models*, Motorbooks International, 1980.

Yovovich, Bozidar. *Chicago, the Next Frontier*, Chatsworth CA., Windsor Publications, 1988.

INDEX